Stock Market Analysis Using the SAS® System: Portfolio Selection and Evaluation

Version 6
First Edition

SAS Institute Inc.
SAS Campus Drive
Cary, NC 27513

The correct bibliographic citation for this manual is as follows: SAS Institute Inc.,
Stock Market Analysis Using the SAS® System: Portfolio Selection and Evaluation, Cary,
NC: SAS Institute Inc., 1994. 243 pp.

Stock Market Analysis Using the SAS® System

Contents

Credits

Design and Production	Design, Production, and Printing Services
Style Programming	Publications Technology Development
Technical Review	James J. Ashton, Darius S. Baer, John C. Brocklebank, Brent L. Cohen, Mark W. Craver, Anwar El-Jawhari, Benno Kurch, Tae Yoon Lee, W. Lee Richardson, Mike Stockstill
Writing and Editing	N. Elizabeth Malcom, Susan H. McCoy, Patsy J. Poole, Josephine P. Pope, James D. Seabolt, Joan M. Stout

Using This Book

Purpose

Stock Market Analysis Using the SAS System: Portfolio Selection and Evaluation provides a set of example analyses using SAS software to analyze the return and risk of stocks, singly and in portfolios. This book is a task-oriented applications guide that shows how to use the SAS System to analyze risk and return of stocks, create and maintain portfolios, and value stock options. The guide explains how to use features of base SAS software, the REG and CLUSTER procedures from SAS/STAT software, and the LP procedure from SAS/OR software for stock market analysis. Several theoretical approaches are presented: Discounted Cash Flow (DCF) Analysis, the Capital Asset Pricing Model (CAPM), Linear Programming Models, and the Markowitz Model. This book does not include technical analysis, which will be presented in a second volume of techniques for stock market analysis.

"Using This Book" contains important information to assist you as you read this book. This information describes the intended audience, prerequisites, and the book's organization and conventions. "Using This Book" also has an "Additional Documentation" section that provides references to other books containing information on related topics.

Audience

Stock Market Analysis Using the SAS System: Portfolio Selection and Evaluation is intended for those with interest in analyzing the risk and return of stocks, including finance professionals and the interested nonspecialist, as well as university students at the master's level and upper-level undergraduates. Minimal knowledge of computing, statistics, and mathematical programming is required to work through the examples. Knowledge of finance at the level of *Modern Portfolio Theory and Investment Analysis*, by Elton and Gruber, is suggested but not required.

Prerequisites

Little or no experience with the SAS System is required to use *Stock Market Analysis Using the SAS System: Portfolio Selection and Evaluation*. The following table summarizes the SAS System concepts you need to use this book:

You need to know how to ...	Refer to ...
invoke the SAS System at your site	instructions provided by the SAS Software Consultant at your site.
have a basic understanding of SAS System concepts, such as the DATA step	*SAS Language and Procedures: Introduction, Version 6, First Edition* for a brief introduction, or *SAS Language and Procedures: Usage, Version 6, First Edition* and *SAS Language and Procedures, Usage 2, Version 6, First Edition* for a more thorough introduction.

Readers of *Stock Market Analysis Using the SAS System: Portfolio Selection and Evaluation* are assumed to be familiar with the computer platform they use, but no formal computing background or graduate level statistical training is assumed. Readers are assumed to be familiar with basic statistical concepts of mean and variance, and have been exposed to regression analysis and hypothesis testing at an introductory level.

What You Should Read

The following table lists some of the stock market analysis tasks you may want to perform and the appropriate chapters to read to accomplish those tasks:

If you want to ...	Read ...
calculate risk and return measures	Chapter 1, "Background Topics" and Chapter 7, "Evaluating Portfolios"
value stocks	Chapter 2, "Discounted Cash Flow (DCF) Analysis"
sort and cluster stocks	Chapter 3, "Sorting and Clustering Stocks"
perform Capital Asset Pricing Model analysis of stocks	Chapter 4, "The Capital Asset Pricing Model (CAPM)"
calculate portfolio weights	Chapter 5 "Portfolio Creation with Linear Programming" and Chapter 6, "The Markowitz Model, Portfolio Creation with Nonlinear Programming"
evaluate portfolio performance	Chapter 7, "Evaluating Portfolios"
value stock options	Chapter 8, "Valuing Stock Options"

Conventions

This section explains the various conventions used to present text and examples in this book.

Typographical Conventions

Stock Market Analysis Using the SAS System: Portfolio Selection and Evaluation uses several type styles for presenting information. The following list explains the meaning of the typographical conventions used in this book.

roman   is the standard type style used for most text in this book.

UPPERCASE ROMAN   is used for SAS language elements.

bold	is used for headings, matrices, and vectors.
bold italics	is used for italicized words when they appear in headings.
italic	is used for terms that are defined in text, for emphasis, for user-supplied values (in text or syntax), and for references to publications.
`code`	is used to show example code and SAS System messages that are set off from the text. In most cases, this book uses lowercase type for SAS code, with the exception of some title characters. SAS System messages appear in mixed case.

Example Conventions

Most examples in *Stock Market Analysis Using the SAS System: Portfolio Selection and Evaluation* build upon previous examples. Except where it would be redundant, each example contains

- □ an explanation of the nature of the example

- □ an explanation of the SAS statements and options

- □ the SAS program for you to submit during your interactive SAS session

- □ a sample of the output you should see on your display

- □ a description or an interpretation of the results.

Feedback

If you have comments or suggestions about this book, any other SAS software manual, or the software, we would like to hear from you. You may write us at the Institute or contact us by using one of our electronic mail addresses. Refer to the Your Turn page at the end of this book for information on how to forward your comments to the appropriate division.

Additional Documentation

SAS Institute provides many publications about products of the SAS System and how to use them on specific hosts. For a complete list of SAS publications, you should refer to the current *Publications Catalog*. The catalog is produced twice a year. You can order a free copy of the catalog by writing, calling, or faxing the Institute:

> SAS Institute Inc.
> Book Sales Department
> SAS Campus Drive
> Cary, NC 27513
> Telephone: 919-677-8000
> Fax: 919-677-8166

SAS Software Documentation

In addition to *Stock Market Analysis Using the SAS System: Portfolio Selection and Evaluation* , you will find these other documents helpful when using SAS/STAT and SAS/OR software for stock market analysis:

☐ *SAS/STAT User's Guide, Version 6, Fourth Edition, Volume 1* and *Volume 2* (order #A56045) documents all procedures in Release 6.06 SAS/STAT software.

☐ *SAS/OR User's Guide, Version 6, First Edition* (order #A5850) documents all procedures in Release 6.06 SAS/OR software.

Documentation for Other SAS Software Products

The SAS System includes many software products in addition to SAS/STAT software and SAS/OR software. Several books about other software products that may be of particular interest to you are listed here:

☐ *SAS Language and Procedures: Introduction, Version 6, First Edition* (order #A56074) gets you started if you are unfamiliar with the SAS System.

☐ *SAS Language and Procedures: Usage, Version 6, First Edition* (order #A56075) provides task-oriented examples of the major features of base SAS software.

☐ *SAS Language and Procedures: Usage 2, Version 6, First Edition* (order #A56078) provides additional task-oriented examples of the major features of base SAS software.

☐ *SAS Language: Reference, Version 6, First Edition* (order #A56076) provides detailed reference information about all elements of base SAS software except procedures.

☐ *SAS Procedures Guide, Version 6, Third Edition* (order #A56080) provides detailed reference information about the procedures in base SAS software.

Chapter 1 Background Topics

Introduction

This chapter introduces basic concepts of stock market analysis and discusses stock markets, stock market data, and measures of risk and return.

Typically, the process of stock market analysis follows these general steps:

1. collecting data

2. creating a SAS data set containing your data

3. calculating measures of stock return and risk

4. sorting and clustering stocks by desired financial characteristics

5. assessing the stock's performance in relation to the market portfolio and to other stocks

6. calculating solution values for portfolio weights

7. deciding in which portfolio to invest

8. evaluating the performance of your portfolio.

This chapter shows you how to use the SAS System to perform the first three steps of this analysis. Other chapters discuss the remaining steps.

Hardcopy Data Sets

You can collect stock data and financial information and then create data sets from any source of financial data, including newspapers and magazines, corporate reports, brokerage firm research reports, investment services reports and newsletters, and government publications.

Depending on the intended purpose for your analysis, you may want to create *time-series data sets* (consisting of observations on a single stock across time), *cross-sectional data sets* (consisting of observations at one point in time across many stocks), and *time-series cross-sectional data sets*, also known as *panel data sets* (consisting of observations on multiple stocks across time).

A typical financial page of a major newspaper contains a variety of financial information, including

□ quotations for stocks, stock options, and mutual funds

□ bond yields

□ yields of U.S. Treasury Securities

□ interest rates

□ exchange rates.

Stocks are listed on a variety of exchanges. The exchange on which a stock or mutual fund is listed depends on the dollar value of the firm, its history of earnings, and the number of shares held publicly as well as their market value. The largest firms (in terms of dollar value) are listed on the New York Stock Exchange (NYSE); medium-sized firms are listed on the American Stock Exchange (AMEX); and small firms traded over-the-counter (OTC) are listed by the National Association of Securities Dealers Automated Quotations (NASDAQ). Transactions are regulated by the Securities and Exchange Commission (SEC).

Stock and mutual fund quotations listed in the financial pages of major newspapers often have the following form:

```
Stock   High    Low     Close   Change
XYZ     50 1/8  48      49 1/2  +5/8
```

The quotation is interpreted as follows:

XYZ	is the exchange abbreviation for the XYZ company.
50 1/8	is the daily high price for stock of firm XYZ.
48	is the daily low price for stock of firm XYZ.
49 1/2	is the daily closing price for stock of firm XYZ.
+5/8	indicates that the stock of firm XYZ closed +5/8 higher today than the previous trading day.

Some newspapers and daily journals also list additional information, including the number of shares traded (*volume*), the 52-week high and low, and the rankings based on earnings per share, relative price volatility measures, and relative price-earnings measures.

Data sets in hardcopy form can be typed into or electronically scanned into SAS data sets.

Electronically Stored Data Sets

Data sets created by a variety of software products can be converted to SAS data sets in a SAS DATA step. For examples and discussion, see *SAS Language and Procedures, Usage, Version 6, First Edition* and *SAS Language and Procedures, Usage 2, Version 6, First Edition.*

Economic and financial data files can be read and stored as SAS data sets by the SAS/ETS CITIBASE and DATASOURCE procedures. Data files supported by PROC DATASOURCE include

□ U.S. Bureau of Economic Analysis data files

□ U.S. Bureau of Labor Statistics data files

□ Standard & Poor's Compustat Services Financial Database Files

□ FAME Software Corporation's CITIBASE data files (tape format, old format, and PC diskette format)

□ Center for Research in Security Prices (CRSP) data files

□ Haver Analytics data files

□ International Monetary Fund data files

□ Organization for Economic Cooperation and Development data files.

PROC CITIBASE reads time series from the CITIBASE files and converts them into a SAS data set. Note that the capabilities of PROC CITIBASE are a subset of PROC DATASOURCE. PROC CITIBASE can read

□ tape-format CITIBASE data files

□ diskette-format CITIBASE databases

□ Haver Analytics data files

For more information on the CITIBASE and DATASOURCE procedures, see *SAS/ETS User's Guide, Version 6, Second Edition.*

Single-Period Return Measure

Single-period return measures consist of two parts: income derived from dividends and capital gains (or losses) derived from selling the stock at a greater (lesser) price than the purchase price. When you buy shares of stock (at time $t - 1$), hold them, then sell them (at time t), you earn the difference between the buying price (P_{t-1}) and the selling price (P_t) plus any dividends (D_t) issued for that stock. Returns can be measured as dollar earnings or as a percentage of the amount invested.

Thus, the stock return for the ith stock for the tth period ($R_{i,t}$) is measured as follows (ignoring commission and other brokerage firm charges):

$$R_{i,t} = \frac{P_{i,t} - P_{i,t-1} + D_{i,t}}{P_{i,t-1}}$$

When you expect a stock price to fall, you can sell it, even though you do not own it. Sales of this type are known as *short sales*. Typically, stockbrokers provide the stock required for the short sale, and they request collateral for the period the stock remains short. When you believe the stock price has reached its lowest point, you purchase shares at the lower price. The return on your short sale is calculated as shown in the previous equation.

Introducing the SP1 Data Set

The SP1 data set consists of the Standard and Poor's (S&P) 500 Composite Stock Index for the years 1970 through 1989, where the period 1941 through 1943 is equal to 10 and the stock dividends are in index form. Note that indexes of stocks are typically weighted by dollar value of outstanding shares.

The following DATA step creates the SP1 data set and labels the variables.

Explanation of Syntax

DATA *data-set-name*
> begins the DATA step and creates a SAS data set named by the specified *data-set-name*. For this example, the data set is named SP1.

INPUT
> reads the input data, then creates and names the SAS variables. For this example, the INPUT statement reads the values of the S&P index and creates the variables V and D. The double trailing at symbol (@@) indicates that each line of data contains more than one observation.

LABEL
> labels the variables.

CARDS
> indicates that data lines follow. The semicolon that follows the data lines causes the DATA-step statements to execute.

Example code

```
data sp1;
    input year v d @@;
    label v='End-of-Year Index Value'
          d='Dividends';
cards;
1970  92.15  3.14  1971 102.09  3.07  1972 118.05  3.15
1973  97.55  3.38  1974  68.56  3.60  1975  90.19  3.68
1976 107.46  4.05  1977  95.10  4.67  1978  96.11  5.07
1979 107.94  5.70  1980 135.76  6.16  1981 122.55  6.63
1982 140.64  6.87  1983 164.93  7.09  1984 167.24  7.53
1985 211.28  7.90  1986 242.17  8.28  1987 247.08  8.81
1988 277.72  9.73  1989 353.40 11.05
;
run;
```

You print variables in the SP1 data set with the PRINT procedure. The following statements print the first five observations. The results are shown in Output 1.1.

Explanation of syntax

PROC PRINT
>invokes the PRINT procedure. The following options of the PROC PRINT statement are specified:

>DATA=   specifies the data set to be printed. This example specifies the SP1 data set. The OBS=*n* option specifies that the first *n* observations be printed. In this example, the OBS= option specifies that the first five observations be printed.

>LABEL   specifies that the variable labels be printed.

VAR
>specifies the variables to be printed.

TITLE
>titles the output. In this example, three title statements are used; however, you can use up to ten title statements. In interactive SAS sessions, TITLE statements remain in effect until they are changed or until the SAS session ends.

Example code

```
proc print data=sp1(obs=5) label;
   var year v d;
   title 'Background Topics';
   title2 'Printing the SP1 Data Set';
   title3 'First Five Observations';
run;
```

Output 1.1
First Five
Observations of the
SP1 Data Set

```
                        Background Topics
                     Printing the SP1 Data Set
                      First Five Observations


                            End-of-Year
          OBS    YEAR      Index Value    Dividends

           1     1970         92.15         3.14
           2     1971        102.09         3.07
           3     1972        118.05         3.15
           4     1973         97.55         3.38
           5     1974         68.56         3.60
```

Interpretation of output

In Output 1.1, the values of the first five observations of the variables YEAR, V, and D are printed. By printing data sets, you can check for coding errors in the input values and for the appropriate number of observations.

Plotting the SP1 Data Set

Plotting the data versus time is often the first step in analyzing a time-series data set. You use the PLOT procedure to create scatter plots. The following PROC PLOT statements plot the Standard and Poor's Index values and the dividend values versus time in years. The results are printed in Output 1.2.

Explanation of syntax

PROC PLOT
> invokes the PLOT procedure. The following options of the PROC PLOT statement are specified.

> DATA=   specifies the data set to be used.

> VPCT=   specifies the percentage of the SAS output page for the vertical height of the plot.

PLOT
> specifies the vertical axis variable to be plotted versus the horizontal axis variable. In this example, two PLOT statements are used to request one plot each.

Example Code

```
proc plot data=sp1 vpct=150;
   plot v*year;
   plot d*year;
   title2 'Plotting Data Values versus Year';
   title3;
run;
```

Output 1.2
Plotting Index and
Dividend Values
versus Time in Years

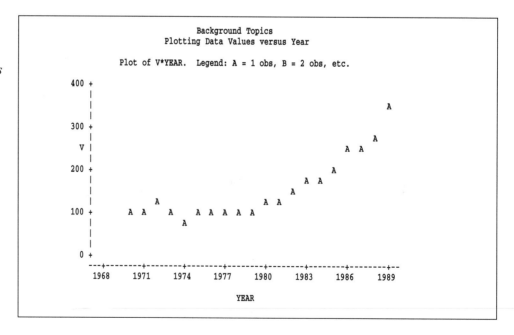

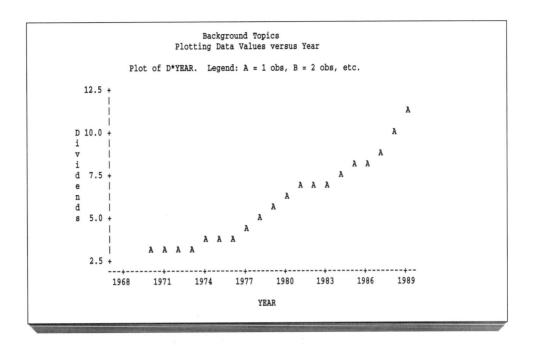

Interpretation of output

The two plots in Output 1.2 indicate that both the Index values and the dividend values are following an overall upward trend. In general, plotting data can reveal trends and seasonal variation, which may be important for later analysis.

Calculating Single-Period Returns

You calculate the single-period returns in a DATA step. The SET statement reads observations from the specified data set. In the following example, observations are read from the SP1 data set. The assignment statements create new variables using the previously created variables and DATA-step functions. In this example, three new variables are created: V_1, R, and R_PER. V_1 is the lagged value of V; R is the returns; and R_PER is R in percentage terms. The input data, the variables used for intermediate calculations, and the returns are printed in Output 1.3.

```
    /* Calculating the Single Period Returns */
data sp2;
   set sp1;
   v_1=lag(v);
   r=(v-v_1+d)/v_1;
   r_per=r*100;
   label v_1='Lagged Index Value'
         r='Returns'
         r_per='Percentage Returns';
run;

    /* Printing Single Period Returns */
proc print data=sp2 label;
   var year v v_1 d r r_per;
   title2 'Printing the Single Period Returns';
run;
```

Output 1.3
Raw Data,
Intermediate Steps,
and Single-Period
Returns

```
                              Background Topics
                      Printing the Single Period Returns

                                   Lagged
                     End-of-Year    Index                        Percentage
     OBS    YEAR     Index Value    Value    Dividends  Returns    Returns

      1     1970       92.15          .        3.14        .           .
      2     1971      102.09        92.15      3.07     0.14118     14.1183
      3     1972      118.05       102.09      3.15     0.18719     18.7188
      4     1973       97.55       118.05      3.38    -0.14502    -14.5023
      5     1974       68.56        97.55      3.60    -0.26028    -26.0277
      6     1975       90.19        68.56      3.68     0.36917     36.9166
      7     1976      107.46        90.19      4.05     0.23639     23.6390
      8     1977       95.10       107.46      4.67    -0.07156     -7.1562
      9     1978       96.11        95.10      5.07     0.06393      6.3933
     10     1979      107.94        96.11      5.70     0.18240     18.2395
     11     1980      135.76       107.94      6.16     0.31480     31.4805
     12     1981      122.55       135.76      6.63    -0.04847     -4.8468
     13     1982      140.64       122.55      6.87     0.20367     20.3672
     14     1983      164.93       140.64      7.09     0.22312     22.3123
     15     1984      167.24       164.93      7.53     0.05966      5.9662
     16     1985      211.28       167.24      7.90     0.31057     31.0572
     17     1986      242.17       211.28      8.28     0.18539     18.5394
     18     1987      247.08       242.17      8.81     0.05665      5.6654
     19     1988      277.72       247.08      9.73     0.16339     16.3388
     20     1989      353.40       277.72     11.05     0.31229     31.2293
```

Interpretation of output

In Output 1.3, the values of the input data and the annual returns are printed. Note that missing values are represented by a period ("."). Missing values appear for the 1970 values of the return and percentage return because those values depend on the lagged index value, which is also missing.

Also note that the Standard and Poor's 500 Composite Index has annual returns that range from a low of -.26028 (in 1974) to a high of .36917 (in 1975). Holding stocks (or a portfolio of stocks) over time raises questions such as "What is the average return over multiple periods?" and "How does compounding affect the average return over multiple periods?" The section "Multiple-Period Return Measures," later in this chapter, presents multiple-period return measures.

Plotting Returns

After calculating returns, you may want to use PROC PLOT to plot them versus time to visually assess trends across time. The following PROC PLOT statements plot the returns versus time in years. The VREF= option specifies that a vertical reference line be drawn perpendicular to the vertical axis at the specified value, which for this example is zero. The results are shown in Output 1.4.

```
proc plot data=sp2 vpct=150;
   plot r*year / vref=0;
   title2 'Plotting Returns versus Year';
run;
```

Output 1.4
Plotting Returns
versus Time in Years

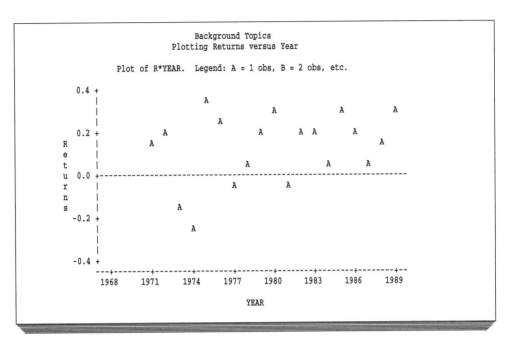

Interpretation of output

In Output 1.4, the plot of the returns versus time shows that there are more positive returns than negative returns and that there are no obvious trends across time. The plot also suggests the possibility of greater dispersion in the data in the 1970s than in the 1980s, and further analysis would be required to corroborate the visual assessment.

Multiple-Period Return Measures

Multiple-period return measures involve calculating arithmetic and geometric averages from the single-period returns. Thus, in assessing stock returns over several periods, the following measures are of interest.

□   The *arithmetic mean* (AM) is simply the sum of the returns over several time periods divided by the number of individual returns (T). The arithmetic mean measures the average (or typical) return over individual periods.

$$AM = \frac{1}{T} \sum_{i=1}^{T} R_i$$

□   The *wealth index* (WEALTH) indicates the wealth generated (or lost) by investing. For example, if you invest \$1 in shares of a stock at the beginning of the year, the wealth index (over the 12 monthly returns or 52 weekly returns) indicates the value at the end of the year. If the wealth index is greater than unity, the value of the portfolio increased. If the wealth index is less than unity, the value of the portfolio decreased. The wealth index for T periods is calculated by the following equation:

$$WEALTH = \left(1 + R_1\right) \times \left(1 + R_2\right) \times \ldots \times \left(1 + R_T\right)$$

Note that the wealth index is also equal to the ending-period value of the investment (W_T) divided by the initial investment (W_0):

$$WEALTH = \frac{W_T}{W_0}$$

□ The *geometric mean* reflects compound, cumulative returns over time and, over *T* periods, is defined as follows:

$$Geometric\ Mean = \left[\left(1 + R_1\right) \times \left(1 + R_2\right) \times \ldots \times \left(1 + R_T\right)\right]^{1/T}$$

$$Geometric\ Mean = \left(WEALTH\right)^{1/T}$$

You use the geometric mean of the returns to calculate the average rate of return over multiple periods. The average compound return (GM) measure for *T* periods is calculated as follows:

$$GM = \left[\left(1 + R_1\right) \times \left(1 + R_2\right) \times \ldots \times \left(1 + R_T\right)\right]^{1/T} - 1$$

$$GM = \left(WEALTH\right)^{1/T} - 1$$

Calculating Multiple-Period Return Measures

You can calculate multiple-period return measures for the SP2 data set. For example, suppose you want to calculate the wealth index, the arithmetic and geometric mean measures, and the percentage values of the mean measures for the period 1985 through 1989 for the data in the SP2 data set. To perform this task,

1. use a DATA step to create a new data set containing the proper subset of the data

2. use the TRANSPOSE procedure to transpose the data for ease in calculation

3. use a second DATA step to calculate the return measures.

Subsetting a Data Set

The following DATA step creates a new data set containing the data for the years 1985 through 1989.

Explanation of syntax

DATA
    begins the DATA STEP and creates a new data set named SP3.

SET
    reads observations from the specified data set. In this example, observations are read from the SP2 data set.

WHERE
    specifies a condition that the data must satisfy before the observations are processed. Using the WHERE statement improves the efficiency of your SAS programs because

only the qualifying observations are read from the input data set. In this example, the where condition for reading observations is that the value for the variable YEAR be greater than or equal to 1985.

Example code

```
data sp3;
   set sp2;
   where year ge 1985;
run;
```

These statements produce no printed output.

Transposing a Data Set

You use PROC TRANSPOSE to transpose data sets. When a data set is transposed, its rows become columns and its columns become rows. In terms of SAS data sets, the observations become variables and the variables become observations. The following statements transpose the SP3 data set.

Explanation of syntax

PROC TRANSPOSE
   invokes the TRANSPOSE procedure.

   DATA=   specifies the data set to be transposed.

   OUT=   creates and names the output data set.

VAR
   specifies the variables to be transposed.

Example code

```
proc transpose data=sp3 out=sp4;
   var r;
run;
```

You print the SP4 data set with the following PROC PRINT statements. Output 1.5 shows the results of this example.

```
proc print data=sp4;
   title2 'Printing the SP4 Data Set';
run;
```

Output 1.5
Printing the SP4
Data Set

```
                              Background Topics
                           Printing the SP4 Data Set

    OBS    _NAME_    _LABEL_     COL1      COL2       COL3      COL4      COL5

     1       R       Returns    0.31057   0.18539   0.056654   0.16339   0.31229
```

Interpretation of output

In Output 1.5, the values of the SP4 data set are printed. PROC TRANSPOSE labels the columns (that is, the variables) of the transposed data set, COL1 through COL*n*. For this example, the variables labeled COL1 through COL5 represent the index returns from 1985 through 1989.

Calculating Return Measures

You can calculate the following multiple-period measures of return using a DATA step and the SP4 data set:

□ wealth index (WEALTH)

□ arithmetic mean in level form (AM)

□ arithmetic mean in percentage form (AM_PCT)

□ average compound rate of return in level form (GM)

□ average compound rate of return in percentage form (GM_PCT)

The following DATA step performs these calculations. The variables C1 through C5 are created for ease in calculating the wealth index and the average compound rate of return.

```
data sp5;
   set sp4;
   t=5;
   c1=col1+1;
   c2=col2+1;
   c3=col3+1;
   c4=col4+1;
   c5=col5+1;
   wealth=(c1*c2*c3*c4*c5);
   gm=((wealth)**(1/t))-1;
   gm_pct=gm*100;
   am=mean(of col1-col5);
   am_pct=am*100;
run;
```

For larger numbers of variables, array processing is a more efficient way of coding. The following DATA step performs the same tasks using array processing in an iterative DO loop. The variables C1 through C5 are created from the variables COL1 through COL5.

Explanation of syntax

ARRAY

creates a temporary grouping of variables. Arrays enable you to efficiently apply the same process to each of the variables in the group. A simple ARRAY statement has the following form:

ARRAY *array-name* {*number-of-elements*} *list-of-variables*;

In this example, two arrays are created (COL and C); each consists of five variables.

DO ... END

specifies that the same action be performed several times. An iterative DO loop begins with an iterative DO statement, contains other SAS statements, and ends with an END statement, as shown in the following syntax:

DO *index-variable=1* TO *number-of-variables-in-array*;
  more SAS statements
END;

Example code

```
data sp5a;
   set sp4;
   t=5;
   array col(5) col1-col5;
   array c(5) c1-c5;
   do i=1 to 5;
      c(i) = col(i) + 1;
   end;
   wealth=(c1*c2*c3*c4*c5);
   gm=(wealth**(1/t))-1;
   gm_pct=gm*100;
   am=mean(of col1-col5);
   am_pct=am*100;
run;
```

For more information on ARRAY processing in iterative DO loops, see *SAS Language, Reference, Version 6, First Edition* (pages 160-171) and *SAS Language and Procedures, Usage* (pages 178-182), and *SAS Language and Procedures, Usage 2* (pages 143 and 144).

The following PROC PRINT statements print the multiple-period return measures.

```
proc print data=sp5;
   var wealth gm gm_pct am am_pct;
   title2 'Multiple Period Return Measures';
run;
```

Output 1.6
Multiple-Period
Return Measures

```
                              Background Topics
                        Multiple Period Return Measures

        OBS     WEALTH      GM       GM_PCT      AM       AM_PCT

         1     2.50618   0.20172   20.1717   0.20566   20.5660
```

Interpretation of output

In Output 1.6, the return measures are printed. The wealth index value (WEALTH) of 2.50618 indicates that $1 invested in the Standard & Poor's 500 Composite Stock Index in 1985 would have grown to about $2.51 by 1989. So for example, if you had invested $25,000 in the S&P Index in 1985, your investment would have grown to $62,654.50 in 1989.

Both the arithmetic mean (AM) and the average compound growth rate (GM) are over .20, while the percentage values (AM_PCT and GM_PCT) are over 20 percent. These values indicate that the average growth rate for an investment in the S&P Index was over 20 percent per year.

Calculating Expected Returns

Stock analysts calculate past stock returns to evaluate the historical performance of stocks, which provides a benchmark measure for future returns. But for the purpose of investment, stock analysts need to estimate future returns.

You can pursue many approaches for estimating the level of future returns, including those in the following table:

Table 1.1   *Approaches for Calculating Expected Returns*

Approach	Appropriate if research indicates...	To follow this approach, use...
Use the mean value of past returns.	distribution of returns is constant and future returns are expected to be quite similar to the average of past returns.	PROC MEANS
Calculate the mean value from a discrete distribution.	a set of particular values and probabilities for their occurrence.	DATA step and PROC MEANS
Calculate a growth rate and extrapolate into the future.	past growth trends are stable and will continue in the future.	DATA step
Fit a regression model and use the forecasted values.	returns are correlated with one or more variables so that as these variables change, the returns also change.	PROC REG, PROC MODEL, or PROC SYSLIN
Fit a time series model to the past values and forecast future values.	returns have seasonal patterns or identifiable trends over time.	PROC ARIMA, PROC AUTOREG, or PROC FORECAST

This section discusses the first three approaches, while the fourth approach is discussed in Chapter 4, "The Capital Asset Pricing Model (CAPM)." (The last approach is beyond the scope of this text.)

Calculating Mean Return Values

You can use the MEANS procedure to calculate the mean and other statistical summary measures. The following statements calculate the mean values for the variables R and R_PER from the SP3 data set. The results are shown in Output 1.7.

Explanation of syntax

PROC MEANS
invokes the MEANS procedure. The following options of the PROC MEANS statement are specified.

DATA=   specfies the data set to be used in the analysis.

MEAN   specifies that the mean values be calculated for the listed variables.

VAR
specifies the variables to be used in the analysis.

Example code

```
proc means data=sp3 mean;
   var r r_per;
   title2 'Mean Returns';
run;
```

Output 1.7
Arithmetic Mean
Return in Level and
Percentage Form

```
                        Background Topics
                          Mean Returns

         Variable  Label                      Mean
         -----------------------------------------
         R         Returns              0.2056602
         R_PER     Return Percentage   20.5660235
         -----------------------------------------
```

Interpretation of output

In Output 1.7, the return measures are printed. These are the same values calculated in Output 1.6 for the variables AM and AM_PCT. However, in Output 1.6 additional values were calculated (GM, GM_PCT, and WEALTH). For larger data sets, and for the calculation of summary statistics, PROC MEANS is more efficient.

Calculating the Mean of a Discrete Distribution

Your research may indicate that a stock has returns that follow a discrete distribution. That is, you expect the stock to have returns of various amounts with specified probabilities (and the probabilities are nonnegative and sum to unity). For example, you may expect returns of a stock to be .02 with a 20 percent chance, .015 with a 40 percent chance, and .01 with a 40 percent chance. The mean of this discrete distribution is

$$Mean\,Return = (.02 \times .2) + (.015 \times .4) + (.01 \times .4)$$

$$Mean\,Return = .004 + .006 + .004 = .014 \; or \; 1.4\%$$

The calculations for one stock are trivial; however, your analysis may involve hundreds or even thousands of stocks. The following table shows multiple stocks, where the returns are expected to follow the listed values with the specified probabilities:

Table 1.2
*Discrete
Distribution of Stock
Returns and
Specified
Probabilities*

	Probabilities			
Return	**Stock 1**	**Stock 2**	**Stock 3**	**Stock 4**
-.10	0	.05	0	0
-.05	.05	.10	0	.10
0	.25	.20	.20	.10
.05	.40	.30	.30	.20
.10	.20	.20	.30	.30
.15	.10	.10	.20	.20
.20	0	.05	0	.10

Each stock has its own discrete distribution of returns. The expected return for each stock is the mean of its discrete distribution, which is the sum of a linear combination of the returns ($R_{i,j}$) and their respective probabilities ($P_{i,j}$). Thus, the mean return of a discrete distribution of expected returns for the *i*th stock is

$$Mean\ Return_i = \sum_{j=1}^{J} P_{i,j} \times R_{i,j} \quad .$$

To calculate the mean of a discrete distribution, use the DATA step and PROC MEANS. The following DATA step creates the D1 data set and uses array processing to calculate linear combinations (LC1 through LC4) of the returns (R) and the probabilities (P1 through P4). The results are not shown.

```
data d1;
   input r p1 p2 p3 p4;
   array p(4) p1-p4;
   array lc(4) lc1-lc4;
   do i=1 to 4;
      lc(i)=r*p(i);
   end;
cards;
 -.10   0   .05   0    0
 -.05  .05  .10   0   .10
   0   .25  .20  .20  .10
```

```
.05   .40   .30   .30   .20
.10   .20   .20   .30   .30
.15   .10   .10   .20   .20
.20    0    .05    0    .10
;
```

The following PROC MEANS statements calculate the mean values. The results are shown in Output 1.8.

Explanation of syntax

PROC MEANS
> invokes the MEANS procedure. The following options of the PROC MEANS statement are specified:

> SUM
>> sums the observations of the listed variables. For this example, the variables LC1-LC4 are summed. They are the product of the returns and probabilities.

> NOPRINT
>> suppresses the printed output.

OUTPUT
> creates the output data set OUT_D1, which is named in the OUT= option. OUT_D1 contains the mean values for the variables MEAN1_MEAN4.

Example code

```
proc means data=d1 sum noprint;
   var lc1-lc4;
   output out=out_d1 sum=mean1-mean4;
run;

proc print data=out_d1;
   var mean1-mean4;
   title2 'Discrete Distribution Mean Returns';
run;
```

Output 1.8
Discrete
Distribution Mean
Returns

```
                    Background Topics
              Discrete Distribution Mean Returns

      OBS     MEAN1     MEAN2     MEAN3     MEAN4

       1      0.0525    0.05      0.075     0.085
```

Using a Growth Rate to Calculate Expected Returns

Your research may indicate that the returns of a stock have grown at a constant rate and appear to be continuing at that rate. This growth rate can be used to calculate values for future returns. For example, you can use the last return value in the series and multiply it by the sum of the growth rate plus 1 to calculate the next value in the series.

There are several growth rates that may be appropriate, including the following:

□   arithmetic mean in level form (AM, as discussed previously)

□   average compound rate of return in level form (GM, as discussed previously)

□   linear or higher-order polynomial functions of time

□   nonlinear functions of time; for example, logistic curves.

The first two growth rates listed are calculated in the statements producing Output 1.6; the third approach is discussed in Chapter 2 for dividend growth rates; while the fourth approach is beyond the scope of this book.

This example uses the first two growth rates listed. The SP5 data set is used for illustrative purposes. Note that the returns in the SP5 data set have not grown at a constant rate, as shown previously in the plot of Output 1.4.

Use the following DATA step to calculate these growth rates and to calculate returns for the next year. Note that the variable COL5 contains the return for the last period in the series, 1989. The future return values are printed using PROC PRINT in Output 1.9.

```
   /* Calculating Next Period's Return */
data sp6;
   set sp5;
   r_am = col5*(am+1);
   r_gm = col5*(gm+1);
run;

   /* Printing Calculated Returns */
proc print data=sp6;
   var col5 r_am r_gm;
   title2 'Future Returns';
   title3 'Calculating with Past Growth Rates';
run;
```

Output 1.9
1989 Return (COL5)
and 1990 Returns
Calculated from
Constant Growth
Rate

```
                       Background Topics
                         Future Returns
                Calculating with Past Growth Rates

        OBS      COL5        R_AM        R_GM

         1      0.31229     0.37652     0.37529
```

Interpretation of output

In Output 1.9, the 1989 return value (labeled COL5) and the calculated return values for 1990 (R_AM and R_GM) are printed. By either growth rate (arithmetic average or annually compounded), the future value is the largest in the series over the period 1970-1990, as shown previously in Output 1.3.

This approach should be used with constant-growth return series and for calculating the next-period return value. This approach should **not** be used with return series that grow at different rates, nor for calculating expected returns far into the future. For example, if this approach were used (with this data set) to calculate the return values for the year 2000, the expected returns are well over 225 percent.

Risk Measures

Knowing the past returns and the expected return for financially investing in a stock is rarely sufficient. Stock analysts realize that risk accompanies investments. Investors weigh the expected returns and risk in making investment decisions.

Investment literature classifies risk into categories, including

□ *systematic* or *market risk*, which is risk associated with the movements of the market portfolio (for example, the Standard & Poor's 500 or the Dow Jones Industrials). Systematic risk is also known as *nondiversifiable risk* because owning additional assets cannot reduce this risk; that is, it **cannot** be diversified away.

□ *nonsystematic* or *nonmarket risk*, which is risk associated with factors other than the movement of the market (for example, industry and firm-specific factors that affect stock returns). Nonsystematic risk is also known as *diversifiable risk* because owning additional assets reduces this risk; that is, it **can** be diversified away.

□ additional risk catagories:

Interest Rate Risk
is fluctuations of interest rates that affect the present values of future returns. As interest rates increase (decrease), the present value of a future return decreases (increases). Interest rate fluctuations affect a firm's decision to finance operations by stock issues or bond issues and the mix of the two. In general, the larger and more rapid the shifts in interest rates, the greater the effect on investors' calculations.

Inflation Risk
is fluctuations of inflation rates that affect the purchasing power of currencies. The larger and more unexpected the change in the inflation rate, the greater the impact on investors' decisions and their evaluation of previous investments.

Currency Risk
is fluctuations of relative currency values (through changes in exchange rates) that affect international investing decisions. Currency appreciation and depreciation can greatly affect the returns received by the investor.

Total risk includes all the components of risk and is typically measured by the standard deviation of the distribution of returns. Often, investors use past returns as a representative sampling of the distribution of returns. Alternatively, you may want to use a discrete distribution of future returns (that is, specific returns with specified probabilities). The following sections present an example of each.

Calculating Risk from Historical Data

For stock analysts, risk is most often measured by the standard deviation of a stock's returns. The standard deviation is the square root of the variance, and the sample variance is defined as follows:

$$\sigma^2 = \frac{1}{T-1} \sum_{t=1}^{T} \left(R_t - \overline{R} \right)^2$$

You can calculate the standard deviation of the returns in the SP3 data set using PROC MEANS. The following PROC MEANS statements calculate the mean, variance, and standard deviation with the MEAN, VAR, and STD options, respectively. The results are printed in Output 1.10.

```
proc means data=sp3 mean var std;
    var r;
    title2 'Mean, Variance, and Standard Deviation';
    title3;
run;
```

Output 1.10
Mean, Variance,
and Standard
Deviation

```
                        Background Topics
                 Mean, Variance, and Standard Deviation

                 Analysis Variable : R Returns

                     Mean       Variance      Std Dev
              ----------------------------------------
                 0.2056602     0.0116943     0.1081403
              ----------------------------------------
```

Calculating Risk from Discrete Distribution

A measure of expected risk can be obtained by listing the expected returns ($R_{i,j}$) and the probabilities (P) of achieving them and then calculating the standard deviation of the distribution. For example, you calculate the risk (standard deviation) of the stock returns listed in the D1 data set with the following formula:

$$Risk = \sigma = \sqrt{\sum_{j=1}^{J} P_{i,j} \times \left(R_{i,j} - \overline{R}_{i,j}\right)^2}$$

You use the DATA step and PROC MEANS in the following steps to calculate the risk level (standard deviation) of a discrete distribution of expected returns. For this example, you use the returns and probabilities of the four stocks in the D1 data set and the distribution mean values contained in the OUT_D1 data set:

Tasks performed by the Program

1. Use a DATA step to create additional observations of the OUT_D1 data, which contains the mean values. For this example, there are seven observations in the D1 data set; therefore, you need seven observations in the OUT_D1 data set.

2. Use another DATA step to merge the D1 and OUT_D2 data sets, and use array processing in an iterative DO LOOP to create the intermediate-step variables VV1 through VV4.

3. Use PROC MEANS to sum the intermediate-step variables for calculating the variances and to store them in an output data set, OUT_D3.

4. Use array processing in a third DATA step to calculate the square root of the variances, which are the standard deviations.

5. Use PROC PRINT to print the variances and standard deviations.

Example code

```
     /* Creating Additional Observations of Mean Values */
data out_d2;
   set out_d1;
   do i=1 to 7;
      output;
   end;
run;

     /* Merging Data Sets */
data d2;
   merge d1 out_d2;
   array p(4) p1-p4;
   array m(4) mean1-mean4;
   array vv(4) vv1-vv4;
   do i=1 to 4;
      vv(i)=p(i)*(r-m(i))**2;
   end;
run;

     /* Calculating Variances */
proc means data=d2 sum noprint;
   var vv1-vv4;
   output out=out_d3 sum=var1-var4;
run;

     /* Printing the Variances */
proc print data=out_d3;
   var var1-var4;
   title2 'Discrete Distribution Variance';
run;
```

Output 1.11
Discrete
Distribution
Variances

```
                        Background Topics
                 Discrete Distribution Variance

        OBS      VAR1       VAR2       VAR3       VAR4

         1      .0026188    .00525    .002625    .005025
```

```
     /* Calculating Standard Deviations */
data d3;
   set out_d3;
   array vv(4) var1-var4;
   array stt(4) std1-std4;
   do i=1 to 4;
      stt(i)=sqrt(vv(i));
```

```
        end;
    run;

        /* Printing Standard Deviations */
    proc print data=d3;
        var std1-std4;
        title2 'Discrete Distribution Standard Deviation';
    run;
```

Output 1.12
Discrete
Distribution
Standard Deviations

```
                            Background Topics
                Discrete Distribution Standard Deviation

        OBS      STD1       STD2       STD3       STD4

         1     0.051174   0.072457   0.051235   0.070887
```

Interpretation of output

In Outputs 1.11 and 1.12, the variances and standard deviations for the discrete distributions of the D1 data set are printed. The variances are the square of the standard deviations. You can use the expected stock returns and the risk level to analyze investment decisions, compare stocks, and create portfolios. These tasks are discussed in later chapters.

Learning More

□ For more information on the DATA step, see *SAS Language, Reference, Version 6, First Edition*; *SAS Language and Procedures, Usage, Version 6, First Edition*; and *SAS Language and Procedures, Usage 2, Version 6, First Edition*.

□ For more information on the MEANS, PLOT, PRINT, and TRANSPOSE procedures, see *SAS Procedures Guide, Version 6, Third Edition* and *SAS Language and Procedures, Usage 2*.

□ For more information on PROC REG, see *SAS/STAT User's Guide, Version 6, Fourth Edition, Volume 1* and *Volume 2*.

□ For more information on the ARIMA, AUTOREG, CITIBASE, DATASOURCE, FORECAST, MODEL, and SYSLIN procedures, see *SAS/ETS User's Guide, Version 6, Second Edition*; *SAS/ETS Software: Applications Guide 1*; and *SAS/ETS Software: Applications Guide 2*.

References

Elton, E. and Gruber, M. (1987), *Modern Portfolio Theory and Investment Analysis, Third Edition*, New York: John Wiley & Sons, Inc.

Hagin, R. (1979), *Modern Portfolio Theory*, Homewood, Illinois: Dow Jones-Irwin.

Jones, C. (1991), *Investments: Analysis and Management, Third Edition*, New York: John Wiley & Sons, Inc.

Chapter 2 Discounted Cash Flow (DCF) Analysis

Introduction

This chapter discusses discounted cash flow (DCF) analysis of stocks and shows you how to use SAS software to perform DCF analysis. The chapter also shows a technique for identifying undervalued and overvalued stocks.

Discounted cash flow analysis is based on the present value of the company's expected future earnings. Dividends represent the portion of cash flows (earnings) that are distributed to stock holders. The value (or price) of stock reflects the market's expectation of future dividends. In general, the price of a stock is expressed in the following present value (DCF) equation.

$$V = \frac{D_1}{(1 + K)} + \frac{D_2}{(1 + K)^2} + \frac{D_3}{(1 + K)^3} + \ldots + \frac{D_\infty}{(1 + K)^\infty}$$

The variables are defined as follows:

V   represents the value (or price) per share of stock.

D_i represents the dividends for the *i*th period. (Dividends may be constant for all time periods or they may vary.)

K   represents the appropriate discount rate in decimal form. Commonly used discount rates are expected or realized bond yields and the prime interest rate (the interest rate banks offer their largest and best customers).

Note that the general DCF equation is an infinite series. However, if you believe there is a date when the firm will cease to exist, then the series would end at that period. Formulated as an infinite series the DCF equation is difficult to use. But by making assumptions about the firm, its dividend policy, and the future of the firm and the market, the DCF equation can be simplified and used to value securities. The following sections show you how to use the SAS System to value stocks with DCF methodology under the following assumptions:

□   fixed-dollar dividends

□   constant-growth dividends

□   two periods of different dividend growth.

This chapter also shows you how to use calculated dividend growth rates to identify underpriced and overpriced stocks.

Fixed-Dollar Dividends

Some firms have a policy of paying fixed-dollar dividends over time. This policy may be followed to demonstrate financial stability under changing market conditions.

If a firm pays a fixed-dollar dividend, all of the numerator terms of the DCF equation are the same, and summing the infinite series yields

$$V = \frac{D}{K} \quad .$$

Examples of firms paying a fixed-dollar dividend on their common stock are listed in the following table, along with the dividend amount and the time period (ending in 1990):

Table 2.1
Common Stocks with
Fixed-Dollar
Dividends

Firm	Annual Dividend	Time Period
Public Service Colorado	2.00	1986-1990
Puget Sound Power	1.76	1982-1990
WA Water Power	2.48	1983-1990

(continued)

Table 2.1
(continued)

Firm	Annual Dividend	Time Period
Wendy's International	0.24	1987-1990
Westcoast Energy	0.80	1987-1990
Whirlpool	1.10	1987-1990
Williams Companies	1.40	1985-1990
Wyle Laboratories	0.28	1988-1990
Xerox	3.00	1982-1990

DCF analysis can be used to calculate the value of these stocks at the end of 1990.

Calculating DCF Values from Fixed-Dollar Dividends

You can use a DATA step, the PRINT procedure, and the realized yield (.0932) of AAA grade bonds in 1990 as the appropriate discount rate to perform the DCF analysis. The ROUND function rounds the calculated value to the nearest specified amount; for this example, the specified amount is thousandths.

```
data dcf1;
    input firm $20. d hi lo;
        k=.0932;
        v=round(d/k, .001);
    label d='Dividend'
          v='Value'
           hi='High Price 1990'
           lo='Low Price 1990';
    cards;
Pub Service Colorado  2.00 26.500 20.000
Puget Sound Power     1.76 22.500 18.625
WA Water Power        2.48 31.000 26.875
Wendy's               0.24  7.500  3.875
Westcoast Energy      0.80 19.625 16.750
Whirlpool             1.10 33.500 17.500
Williams Companies    1.40 40.625 23.125
Wyle Laboratories     0.28 15.125  8.750
Xerox                 3.00 58.875 29.000
;

proc print data=dcf1 label;
    var firm d hi v lo;
    title 'DCF Analysis';
    title2 'Fixed Dollar Dividends';
run;
```

Output 2.1
DCF Value of
Fixed-Dollar
Dividend Stocks

```
                                    DCF Analysis
                               Fixed Dollar Dividends

                                          High              Low
                                          Price             Price
          OBS    FIRM            Dividend  1990     Value    1990

           1   Pub Service Colorado  2.00   26.500  21.459  20.000
           2   Puget Sound Power     1.76   22.500  18.884  18.625
           3   WA Water Power        2.48   31.000  26.609  26.875
           4   Wendy's               0.24    7.500   2.575   3.875
           5   Westcoast Energy      0.80   19.625   8.584  16.750
           6   Whirlpool             1.10   33.500  11.803  17.500
           7   Williams Companies    1.40   40.625  15.021  23.125
           8   Wyle Laboratories     0.28   15.125   3.004   8.750
           9   Xerox                 3.00   58.875  32.189  29.000
```

Interpretation of output

Output 2.1 shows the value of the fixed-dollar dividend common stocks as well as a comparison of the 1990 high and low values.

Notice that the DCF values of three firms (Public Service of Colorado, Puget Sound Power, and Xerox) are between the 1990 high and low prices, and the DCF values of the remaining six firms are below the 1990 low prices. These DCF values are based on the assumption that dividends are a fixed-dollar amount while all DCF values are sensitive to the discount rate used.

If you are satisfied with the DCF analysis and believe that these are the correct values, you can draw conclusions about the prices of these stocks and formulate investment strategies. For example, if you believe that Wyle Laboratories will again pay annual dividends of $.28, and the appropriate discount rate is the realized yield .0932 on AAA bonds, you can conclude that the stock's intrinsic value is about $3.00 per share. Under these assumptions, Wyle Laboratories stock is sold at prices higher than expected. If you believe the stock is actually overpriced and a market correction is due, then you can profit from selling it short.

Constant-Growth Dividends

Some firms maintain a policy of constant dividend growth over time. Each year, such a firm increases dividends by a certain amount or by a certain percentage. If a firm tends to pay out the same percentage of earnings as dividends and earns a stable return on new equity investments over time, the DCF model can be simplified to the constant dividend growth form.

Under these conditions, the general DCF equation can be summed to yield

$$V = \frac{D_1}{K - G} \quad .$$

In this equation, G is the constant growth rate of dividends, and the numerator is the next-period dividend D_1. If G is known, then D_1 is the product of the current dividend D_0 times the sum of G plus one:

$$D_1 = D_0 \times (G + 1)$$

The DCF values generated by this methodology depend on the calculated dividend growth rate and the discount rate. There are several approaches to calculating dividend growth rates, including

□ fitting a polynomial regression model of dividends (in levels) to time. The simplest polynomial model is a linear model, in which the estimated slope parameter associated with the independent variable is the growth rate. For higher-order polynomial models, the derivative of dividends with respect to time is the growth rate. This method is appropriate if your research shows that dividends grow over time by a constant dollar amount or by an amount defined by a functional form of time.

□ fitting a semi-log regression model of dividends to time, where the natural logarithm of dividends is regressed against time in years. The estimated slope parameter is the growth rate. This method is appropriate if your research shows that dividends grow over time at a constant percentage.

□ calculating the compound growth rate over the period. This approach is appropriate if your research shows that dividends grow at a compound rate.

The next section explores which growth-rate approach is appropriate based on visual and statistical evidence.

Plotting Dividends

Plotting the dividends in levels and in natural logarithms versus time provides visual evidence as to the choice of approach for calculating dividend growth rates. This section shows you how to use the PLOT procedure to create scatter plots.

Plotting Dividends in Levels

To begin the constant-dividend, growth rate DCF analysis, you use the DATA step to create a data set, named DCF2, containing the dividends. Natural logarithms of the dividends are created in the DATA step for use in the section, "Plotting Dividends in Semi-Log Form." Then you use the PLOT procedure to plot dividends versus time.

The following statements are used to create the DCF2 data set, which contains annual stock dividends for 23 firms for the period 1981-1990.

Explanation of syntax

DATA
> begins a DATA step and provides names for any output SAS data sets. In this example, the SAS data set DCF2 is created.

INPUT
> describes the arrangement of values in observations and assigns input values to the corresponding SAS variables. In this example, the input variables are YEAR and STOCK1-STOCK23.

ARRAY
> defines the elements of an explicit array. You use array processing to apply the same process to a group of variables. In this example, arrays are created for the variables STOCK1-STOCK23 and the natural logarithmic transformations LSTOCK1-LSTOCK23.

DO . . . END

The iterative DO statement causes the statements between DO and END statements to be executed repetitively based on the value of the index variable. In the following example, the index variable is I, and I ranges from 1 to 23. This example uses an iterative DO loop, array processing, and the LOG function to transform the level variables STOCK1-STOCK23 to the natural logarithms variables LSTOCK1-LSTOCK23.

assignment statement

appears between the iterative DO loop and the LABEL statement. This statement creates a quadratic time trend for later use.

LABEL

labels the variables.

CARDS

indicates that data lines follow. In the program that follows, the 20 data lines in the CARDS statement contain the annual dividends.

Example code

```
data dcf2;
    input year stock1 stock2 stock3 stock4 stock5 stock6
        stock7 stock8 stock9 stock10 stock11 stock12
        stock13 stock14 stock15 stock16 stock17 stock18
        stock19 stock20 stock21 stock22 stock23;
    array stock(23) stock1-stock23;
    array lstock(23) lstock1-lstock23;
    do i=1 to 23;
        lstock(i)=log(stock(i));
    end;
    year2=year*year;
label stock1='3M Company'
    stock2='Allegheny Power'
    stock3='Cincinnati G&E'
    stock4='Detroit Edison'
    stock5='Dominion Resources'
    stock6='Duke Power'
    stock7='Eli Lilly'
    stock8='Green Mountain Power'
    stock9='Iowa-Ill Gas & Electric'
    stock10='Kansas Power & Light'
    stock11='Kentucky Utilities'
    stock12='Minnesota Power & Light'
    stock13='Northern States Power'
    stock14='Oklahoma Gas & Electric'
    stock15='Orange & Rockland Utilities'
    stock16='Pennsylvania Power & Light'
    stock17='Piedmont Natural Gas'
    stock18='Potomac Electric Power'
    stock19='TECO Energy'
    stock20='Texas Utilities'
    stock21='Union Electric'
    stock22='Wisconsin Energy'
    stock23='Wicor'
```

```
           lstock1='Natural Log 3M Company'
           lstock2='Natural Log Allegheny Power';
        cards;
   81 1.50 2.01 2.07 1.62 1.43 1.04  .58 1.44 1.10 1.08 1.06
    1.06 1.25 1.68 1.64 2.21  .87  .79  .84 1.85 1.52  .88 1.05
   82 1.60 2.28 2.12 1.68 1.53 1.12  .67 1.52 1.18 1.18 1.10
    1.14 1.33 1.76 1.74 2.30  .93  .84  .92 2.00 1.58  .95 1.07
   83 1.65 2.50 2.16 1.68 1.63 1.16  .69 1.60 1.24 1.26 1.14
    1.20 1.43 1.84 1.86 2.38  .97  .89 1.00 2.16 1.66 1.03 1.07
   84 1.70 2.63 2.16 1.68 1.73 1.21  .75 1.68 1.30 1.36 1.18
    1.28 1.55 1.92 1.98 2.46 1.07  .97 1.08 2.32 1.72 1.12 1.11
   85 1.75 2.70 2.16 1.68 1.83 1.27  .80 1.74 1.37 1.46 1.22
    1.38 1.69 2.00 2.09 2.56 1.16 1.08 1.16 2.48 1.78 1.22 1.18
   86 1.80 2.86 2.16 1.68 1.91 1.32  .90 1.78 1.45 1.56 1.26
    1.52 1.83 2.08 2.16 2.57 1.19 1.18 1.24 2.64 1.86 1.32 1.28
   87 1.86 2.94 2.18 1.68 1.99 1.37 1.00 1.83 1.52 1.63 1.29
    1.66 1.96 2.18 2.20 2.66 1.29 1.30 1.32 2.77 1.92 1.42 1.30
   88 2.12 3.02 2.23 1.68 2.07 1.44 1.15 1.89 1.59 1.70 1.34
    1.72 2.07 2.28 2.24 2.74 1.44 1.38 1.40 2.86 1.94 1.52 1.32
   89 2.60 3.10 2.30 1.68 2.15 1.52 1.35 1.95 1.63 1.75 1.40
    1.78 2.17 2.38 2.28 2.84 1.57 1.46 1.50 2.91 2.02 1.63 1.37
   90 2.82 3.16 2.40 1.76 2.23 1.60 1.64 2.00 1.67 1.79 1.46
    1.86 2.27 2.48 2.32 2.95 1.66 1.52 1.60 2.96 2.10 1.74 1.42
   ;
```

The following PROC PLOT statements plot the dividends of the 3M Company, Allegheny Power, and Cincinnati Gas & Electric versus time in years. The results are shown in Output 2.2.

```
proc plot data=dcf2 vpct=110;
   plot (stock1-stock3)*year;
   title2;
run;
```

For this example, only three firm's dividends are plotted in separate scatter plots. You may want to plot the dividends of all the firms. In that case, the PLOT statement would become:

```
plot (stock1-stock23)*year;
```

Output 2.2
Scatter Plot of
Dividends Versus
Year

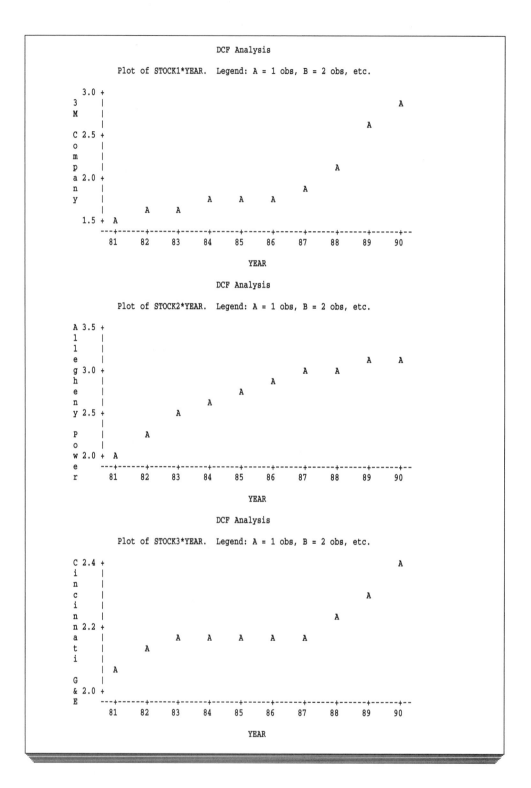

Interpretation of output

In Output 2.2, three scatter plots of dividends versus time are shown. In order, they are the 3M Company, Allegheny Power, and Cincinnati Gas & Electric. The scatter plot of the 3M Company's dividends appears to grow at an increasing rate, which indicates an exponential growth rate or a compound growth rate. The scatter plot of Allegheny Power's dividends appears to follow a quadratic curve while the scatter plot of Cincinnati G&E dividends appears to follow a cubic curve.

The visual evidence of scatter plots can assist you in selecting a growth model for dividends.

Plotting Dividends in Semi-Log Form

For stocks that appear to grow at an increasing rate when plotted in level form, you may want to transform the dividends by taking natural logarithms and then plotting the natural logs versus time. This is a *semi-log scatter plot*, which provides visual evidence as to the appropriateness of the semi-log dividend growth model.

You can use PROC PLOT and the DCF2 data set to plot the natural logs of the 3M Company dividends versus time. The following PROC PLOT statements perform this task. The results are not shown.

```
proc plot data=dcf2 vpct=110;
   plot lstock1*year;
   title2 'Semi-Log Plot';
   title3 '3M Company Dividends';
run;
```

Fitting Quadratic Regression Models

As shown in the scatter plots in Output 2.2, dividends may grow over time at different rates. Polynomial models can be used to approximate many functional forms. After the polynomial model is estimated, the derivative with respect to time may be taken to estimate the growth rate. This section explores a quadratic model of dividend growth.

Model theory

Applying the quadratic polynomial model to the dividends of DCF2 data set implies fitting regression models of the form

$$\text{STOCK} = a + f \times \text{YEAR} + h \times \text{YEAR2} + \epsilon \quad .$$

The variable YEAR is a linear time trend, and YEAR2 is a quadratic time trend. The ϵ terms are the random errors and are assumed to conform to the usual ordinary least squares (OLS) regression error term assumptions. There is one equation to be fit for each stock.

The derivative of dividends with respect to time is an estimate of the growth rate; that is, the change in dividends over time:

$$\frac{\partial\,\text{STOCK}}{\partial\,\text{YEAR}} = f + 2 \times h \times \text{YEAR}$$

You can use the SAS/STAT REG procedure to fit polynomial regression models to the DCF2 data set. From the estimated parameters, the growth rate of dividends at the end of 1990 can be calculated in a DATA step.

Explanation of syntax

PROC REG
> invokes the REG procedure. The following options of the PROC REG statement are specified.

> | | |
> |---|---|
> | DATA= | specifies the data set to be used. |
> | OUTEST= | creates a data set that contains parameter estimates. In this example, the OUTEST= data set is named DCF_EST1. The RENAME= option is used to rename the slope parameters. |
> | NOPRINT | suppresses the printed output. |

MODEL
> specifies the model to be fit. The dependent variable is to the left of the equal sign; the independent variables are to the right. In the polynomial models, each of the dependent variables are the dividends, and the independent variables are YEAR (the linear time trend) and YEAR2 (the quadratic time trend). Note that each model is fit separately. The option ADJRSQ specifies that the R-Square and Adjusted R-Square be calculated and included in the OUTEST= data set.

Tasks performed by the program
The following SAS statements,

□   fit the quadratic models.

□   create an output data set named DCF_EST1 containing the parameter estimates for the models.

□   calculate the growth rate at the end of 1990 in a DATA step. Also, this DATA step creates a caution variable, CAUTION1, which indicates if the dividend growth rate is greater than or equal to the discount rate K.

> Note that the SET statement reads all variables and observations from the specified input data set. In this example, the DCF_EST1 data set is read in, and the variable GQ is added to create the DCF_EST2 data set.

□   print the estimated parameters and the growth rates from the quadratic models.

Example code

```
      /* Fitting the Quadratic Models */
    proc reg data=dcf2 outest=dcf_est1(rename=(year=f year2=h))
          noprint;
      model stock1=year year2 / adjrsq;
      model stock2=year year2 / adjrsq;
      model stock3=year year2 / adjrsq;
                     .
                     .
                     .
      more MODEL statements of same form, 23 in all
                     .
                     .
                     .
      model stock22=year year2 / adjrsq;
      model stock23=year year2 / adjrsq;
```

```
run;

       /* Calculation of Growth Rate at End of 1990 */
data dcf_est2;
   set dcf_est1;
   k=.0932;

       /* Derivative of Quadratic Growth Model */
       /* with respect to YEAR is Growth Rate   */
       /* GQ is Growth Rate at the End of 1990 */
   gq=f+2*h*90;

       /* Caution Variable */
   if gq ge k then caution1 = 'YES';
   else caution1 = 'NO ';
run;

       /* Printing Fitted Quadratic Models and Growth Rates */
proc print data=dcf_est2;
   var _depvar_ _rsq_ _adjrsq_ intercep f h gq caution1;
   title2 'Fitted Quadratic Models';
   title3 'and Growth Rate of Dividends';
run;
```

The output from PROC REG is not shown. You may want to print the fitted models (in the DCF_EST1 data set with PROC PRINT) and further assess the fit by examining *F*-statistics, *t*-statistics, and *p*-values.

Output 2.3
Quadratic Regression Models of Dividend Growth Rates

```
                        DCF Analysis
                   Fitted Quadratic Models
                  and Growth Rate of Dividends

OBS _DEPVAR_  _RSQ_    _ADJRSQ_ INTERCEP    F        H        GQ     CAUTION1

  1 STOCK1   0.95613  0.94360  147.491  -3.54073  0.021477  0.32517  YES
  2 STOCK2   0.99186  0.98953  -81.933   1.86227 -0.010189  0.02817  NO
  3 STOCK3   0.89744  0.86813   26.619  -0.60017  0.003674  0.06119  NO
  4 STOCK4   0.49398  0.34940    4.348  -0.07009  0.000455  0.01173  NO
  5 STOCK5   0.99974  0.99967  -19.545   0.41235 -0.001894  0.07144  NO
  6 STOCK6   0.99636  0.99532    7.859  -0.21283  0.001591  0.07353  NO
  7 STOCK7   0.98786  0.98440   87.888  -2.14186  0.013144  0.22405  YES
  8 STOCK8   0.99693  0.99606  -17.816   0.39736 -0.001970  0.04282  NO
  9 STOCK9   0.99680  0.99588  -13.303   0.27902 -0.001250  0.05402  NO
 10 STOCK10  0.99749  0.99678  -31.236   0.68414 -0.003523  0.05005  NO
 11 STOCK11  0.99704  0.99619    6.156  -0.15795  0.001174  0.05342  NO
 12 STOCK12  0.98826  0.98490   -6.050   0.08135  0.000076  0.09498  YES
 13 STOCK13  0.99645  0.99543   -8.140   0.11249  0.000038  0.11931  YES
 14 STOCK14  0.99974  0.99967    8.324  -0.23538  0.001894  0.10553  YES
 15 STOCK15  0.99626  0.99519  -55.3345  1.26776 -.0069697  0.01321  NO
 16 STOCK16  0.99168  0.98930    2.5465 -0.07758  0.0009091  0.08606  NO
 17 STOCK17  0.99392  0.99218   29.3142 -0.74690  0.0048864  0.13264  YES
 18 STOCK18  0.99143  0.98898    3.0574 -0.13265  0.0012879  0.09917  YES
 19 STOCK19  0.99949  0.99935    1.8515 -0.09833  0.0010606  0.09258  NO
 20 STOCK20  0.99614  0.99504  -66.3860  1.48327 -.0079167  0.05827  NO
 21 STOCK21  0.99541  0.99409   -7.9942  0.16655 -.0006061  0.05745  NO
 22 STOCK22  0.99974  0.99966    8.2305 -0.25958  0.0020833  0.11542  YES
 23 STOCK23  0.96548  0.95561    4.0465 -0.11091  0.0009091  0.05273  NO
```

Interpretation of output

Each observation in Output 2.3 corresponds to a fitted quadratic model. The columns labeled _RSQ_ and _ADJRSQ_ contain the R-Square and Adjusted R-Square for each model. Notice that only the R-Square values for the STOCK3 and STOCK4 models are below .9. R-Square is interpreted as the percentage of the variation in the dependent variable that is accounted for by the model. For this example, an R-Square of .99 implies that 99 percent of the variation in dividends is accounted for by the quadratic model.

Notice that the caution variable (CAUTION1) indicates that the calculated growth rates of stocks 1, 7, 12, 13, 14, 17, 18, and 22 are greater than the realized return (K = .0932) on AAA bonds in 1990, which has been used as the discount rate. If the calculated growth rate is greater than the discount rate, then the denominator of the constant-growth DCF model is negative, which in turn produces a negative DCF value. (See Output 2.9 for examples.) This is a shortcoming of the DCF methodology. In this case, you should use another method to analyze the value of this stock.

Although this example shows you how to fit quadratic models to estimate the dividend growth rates, you may also want to explore fitting linear models.

Fitting the Semi-Log Models

Another functional form you may want to use to model dividend growth rate is the *semi-logarithmic form* (which is derived from the exponential growth model). In Output 2.2, the scatter plot of the 3M Company dividends appears to follow an exponential growth curve, and if this the case, then the natural logarithmic transformation of the dividends yields a linear growth rate.

An exponential growth curve applied to dividends of the DCF2 data set has the form

$$\text{STOCK} = b \times e^{g \times \text{YEAR}} .$$

In this form, the exponential growth curve is nonlinear and can be fit using the SAS/ETS MODEL procedure. However, you can also transform the nonlinear curve to a linear model by taking natural logarithms of each side, where A is the natural log of B, and G is the constant growth rate:

$$\text{LSTOCK} = a + g \times \text{YEAR}$$

This semi-log model can be applied to the dividends in the DCF2 data set, yielding linear regression models of the form

$$\text{LSTOCK} = a + g \times \text{YEAR} + \epsilon .$$

The slope parameters are the estimated growth rates of the dividends. This can be observed from changes in the dependent variable stemming from changes in the independent variable YEAR.

The ratio of the changes gives the change in dividends per year. This is also the first derivative of the natural log of the dividends (LSTOCK) with respect to time in years (YEAR), as shown in the following equation:

$$G = \frac{\partial \text{LSTOCK}}{\partial \text{YEAR}}$$

In discrete form, the previous equation becomes

$$G = \frac{\Delta D}{D}$$

$$G = \frac{D_t - D_{t-1}}{D_{t-1}} \quad .$$

Thus, the growth rate of semi-log models is a constant-percentage growth rate. Notice that the semi-log model may be easier to fit than the quadratic polynomial model because it has one less parameter to estimate.

You can use PROC REG to fit semi-log regression models to the DCF2 data set. The following statements fit the semi-log models, create an output data set named DCF_EST3 containing the fitted models, and print the fitted models and R-Squares.

The estimated parameters and R-Squares are printed in Output 2.4.

```
    /* Fitting the Semi-log Models */
proc reg data=dcf2 outest=dcf_est3(rename=(year=gl)) noprint;
    model lstock1=year / adjrsq;
    model lstock2=year / adjrsq;
    model lstock3=year / adjrsq;
                    .
                    .
                    .
    more MODEL statements of same form, 23 in all
                    .
                    .
                    .
    model lstock22=year / adjrsq;
    model lstock23=year / adjrsq;
run;

    /* Printing the Fitted Semi-log Models and Growth Rates */
proc print data=dcf_est3;
    var _depvar_ _rsq_ _adjrsq_ intercep gl;
    title2 'Fitted Semi-Log Models';
    title3 'and Growth Rate of Dividends';
run;
```

Output 2.4
Semi-log Regression
Models of Dividend
Growth Rates

```
                              DCF Analysis
                         Fitted Semi-Log Models
                        and Growth Rate of Dividends

      OBS    _DEPVAR_     _RSQ_      _ADJRSQ_     INTERCEP      GL

        1    LSTOCK1     0.86896     0.85258      -4.86705    0.06443
        2    LSTOCK2     0.91515     0.90454      -2.92551    0.04581
        3    LSTOCK3     0.82040     0.79795      -0.29749    0.01266
        4    LSTOCK4     0.48509     0.42072       0.13325    0.00452
        5    LSTOCK5     0.98622     0.98450      -3.55973    0.04872
        6    LSTOCK6     0.99600     0.99550      -3.63236    0.04550
        7    LSTOCK7     0.96603     0.96179      -9.32024    0.10784
        8    LSTOCK8     0.97963     0.97708      -2.46150    0.03523
        9    LSTOCK9     0.98716     0.98556      -3.70474    0.04720
       10    LSTOCK10    0.96947     0.96566      -4.50118    0.05705
       11    LSTOCK11    0.99697     0.99659      -2.72774    0.03441
       12    LSTOCK12    0.98569     0.98390      -5.26502    0.06580
       13    LSTOCK13    0.99105     0.98994      -5.37978    0.06927
       14    LSTOCK14    0.99975     0.99972      -2.96919    0.04309
```

```
15  LSTOCK15  0.92603  0.91678  -2.54858  0.03814
16  LSTOCK16  0.99164  0.99059  -1.66147  0.03041
17  LSTOCK17  0.99183  0.99081  -6.06758  0.07298
18  LSTOCK18  0.98974  0.98845  -6.58797  0.07830
19  LSTOCK19  0.99583  0.99531  -5.82927  0.07014
20  LSTOCK20  0.95511  0.94950  -3.68526  0.05366
21  LSTOCK21  0.99094  0.98981  -2.40791  0.03504
22  LSTOCK22  0.99814  0.99791  -6.33036  0.07667
23  LSTOCK23  0.96230  0.95758  -2.94545  0.03668
```

Interpretation of output

Each observation in Output 2.4 corresponds to a fitted semi-log model. The columns labeled _RSQ_ and _ADJRSQ_ contain the R-Square and Adjusted R-Square for each model. Notice that only three of the R-Squares are below .90. An R-Square of .90 implies 90 percent of the variation in the dependent variable is accounted for by the model.

The estimated parameters for the intercept are in the column labeled INTERCEP, and the estimated parameters for the slope are in the column labeled GL. The variable GL contains the estimates of the dividend growth rates.

Only one of the estimated growth rates (for LSTOCK7) is greater than the discount rate (9.32 percent, the realized return on AAA bonds in 1990), which implies that the constant dividend growth DCF methodology will produce a negative value for shares of this stock.

Calculating Compound Growth Rate

Another model of dividend growth is the *compound growth rate model*. The compound growth rate over T periods, with D_0 as the first period dividend and D_T as the last period dividend, is calculated as follows:

$$G = \left(\frac{D_T}{D_0}\right)^{1/T} - 1$$

You can use the TRANSPOSE procedure and the DATA step to calculate the compound growth rate for the stocks in the DCF2 data set. The TRANSPOSE procedure transposes the data; that is, rows become columns and columns become rows. By transposing the DCF2 data set, you can form the ratio of the last-period dividends to the first-period dividends and then proceed to calculating the compound growth rates.

Explanation of syntax

PROC TRANSPOSE
   invokes the TRANSPOSE procedure. The following options of the PROC TRANSPOSE statement are specified.

   DATA=   specifies the data set to be used. In the example that follows, the data set to be transposed is the DCF2 data set.

   OUT=   creates and names the output data set. In the example that follows, the data set to be created is named DCF_TR1. PROC TRANSPOSE creates variables for the output data set as follows:

             LABEL   contains the name of the variable being transposed.

COL1	contains the values in the first observation (that is, the first row) of the variables being transposed.
COL2	contains the values in the second observation of the variables being transposed. This process continues; one column is created for each row of data.

VAR

specifies the variables to be transposed.

Example code

```
proc transpose data=dcf2 out=dcf_tr1;
   var stock1-stock23;
run;
```

In the DCF_TR1 data set, COL1 contains the 1981 dividends, COL2 contains the 1982 dividends, and so on through COL10, which contains the 1990 dividends. In Output 2.5, the first five observations of the variables _LABEL_, COL1, and COL10 data set are printed.

```
proc print data=dcf_tr1 (obs=5);
   var _label_ col1 col10;
   title2 'First Five Observations';
   title3 'Transposed DCF2 Data Set';
   title4 'Firm, 1981 and 1990 Dividends';
run;
```

Output 2.5
Printing the Data
for Compound
Growth Rate
Calculations

```
                    DCF Analysis
                First Five Observations
               Transposed DCF2 Data Set
              Firm, 1981 and 1990 Dividends

       OBS    _LABEL_              COL1    COL10

         1    3M Company           1.50    2.82
         2    Allegheny Power      2.01    3.16
         3    Cincinnati G&E       2.07    2.40
         4    Detroit Edison       1.62    1.76
         5    Dominion Resources   1.43    2.23
```

You are now ready to use a DATA step to calculate the annually compounded growth rates over the ten-year period 1981-1990. The first ten growth rates are printed in Output 2.6.

```
data dcf_tr2;
   set dcf_tr1;
   t=10;
   gc=((col10/col1)**(1/t))-1;
   label gc='Annually Compounded Growth Rate';
run;

proc print data=dcf_tr2 (obs=10);
   var _label_ gc;
```

```
                    title2 'Annually Compounded Growth Rate';
                    title3;
                    title4;
                run;
```

Output 2.6
Annually
Compounded
Growth Rates

```
                              DCF Analysis
                      Annually Compounded Growth Rate

              OBS    _LABEL_                        GC

               1     3M Company                   0.06516
               2     Allegheny Power              0.04628
               3     Cincinnati G&E               0.01490
               4     Detroit Edison               0.00832
               5     Dominion Resources           0.04543
               6     Duke Power                   0.04402
               7     Eli Lilly                    0.10954
               8     Green Mountain Power         0.03340
               9     Iowa-Ill Gas & Electric      0.04264
              10     Kansas Power & Light         0.05182
```

Calculating DCF Values for Stocks with Constant-Growth Dividends

Thus far, this chapter has shown you how to calculate growth rates by three different approaches. The next section shows you how to calculate DCF values using the constant-growth methodology.

To use this methodology, you use a DATA step to

□ merge the DCF_TR2, DCF_EST2, and DCF_EST3 data sets to create the DCF_CAL1 data set.

□ calculate the next-period dividends for use in the DCF value calculations:

$$D_{1991} = D_{1990} \times (G + 1)$$

□ calculate DCF values using the different growth rates and the corresponding next-period dividends. For this example, the 1990 dividend is the current-period dividend, and the 1991 dividend is the next-period dividend.

Example code

```
    /* Merging Data Sets */
data dcf_cal1;
    merge dcf_tr2 dcf_est2 dcf_est3;
    d0=col10;
    k=.0932;

        /* Calculating D1 and DCF Value */
        /* from Quadratic Model          */
    d1q=round(d0*(1+gq), .001);
    vq=round(d1q/(k-gq), .001);
```

```
    /* Calculating D1 and DCF Value */
    /* from Semi-Log Model          */
dll=round(d0*(1+gl), .001);
vl=round(dll/(k-gl), .001);

    /* Calculating D1 and DCF Value    */
    /* from Compound Growth Rate Model */
dlc=round(d0*(1+gc), .001);
vc=round(dlc/(k-gc), .001);

    /* Labeling the Variables */
label k='Discount Rate'
    d0='1990 Dividend'
    gq='Quadratic Model Growth Rate'
    dlq='Quadratic Model 1991 Dividend'
    vq='Quadratic Model DCF Value'
    gl='Semi-Log Model Growth Rate'
    dll='Semi-Log Model 1991 Dividend'
    vl='Semi-Log Model DCF Value'
    dlc='Compound Growth Rate 1991 Dividend'
    vc='Compound Growth DCF Value';
run;
```

For ease in presentation and comparison, the growth rates and corresponding next-period dividends are presented in three separate outputs. Growth rates and the discount rate are printed in Output 2.7.

```
proc print data=dcf_cal1 label;
    var _label_ gq gl gc k;
    title2 'Growth Rates';
run;
```

Output 2.7
Growth Rates for
DCF Analysis

```
                              DCF Analysis
                              Growth Rates

                          Quadratic  Semi-Log
                            Model      Model
                           Growth     Growth    Annually
                            Rate       Rate    Compounded  Discount
   OBS  LABEL OF FORMER VARIABLE    Rate      Rate     Growth Rate    Rate

     1  3M Company                0.32517   0.06443   0.06516    0.0932
     2  Allegheny Power           0.02817   0.04581   0.04628    0.0932
     3  Cincinnati G&E            0.06119   0.01266   0.01490    0.0932
     4  Detroit Edison            0.01173   0.00452   0.00832    0.0932
     5  Dominion Resources        0.07144   0.04872   0.04543    0.0932
     6  Duke Power                0.07353   0.04550   0.04402    0.0932
     7  Eli Lilly                 0.22405   0.10784   0.10954    0.0932
     8  Green Mountain Power      0.04282   0.03523   0.03340    0.0932
     9  Iowa-Ill Gas & Electric   0.05402   0.04720   0.04264    0.0932
    10  Kansas Power & Light      0.05005   0.05705   0.05182    0.0932
    11  Kentucky Utilities        0.05342   0.03441   0.03253    0.0932
    12  Minnesota Power & Light   0.09498   0.06580   0.05784    0.0932
    13  Northern States Power     0.11931   0.06927   0.06148    0.0932
    14  Oklahoma Gas & Electric   0.10553   0.04309   0.03972    0.0932
    15  Orange & Rockland Utilities 0.01321 0.03814   0.03530    0.0932
    16  Pennsylvania Power & Light 0.08606  0.03041   0.02930    0.0932
    17  Piedmont Natural Gas      0.13264   0.07298   0.06674    0.0932
    18  Potomac Electric Power    0.09917   0.07830   0.06763    0.0932
    19  TECO Energy               0.09258   0.07014   0.06656    0.0932
```

20	Texas Utilities	0.05827	0.05366	0.04812	0.0932
21	Union Electric	0.05745	0.03504	0.03285	0.0932
22	Wisconsin Energy	0.11542	0.07667	0.07055	0.0932
23	Wicor	0.05273	0.03668	0.03065	0.0932

The following PROC PRINT statements print the next-period (1991) dividends generated from the 1990 dividends and the growth rates, as shown in Output 2.8.

```
proc print data=dcf_cal1 label;
   var _label_ d0 d1q d1l d1c;
   title2 'Next Period (1991) Dividends';
run;
```

Output 2.8
Dividends Generated from Different Growth Rates

DCF Analysis
Next Period (1991) Dividends

OBS	LABEL OF FORMER VARIABLE	D0	Quadratic Model Next Dividend	Semi-Log Model Next Dividend	Compound Growth Rate Next Dividend
1	3M Company	2.82	3.737	3.002	3.004
2	Allegheny Power	3.16	3.249	3.305	3.306
3	Cincinnati G&E	2.40	2.547	2.430	2.436
4	Detroit Edison	1.76	1.781	1.768	1.775
5	Dominion Resources	2.23	2.389	2.339	2.331
6	Duke Power	1.60	1.718	1.673	1.670
7	Eli Lilly	1.64	2.007	1.817	1.820
8	Green Mountain Power	2.00	2.086	2.070	2.067
9	Iowa-Ill Gas & Electric	1.67	1.760	1.749	1.741
10	Kansas Power & Light	1.79	1.880	1.892	1.883
11	Kentucky Utilities	1.46	1.538	1.510	1.508
12	Minnesota Power & Light	1.86	2.037	1.982	1.968
13	Northern States Power	2.27	2.541	2.427	2.410
14	Oklahoma Gas & Electric	2.48	2.742	2.587	2.578
15	Orange & Rockland Utilities	2.32	2.351	2.408	2.402
16	Pennsylvania Power & Light	2.95	3.204	3.040	3.036
17	Piedmont Natural Gas	1.66	1.880	1.781	1.771
18	Potomac Electric Power	1.52	1.671	1.639	1.623
19	TECO Energy	1.60	1.748	1.712	1.706
20	Texas Utilities	2.96	3.132	3.119	3.102
21	Union Electric	2.10	2.221	2.174	2.169
22	Wisconsin Energy	1.74	1.941	1.873	1.863
23	Wicor	1.42	1.495	1.472	1.464

You may want to compare and contrast the calculated dividends for 1991 with the actual 1990 dividends labeled D0. Previous research about the particular firm and other forecasts of dividends may help you in assessing the usefulness of these values.

The following PROC PRINT statements print the DCF values, as shown in Output 2.9.

```
proc print data=dcf_cal1 label;
   var _label_ vq vl vc;
   title2 'DCF Values';
run;
```

Output 2.9
DCF Values
Generated from
Different Dividend
Growth Rates

```
                            DCF Analysis
                             DCF Values

                                 Quadratic    Semi-Log    Compound
                                 Model DCF    Model DCF   Growth DCF
        OBS  LABEL OF FORMER VARIABLE  Value     Value       Value

         1   3M Company              -16.11    104.351     107.141
         2   Allegheny Power          49.97     69.745      70.465
         3   Cincinnati G&E           79.57     30.171      31.112
         4   Detroit Edison           21.86     19.937      20.913
         5   Dominion Resources      109.79     52.580      48.801
         6   Duke Power               87.34     35.071      33.957
         7   Eli Lilly               -15.34   -124.100    -111.407
         8   Green Mountain Power     41.40     35.707      34.563
         9   Iowa-Ill Gas & Electric  44.92     38.022      34.431
        10   Kansas Power & Light     43.57     52.336      45.509
        11   Kentucky Utilities       38.66     25.684      24.858
        12   Minnesota Power & Light -1141.27   72.326      55.659
        13   Northern States Power   -97.32    101.422      75.976
        14   Oklahoma Gas & Electric -222.38    51.627      48.200
        15   Orange & Rockland Utilities 29.39  43.731      41.482
        16   Pennsylvania Power & Light 448.78  48.418      47.514
        17   Piedmont Natural Gas    -47.66     88.095      66.933
        18   Potomac Electric Power  -280.06   110.001      63.478
        19   TECO Energy            2800.19     74.224      64.032
        20   Texas Utilities          89.65     78.871      68.815
        21   Union Electric           62.13     37.381      35.941
        22   Wisconsin Energy        -87.37    113.332      82.249
        23   Wicor                    36.94     26.044      23.404
```

Interpretation of Output 2.9

Output 2.9 shows the constant growth DCF values. You can assess the quality of these values as follows:

□ Negative values are nonsense. They occur because calculated growth rates are greater than the discount rate. For example, the quadratic dividend growth model generates a value of -$1141.27 per share of Minnesota Power & Light stock. Obviously, no investor would be willing to pay over $1100 per share for others to accept the stock. This is a limitation of the constant growth DCF approach.

In this case, you may want to use a different DCF methodology or reconsider which discount rate is appropriate, or both. For example, the realized 1990 yield on AAA bonds is used as the discount rate in this example. If a firm has a BBB bond rating, then the AAA bond yield might be inappropriate.

□ Extremely high values are probably inaccurate. For example, the quadratic dividend growth model yields a DCF value of $2800.19 per share for TECO Energy stock. In 1990, the price of TECO stock fluctuated between $26.25 and $33.875 per share. Thus, the value of $2800.19 per share is unlikely to be accurate.

□ The observed price range of each stock for the previous year can be used as benchmarks. You may expect a stock value close to this range. Many other investors are actively searching for overpriced and underpriced stocks. Studies have shown that stock markets are efficient; typically, price discrepancies are quickly arbitraged.

□ Verify your assumptions about the economy, the industry, the firm, and its dividend policy. Changes or adjustments to your assumptions of the appropriate discount rate, growth model for dividends, and your expectations for future dividends can yield a different DCF value.

▶ *Caution* . . . . *Use DCF Value Calculations with Care*
Only when you are fully satisfied with DCF stock-value calculations should you consider basing your investment strategies upon them. ▲

Multiperiod DCF Methodology

The DCF methodology presented thus far enables you to apply the general DCF equation to stocks paying fixed-dollar dividends or to stocks paying dividends that grow at a constant rate over time. Your research may indicate that these approaches are too restrictive for some stocks.

More flexible models of growth patterns for future dividends include

☐ two-period models of fixed-dollar dividends. Perhaps the fixed-dollar dividends are set at a low level, but may soon rise to a higher-fixed level. Alternatively, the fixed-dollar dividends may be currently set at a higher level, and future dividends are expected to be set at a lower fixed level.

☐ three or more periods of different fixed-dollar dividends.

☐ two periods of fixed-dollar dividends with a transition period in between. The transition period may follow a constant growth rate model or some other function.

☐ many distinct periods that characterize expected future dividends. For example, dividends may be fixed at an initially low level, and you expect a transition period to a higher-fixed level, followed by a transition period back to a lower level.

This section shows you how to use the SAS System to perform DCF multiperiod methodology.

Two-Period DCF Analysis, Fixed-Dollar Dividends

Suppose it is the end of 1987, and you are analyzing the dividends of the Detroit Edison Company, an electric utility. You know that Detroit Edison has followed a fixed-dollar dividend policy, having paid $1.68 per share of common stock in annual dividends since 1982. You also know that the firm is working to reduce indebtedness, has little need for immediate additions to generating capacity, and expects continued growth in electricity sales.

Your research might lead you to conclude that in 1990 Detroit Edison will increase the fixed dividend of its common stock to $1.76, and this higher level of fixed dividends will continue in the future. Under these assumptions, what is the DCF value of Detroit Edison common stock at the end of 1987?

The following sections show you how to perform this analysis.

Plotting Dividends Over Two Periods

By creating the DCF3 data set in a DATA step, you can plot the dividends over time with PROC PLOT and identify the two periods. The HREF= option of the PLOT statement in

PROC PLOT creates a horizontal reference line at the value of 90 on the horizontal axis (YEAR). The following statements perform these tasks, and the results are printed in Output 2.10.

```
data dcf3;
    input year d @@;
    label d='Detroit Edison Dividends';
    cards;
82 1.68   83 1.68   84 1.68   85 1.68   86 1.68
87 1.68   88 1.68   89 1.68   90 1.76   91 1.76
92 1.76   93 1.76
;

proc plot data=dcf3 vpct=110;
    plot d*year='*' / href=90;
    title2 'Dividends Versus Time';
run;
```

Output 2.10
Scatter Plot of
Dividends Versus
Time

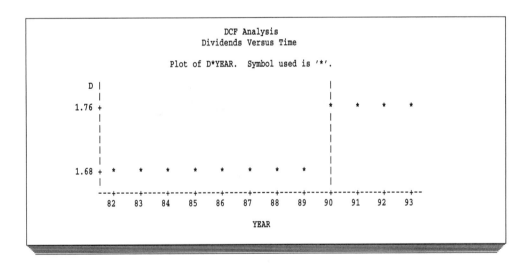

Calculating the DCF Value

To calculate the DCF value of the common stock, you can use expectations about the future and the general DCF equation described in the introduction of this chapter to calculate the DCF value of the common stock.

For this example, the realized yield of AAA bonds in 1987 is used as the appropriate discount rate. In 1987, AAA bonds yielded 9.38 percent, or .0938.

Using the above expectations about Detroit Edison at the end of 1987 implies the DCF equation has the form:

$$V = \frac{\$1.68}{(1 + .0938)} + \frac{\$1.68}{(1 + .0938)^2} + \frac{\$1.76}{(1 + .0938)^3} + \frac{\$1.76}{(1 + .0938)^4} + \dots + \frac{\$1.76}{(1 + .0938)^\infty}$$

In this equation, the first term represents the discounted (or present) value of the expected dividends in 1988; the second term represents the discounted value of the expected dividends in 1989; the third term represents the discounted value of the expected higher dividends in 1990; and so on to infinity.

The DCF equation for Detroit Edison can be summed as two parts. The first part to be summed is the 1988 and 1989 terms, which represent the period of lower fixed dividends. The second part is the infinite series starting in 1990, which represents the period of higher fixed dividends. The second part can be summed as an infinite series then discounted back to the present.

The calculations are as follows:

$$V = \frac{\$1.68}{(1 + .0938)} + \frac{\$1.68}{(1 + .0938)^2} + \frac{\$1.76}{.0938 \times (1 + .0938)^2}$$

The first two terms are the discounted values of the expected 1988 and 1989 dividends; the third term is the summation of the infinite series discounted back two years. The equation becomes

$$V = \$1.54 + \$1.40 + \$15.68 = \$18.62 \qquad .$$

This model can be generalized for any length first and second periods with dividends D1 and D2, respectively. In general form, the two-period DCF approach becomes

$$V = \sum_{i=1}^{N} \frac{D_1}{(1 + K)^i} + \frac{D_2}{K \times (1 + K)^N} \qquad .$$

In this equation, the first period is from 1 to N, and the second period is from $N + 1$ onward. Further generalizations can also be made to 3, 4, 5, or more periods of fixed-dollar dividends.

You can calculate the two-period DCF value for Detroit Edison in the following DATA step. The results are printed in Output 2.11.

```
data dcf_cal1;
   k=.0938;
   d1=1.68;
   d2=1.76;
   v0=round(d1/k, .01);
   v1=round(d1/(1+k), .01);
   v2=round(d1/((1+k)**2), .01);
   v3=round(d2/(k*(1+k)**2), .01);
   v=v1+v2+v3;
   label v0='DCF Value for $1.68 Dividend Series'
         v1='Discounted Value for 1988'
         v2='Discounted Value for 1989'
         v3='DCF Value for $1.76 Dividend Series'
         v='DCF Value for Two Periods';
run;

proc print data=dcf_cal1 label;
   var v0 v1 v2 v3 v;
   title2 'Discounted Cash Flow Values';
run;
```

Output 2.11
DCF Values for
Series and
Individual Periods

```
                                    DCF Analysis
                             Discounted Cash Flow Values

               DCF Value                              DCF Value
               for $1.68    Discounted   Discounted   for $1.76   DCF Value
               Dividend     Value for    Value for    Dividend    for Two
        OBS    Series       1988         1989         Series      Periods

         1     17.91        1.54         1.4          15.68       18.62
```

Interpretation of output

Output 2.11 shows the following DCF values, discounted back to the end of 1987:

□ for the case where dividends remain fixed at $1.68

□ the individual discounted (or present) values for 1988 and 1989

□ the DCF value for the fixed $1.76 dividends

□ the DCF value, $18.62 per share of Detroit Edison common stock, for the two-period approach. This value is the sum of the 1988 and 1989 values and the new higher level of fixed dividends from 1990 onward.

Two-Period DCF Analysis, Growing Dividends and Fixed-Dollar Dividends

DCF analysis can be performed on common stocks that are in transition from one level of fixed dividends to another. For example, at the end of 1989, you might have been analyzing the common stock dividends of AT&T.

In 1983, AT&T paid $5.85 in dividends. After divestiture of regional telephone companies in 1984, AT&T's common stock dividends fell to $1.20 in 1985 and remained at $1.20 through 1989. Suppose now at the end of 1990, AT&T has paid $1.29 in annual dividends. Your research into the fundamentals of AT&T leads you to believe that AT&T will continue to increase its dividends over the next five years and then will become fixed at the predivestiture level of $5.85. What is the DCF value of a share of AT&T common stock given these expectations?

Before you can perform the DCF valuation analysis, you want to model the growth process of dividends from the end of 1990-1995. The rate at which dividends grow affects the DCF value.

There are several growth models that may be appropriate for this stock. You may want to fit one or more of the following growth models:

□ annually compounded growth:

$$D_i = D_{1990} \times gc1^{\,YEAR_i - 1990}$$

In this equation, the annually compounded growth rate (plus one) over the five-year period is

$$GC1 = \left(\frac{D_{1995}}{D_{1990}} \right)^{1/5} .$$

□ linear growth model:

$$D_i = a + b \times \text{YEAR}_i$$

□ quadratic growth model:

$$D_i = a + b \times \text{YEAR}_i + c \times \text{YEAR}_i^2$$

In this equation, the first derivative with respect to time (in years) is expected to be positive, and the second derivative can be positive or negative, depending on your expectations of dividend growth.

After fitting the model, you can use the predicted values as the expected dividends.

Fitting Linear and Compound Growth Models

In this example, the fundamental analysis provides a level of dividends for a beginning year and an ending year, as shown in this table:

Point	D	End of YEAR
Begin	1.29	1990
End	5.85	1995

These two points can be used to calculate an annually compounded growth rate and to fit a linear growth model. To calculate the dividends for the compound growth rate and the linear model you follow these steps.

1. In a DATA step,

   □ create the DCF4 data set containing the beginning and ending dividend values

   □ calculate the compound growth rate

   □ use the compound growth rate to calculate the first growth pattern of dividends.

2. Use PROC REG to

   □ fit the linear model

   □ calculate predicted values

   □ create an output data set

   □ store the predicted values in the output data set.

3. Use PROC PRINT to print the calculated values.

The dividend values are printed in Output 2.12.

Example code

```
/* Creating DCF4 Data Set */
/* Calculating Compound Growth Rate and Dividends, D1 */
data dcf4;
    input year d @@;
    t=5;
    d1990=1.29;
    d1995=5.85;
    gc1=(d1995/d1990)**(1/t);
    d1=round(d1990*(gc1**(year-90)), .001);
    cards;
1990 1.29 1991 .  1992 .  1993 .  1994 . 1995 5.85
;

    /* Fitting the Linear Growth Rate Model */
    /* Creating Output Data Set, DCF_OUT1 */
    /* Calculating Dividends, D2 */
proc reg data=dcf4 noprint;
    model d=year;
    output out=dcf_out1 p=d2;
run;

    /* Printing Predicted Dividends */
proc print data=dcf_out1;
    var year d d1 d2;
    title2 'Predicted Dividends Over Time';
    title3 'Compound Growth Rate and Linear Trend';
run;
```

Output 2.12
Expected Dividends from Linear and Compound Growth Rates

```
                        DCF Analysis
                 Predicted Dividends Over Time
              Compound Growth Rate and Linear Trend

        OBS    YEAR     D       D1      D2

         1     1990    1.29    1.290   1.290
         2     1991     .      1.745   2.202
         3     1992     .      2.362   3.114
         4     1993     .      3.195   4.026
         5     1994     .      4.324   4.938
         6     1995    5.85    5.850   5.850
```

Interpretation of output

In Output 2.12, the dividend values are printed for the following cases:

□ beginning and ending dividend growth values based on fundamental analysis, contained in the variable labeled D

□ expected dividends based on annually compounded growth, labeled D1

□ expected dividends based on linear growth, labeled D2.

Fitting Quadratic Growth Models

To fit the quadratic dividend growth models, you must have one further expectation about the path the dividends follow over time. That is, you must provide an intermediate dividend level in addition to the first-year dividends and the new level of fixed-dollar dividends. The intermediate dividend level provided affects the shape of the growth curve, the remaining dividend values, and ultimately the calculated DCF value for the stock.

In this example, two data sets are created, DCF5 and DCF6, in two DATA steps. The two data sets have different intermediate values. The DCF5 data set includes the value $4.24 for 1992, implying rapid initial growth of dividends and then growth tapering off to the higher fixed level of $5.85. The DCF6 data set includes the $4.76 for 1994, implying slower initial growth and then more rapid growth until the higher fixed dividend level is reached.

You fit the two quadratic dividend growth models with PROC REG and create output data sets containing the predicted dividends. The predicted values are printed with PROC PRINT. The results are shown in Output 2.13.

```
        /* Creating DCF5 Data Set */
data dcf5;
   set dcf4;
   if year=1992 then d=4.24;
   year2=year*year;
run;

        /* Creating DCF6 Data Set */
data dcf6;
   set dcf4;
   if year=1994 then d=4.76;
   year2=year*year;
run;

        /* Fitting 1st Quadratic Dividend Growth Model */
        /* Rapid Initial Growth Rate */
        /* Creating Output Data Set DCF_OUT2 */
        /* Calculating Dividends, D3 */
proc reg data=dcf5 noprint;
   model d=year year2;
   output out=dcf_out2 p=d3;
run;

        /* Fitting 2nd Quadratic Dividend Growth Model */
        /* Slower Initial Growth Rate */
        /* Creating Output Data Set DCF_OUT3 */
        /* Calculating Dividends, D4 */
proc reg data=dcf6 noprint;
   model d=year year2;
   output out=dcf_out3 p=d4;
run;

proc print data=dcf_out2;
   var year d d3;
   title2 'Predicted Dividends Over Time';
   title3 'Rapid Initial Growth Quadratic Model';
run;
```

```
proc print data=dcf_out3;
   var year d d4;
   title3 'Slow Initial Growth Quadratic Model';
run;
```

Output 2.13
Expected Dividends
from Quadratic
Growth Rates

```
                    DCF Analysis
            Predicted Dividends Over Time
          Rapid Initial Growth Quadratic Model

        OBS    YEAR      D        D3

         1     1990     1.29    1.73447
         2     1991      .      2.61684
         3     1992     4.24    3.49921
         4     1993      .      4.38158
         5     1994      .      5.26395
         6     1995     5.85    6.14632


                    DCF Analysis
            Predicted Dividends Over Time
          Slow Initial Growth Quadratic Model

        OBS    YEAR      D        D4

         1     1990     1.29    1.26881
         2     1991      .      2.16810
         3     1992      .      3.06738
         4     1993      .      3.96667
         5     1994     4.76    4.86595
         6     1995     5.85    5.76524
```

Calculating DCF Values from Dividend Growth Models

You can calculate the DCF Values for AT&T common stock in a DATA step, using the dividends generated by the different growth models. First, the data sets containing the dividend values are merged; then, the DCF values are calculated. The PROC TRANSPOSE statements are interpreted in the example code producing Output 2.5. The results from this example code are printed in Output 2.14.

```
   /* Merging Data Sets */
data dcf7;
   merge dcf_out1 dcf_out2 dcf_out3;
   by year;
run;

   /* Transposing Data for Ease in DCF Calculations */
proc transpose data=dcf7 out=dcf_tr3;
   var d1-d4;
run;

   /* Calculating Present Value of Future Dividends */
   /* Calculating DCF Values for Different Growth Rate Models */
data dcf8;
   set dcf_tr3;
   k=.0932;                /* actual AAA bond yield at end of 1990 */
   yr91=col2/(1+k);        /* 1990 Present Value of 1991 Dividend */
```

```
            yr92=col3/((1+k)**2);  /* 1990 Present Value of 1992 Dividend */
            yr93=col4/((1+k)**3);  /* 1990 Present Value of 1993 Dividend */
            yr94=col5/((1+k)**4);  /* 1990 Present Value of 1994 Dividend */

            yr95=col6/(k*((1+k)**4));  /* 1990 PV of Fixed Dividends */
                                       /* Starting in 1995 */
            v=sum(of yr91-yr95);
        run;


            /* Printing Present Values of Predicted Dividends */
            /* Printing Calculated DCF Values */
        proc print data=dcf8;
            var yr91-yr95 v;
            title2 'Calculated DCF Values';
            title3 'and Predicted Dividends Over Time';
        run;
```

Output 2.14
Calculated DCF
Values from
Different Dividend
Growth Models

```
                              DCF Analysis
                       Predicted Dividends Over Time

       OBS    YR91      YR92      YR93      YR94      YR95       V

        1    1.59623   1.97643   2.44552   3.02752   43.9482   52.9939
        2    2.01427   2.60567   3.08159   3.45742   43.9482   55.1072
        3    2.70094   3.54786   3.94346   3.98302   43.9482   58.1235
        4    1.85145   2.38225   2.87722   3.33279   43.9482   54.3920
```

Interpretation of output

In Output 2.14, the columns (YR91-YR95) contain the discounted (or present) value of the dividends and the DCF values (labeled V). The values in columns YR91-YR94 contain the discounted values of the dividends in the transition period, and the variable YR95 is the discounted value of the summed infinite series for the higher fixed dividend level. Lastly, each DCF value (V) is the sum of the values from YR91-YR95.

The rows in Output 2.14 contain the discounted dividend values and the DCF values for each of the dividend growth rate models. The first row (or observation) contains the values for the compound growth model. The second through fourth rows contain values for the linear trend model, the rapid initial-growth quadratic model, and the slower initial-growth quadratic models, respectively.

Prior to making investment decisions based on these values, you may want to further assess the quality of these values by comparing them with other forecasts and your own intuitive expectations of the future.

Only after you are fully satisfied with your analysis should you use the calculated DCF values for making investment decisions.

Searching For Overpriced and Underpriced Stocks

You can use the DCF calculated growth rates along with other data to identify overpriced and underpriced stocks.

Whitbeck and Kisor (1963) developed a cross-sectional multiple regression model to identify overpriced and underpriced stocks. Their dependent variable was the price earnings ratio, and their independent variables were growth rate, dividend payout rate, and standard deviation of growth rate. This section shows you how to use PROC REG to perform similar analysis on the 23 common stocks listed in the DCF2 data set. You proceed, as follows, using a DATA step and the procedures listed here:

1. Use a DATA step to create the DCF9 data set containing the price earnings ratio (PE) and the 1990 dividend payout ratio (PR).

2. Use PROC MEANS to calculate the standard deviations of the dividend growth rates.

3. Use a DATA step to merge the DCF9 data set, the data set containing the dividend growth rates (DCF_CAL1), and the data set containing the standard deviations of the dividend growth rates (DCF_STD2). This new data set can be used to fit the multiple regression model.

4. Use PROC REG to fit the cross-sectional multiple regression model.

5. Use PROC PLOT to plot the predicted and residual values to identify overpriced and underpriced stocks.

Creating the Data Set for Regression Analysis

The following statements create the DCF9 data set. Note that the dividend payout ratio for Wicor is not meaningful for 1990 and is listed as a missing value.

```
data dcf9;
    input firm $32. pe pr;
    label pe='Price Earnings Ratio 1990'
          pr='Dividend Payout Ratio 1990';
    cards;
3M Company                      14.0  48
Allegheny Power                 10.5  88
Cincinnati G&E                   7.3  58
Detroit Edison                   8.2  54
Dominion Resources              10.3  76
Duke Power                      12.1  67
Eli Lilly                       19.1  42
Green Mountain Power            10.8  87
Iowa-Ill Gas & Electric         10.6  84
Kansas Power & Light            10.0  80
Kentucky Utilities               9.9  74
Minnesota Power & Light         10.5  78
Northern States Power           12.3  81
Oklahoma Gas & Electric         10.7  73
Orange & Rockland Utilities      9.8  78
Pennsylvania Power & Light      10.6  75
```

```
Piedmont Natural Gas        11.3  68
Potomac Electric Power      13.0  94
TECO Energy                 12.3  65
Texas Utilities              8.1  67
Union Electric              10.0  77
Wisconsin Energy            10.7  63
Wicor                       20.9   .
;
```

Calculating Standard Deviation of Dividends

You use the MEANS procedure to calculate the standard deviation of dividends and create an output data set containing these values. The STD= option in the OUTPUT statement specifies that the standard deviations of the listed variables (STOCK1-STOCK23) be stored in the output data set. The 23 standard deviations are to be named STD1-STD23.

```
/* Calculating the Standard Deviations of Dividend Growth Rates */
proc means data=dcf2 noprint;
   var stock1-stock23;
   output out=dcf_std1 std=std1-std23;
run;
```

After calculating the standard deviations and storing them in the DCF_STD1 data set, the DCF_STD1 data set is transposed with PROC TRANSPOSE to facilitate merging with the DCF9 data set.

Note that the OUT= option in the PROC TRANSPOSE statement names the output data set. In this example, the output data set is named DCF_STD2. The RENAME option is used to rename the variable COL1 (as named by PROC TRANSPOSE) to STD.

In this example, the variables STD1-STD23 are specified. Prior to transposing, these 23 values are stored in one observation (1 row) and 23 columns; after transposing, the values are stored in 23 observations (23 rows) and 1 column. PROC TRANSPOSE creates a variable _NAME_ containing the names of the variables being transposed and, for this example, a variable named COL1 containing the values of the transposed variables.

```
/* Transposing the Data Set Containing the Standard Deviations */
proc transpose data=dcf_std1 out=dcf_std2(rename=(col1=std));
   var std1-std23;
run;
```

Lastly, PROC PRINT is used to print the first five observations of the transposed data set.

```
proc print data=dcf_std2 (obs=5);
   var std;
   title2 'Standard Deviations of Dividends';
   title3 'First Five Observations';
run;
```

Output 2.15
Standard Deviations
of Dividends

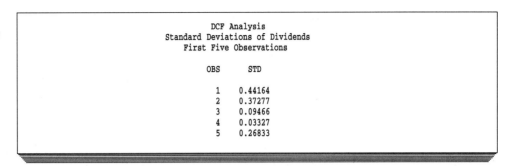

```
                        DCF Analysis
                Standard Deviations of Dividends
                    First Five Observations

                       OBS      STD

                        1     0.44164
                        2     0.37277
                        3     0.09466
                        4     0.03327
                        5     0.26833
```

Merging Data Sets

Prior to performing the regression analysis, you use a DATA step to merge the DCF9, DCF_STD2, and DCF_CAL1 data sets. Merging these data sets produces a single data set containing the dependent and independent variables for the regression analysis. The following statements merge the data sets, and PROC PRINT is used to print the first five observations.

```
data dcf_cal2;
   merge dcf9 dcf_std2 dcf_cal1;
run;

proc print data=dcf_cal2 (obs=5);
   var pe gc pr std;
   title2 'Cross-Sectional Multiple Regression Data';
   title3 'First Five Observations';
run;
```

Output 2.16
Data for
Cross-Sectional
Multiple Regression
Analysis

```
                         DCF Analysis
              Cross-Sectional Multiple Regression Data
                     First Five Observations

         OBS     PE       GC       PR      STD

          1    14.0    0.065162   48    0.44164
          2    10.5    0.046283   88    0.37277
          3     7.3    0.014902   58    0.09466
          4     8.2    0.008323   54    0.03327
          5    10.3    0.045435   76    0.26833
```

Performing Cross-Sectional Multiple Regression Analysis

You use PROC REG to fit the cross-sectional multiple regression model. Cross-sectional analysis is performed at a point in time across several variables. The cross-sectional variables are collected for the end of 1990. Note that cross-sectional analysis is analogous to a photograph, stopping the flow of time for an instant, whereas time series analysis is analogous to a movie, a series of pictures, forming a moving picture.

The model to be fit is of the form

$$PE_i = a + b \times GC_i + c \times PR_i + d \times STD_i + \epsilon_i \quad .$$

The PROC REG statements to fit this model and calculate the predicted and residuals values are shown in the following example. The MODEL statement specifies the model to be fit: the dependent variable (PE) on the left, and the independent variables on the right (GC, PR, STD). The OUTPUT statement creates a new data set containing the specified values and statistics. In this example, the predicted and residual values are included in the output data set, DCF_REG1. The P= and R= options specify that the predicted and residual values, respectively, are included in the output data set. In this example, the predicted values are named P, and the residual values are named R.

```
proc reg data=dcf_cal2;
   model pe=gc pr std;
      output out=dcf_reg1 p=p r=r;
run;
```

Output 2.17
Fitted
Cross-Sectional
Multiple Regression
Model

```
                                DCF Analysis
                   Cross-Sectional Multiple Regression Data

       Model: MODEL1
       Dependent Variable: PE          Price Earnings Ratio 1990

                             Analysis of Variance

                               Sum of        Mean
          Source      DF       Squares       Square      F Value      Prob>F

          Model        3       87.53104     29.17701      16.475      0.0001
          Error       18       31.87851      1.77103
          C Total     21      119.40955


               Root MSE       1.33080      R-square      0.7330
               Dep Mean      11.00455      Adj R-sq      0.6885
               C.V.          12.09318


                             Parameter Estimates

                          Parameter      Standard     T for H0:
          Variable   DF    Estimate         Error    Parameter=0    Prob > |T|

          INTERCEP   1      8.315850     1.93401309       4.300       0.0004
          GC         1    102.156361    19.06432074       5.359       0.0001
          PR         1     -0.017311     0.02332233      -0.742       0.4675
          STD        1     -4.119472     4.14134928      -0.995       0.3331
```

Interpretation of output

In Output 2.17, the fitted model is as follows:

$$PE_i = 8.31585 + 102.15636 \times GC_i - 0.01731 \times PR_i - 4.11947 \times STD_i$$

The overall fit of this model is good, as the following statistics indicate:

□ The *F*-Statistic is 16.475 with 3 and 18 degrees of freedom and is significantly different from 0 at *p*-values (Prob>F) at or below .0001. This *F*-test is a joint test of the model parameters being different from 0.

□ The R-Square is .7330, indicating that over 73 percent of the variation in the dependent variable PE is accounted for by the model.

Only the intercept and GC slope parameter are significantly different from 0 at the .10 level. You may want to drop the variables PR and STD from the model or respecify the model in some other form.

Plotting Residual Values

By plotting the residual values, you can visually assess the fit of the model, and you can visually identify overvalued and undervalued stocks. Each residual value indicates the deviation of the actual price-earnings ratio from the predicted price-earnings ratio.

Residual values are actual values minus predicted values. *Positive residual values* indicate that the stock has a higher price-earnings ratio than would otherwise be expected. You conclude, other things remaining equal, that these stocks are overvalued relative to the other stocks used in the cross-section analysis. *Negative residual values* indicate that the stock has a lower price-earnings ratio than would otherwise be expected, and these stocks are undervalued relative to the other stocks used in the analysis.

You can plot the residual values using the DCF_REG1 data set and the following PROC PLOT statements:

```
proc plot data=dcf_reg1 vpct=125;
   plot r*gc='*' / vref=0;
   title2 'PE Regression Residuals';
   title3 'versus Compound Growth Rate';
run;
```

Output 2.18
Plot of PE
Regression
Residuals versus
Compound Growth
Rate

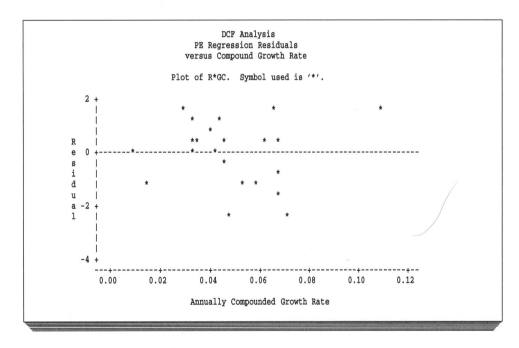

Printing Residual Values

You can print the residual values using PROC PRINT. Prior to printing the residual values, you may want to use a DATA step to create a new variable that assigns an identifying value to each stock, indicating if it is relatively overvalued or undervalued. The following statements perform these tasks. The results are printed in Output 2.19.

```
data dcf_reg2;
   set dcf_reg1;
   if r=. then hi_lo='.....';
   else if r>0 then hi_lo='Over ';
   else if r=0 then hi_lo='0    ';
   else if r<0 then hi_lo='Under';
run;

proc print data=dcf_reg2;
   var firm r hi_lo;
   title2 'Regression Residuals and';
   title3 'Over- and Undervalued Variable, HI_LO';
run;
```

Output 2.19
Printing Regression Residuals

```
                             DCF Analysis
                        Regression Residuals and
                  Over- and Undervalued Variable, HI_LO

       OBS    FIRM                          R       HI_LO

         1    3M Company                 1.67767    Over
         2    Allegheny Power            0.51508    Over
         3    Cincinnati G&E            -1.14418    Under
         4    Detroit Edison             0.10574    Over
         5    Dominion Resources        -0.23625    Under
         6    Duke Power                 1.18870    Over
         7    Eli Lilly                  1.71255    Over
         8    Green Mountain Power       1.33750    Over
         9    Iowa-Ill Gas & Electric    0.19922    Over
        10    Kansas Power & Light      -1.19801    Under
        11    Kentucky Utilities         0.07806    Over
        12    Minnesota Power & Light   -1.19131    Under
        13    Northern States Power      0.59233    Over
        14    Oklahoma Gas & Electric    0.69613    Over
        15    Orange & Rockland Utilities 0.20292   Over
        16    Pennsylvania Power & Light 1.56491    Over
        17    Piedmont Natural Gas      -1.53668    Under
        18    Potomac Electric Power     0.50012    Over
        19    TECO Energy               -0.65344    Under
        20    Texas Utilities           -2.33427    Under
        21    Union Electric             0.44788    Over
        22    Wisconsin Energy          -2.52468    Under
        23    Wicor                         .       .....
```

Interpretation of output

In Output 2.19, the regression residuals and the overvalue and undervalue indicating the variable, HI_LO, are printed. There are 14 stocks that are relatively overvalued in this cross-section and 8 stocks that are undervalued, while the WICOR stock has a missing PE ratio.

When you are fully satisfied with your cross-sectional analysis for identifying overvalued and undervalued stocks, only then do you want to make investment decisions based upon your analysis. An investment strategy you may want to consider is buying and holding stocks that are undervalued, while selling stocks that are overvalued.

Chapter Summary

This chapter presents methods of using SAS software to perform discounted cash flow (DCF) analyses. Examples presented are DCF analyses for various assumptions of dividend growth over time and a cross-sectional multiple regression approach to identifying overvalued and undervalued stocks.

Learning More

□ For more information on the DATA step, see *SAS Language, Reference, Version 6, First Edition*; *SAS Language and Procedures, Usage*; and *SAS Language and Procedures, Usage 2, Version 6, First Edition.*

□ For more information on PROC REG, see *SAS/STAT User's Guide, Version 6, Fourth Edition, Volume 1* and *Volume 2.*

□ For more information on PROC MODEL, see *SAS/ETS User's Guide, Version 6, Second Edition* and *SAS/ETS Software: Applications Guide 2, Econometric Modeling, Simulation, and Forecasting, Version 6, First Edition.*

□ For more information on PROC MEANS, PROC PLOT, PROC PRINT, and PROC TRANSPOSE, see *SAS Procedures Guide, Version 6, Third Edition*; *SAS Language and Procedures, Usage*; and *SAS Language and Procedures, Usage 2.*

□ For more information about regression models, see *SAS System for Regression, Second Edition* by R. Freund and R. Littell.

References

Elton, E. and Gruber, M. (1987), *Modern Portfolio Theory and Investment Analysis, Third Edition*, New York: John Wiley & Sons, Inc.

Jones, C. (1991), *Investments: Analysis and Management, Third Edition*, New York: John Wiley & Sons, Inc.

Whitbeck, V. and Kisor, M. (1963), "New Tool in Investment Decision Making," *Financial Analysts Journal*, May-June, pp. 55-62.

Chapter **3** Sorting and Clustering Stocks

Introduction

This chapter describes approaches to sorting and clustering stocks. Sorting and clustering techniques assist investors with the difficult task of selecting stocks of interest. Consider the magnitude of the selection task given that there are thousands of stocks listed on the major U.S. exchanges: NYSE, AMEX, and NASDAQ (not to mention the stocks and futures traded on local exchanges, plus stock options, international securities, and so on).

Sorting and clustering stocks into groups is intuitively appealing. For example, given expectations of the future, some stocks will generate greater returns per unit of risk and will be preferred by investors. Investment houses often use sorting and clustering techniques to select stocks of interest. Then investors can create portfolios from the resulting set of stocks.

You can sort and cluster stocks by any measurable criteria based on industry type, geographic location, expected future returns, price-earnings ratios, dividend yields, risk level, or any other factors that can be measured or estimated. Which criteria you choose depends on your purpose and use for the analysis.

Sorting Stocks by Financial Characteristics

A wide variety of sorting tasks can be performed with the SORT procedure. For example, you can sort stocks by one or more characteristics and in ascending or descending order. Many financial characteristics can be used to sort stocks into clusters. For example, you may want to sort stocks by price-earnings (PE) ratio, dividend yield, dividend pay-out ratio (PR), trading volume, and so on. As an example of the many sort analyses you may want to perform, this section shows you how to sort stocks by PE ratio and by average dividend yields in ascending and descending orders.

Sorting Stocks by Price-Earnings Ratio

Studies conducted by Basu (1977 and 1983) show that stocks with low PE ratios yielded higher returns, even when adjusted for risk and other characteristics. Thus, as an example of sorting stocks, you can use PROC SORT to sort stocks by PE ratios then narrow the stocks of interest to those with lower PE ratios. This example uses the 23 common stocks introduced in the DCF9 data set of Chapter 2, "Discounted Cash Flow (DCF) Analysis."

The following statements sort the stocks by their 1990 PE ratio. Note that ascending order (lowest to highest) is the default method of sorting in PROC SORT. The first five observations of the sorted data are printed with PROC PRINT and shown in Output 3.1.

```
proc sort data=dcf9 out=dcf9a;
   by pe;
run;

   /* Printing the First Five Observations */
proc print data=dcf9a (obs=5) label;
   title 'Sorting and Clustering Stocks';
   title2 'Sorting Stocks by PE Ratios';
run;
```

Output 3.1
Sorting Stocks by
PE Ratios

```
                    Sorting and Clustering Stocks
                    Sorting Stocks by PE Ratios

                                       Price      Dividend
                                      Earnings     Payout
          OBS   FIRM                    Ratio       Ratio

           1    Cincinnati G&E           7.3         58
           2    Texas Utilities          8.1         67
           3    Detroit Edison           8.2         54
           4    Orange & Rockland Utilities  9.8     78
           5    Kentucky Utilities       9.9         74
```

Subsetting a Data Set

After an initial sorting, you may want to create a data set containing a subset of the sorted observations. You can use a DATA step to create subsets of the sorted observations. For this example, you use a SET statement and the OBS= option in a DATA step to create a data set containing the 15 stocks with the lowest PE ratios. Then, you use PROC PRINT to print the new data set, as shown in Output 3.2.

```
    /* Keeping Stocks with Low PE Ratios */
data dcf9b;
    set dcf9a (obs=15);
run;

    /* Printing Stocks with Low PE Ratios */
proc print data=dcf9b label;
    title2 'Stocks with Lowest PE Ratios';
run;
```

Output 3.2
Printing Stocks with the Lowest PE Ratios

```
                    Sorting and Clustering Stocks
                     Stocks with Lowest PE Ratios

                                      Price      Dividend
                                    Earnings      Payout
         OBS    FIRM                   Ratio       Ratio

           1    Cincinnati G&E            7.3         58
           2    Texas Utilities          8.1         67
           3    Detroit Edison           8.2         54
           4    Orange & Rockland Utilities  9.8     78
           5    Kentucky Utilities       9.9         74
           6    Kansas Power & Light    10.0         80
           7    Union Electric          10.0         77
           8    Dominion Resources      10.3         76
           9    Allegheny Power         10.5         88
          10    Minnesota Power & Light 10.5         78
          11    Iowa-Ill Gas & Electric 10.6         84
          12    Pennsylvania Power & Light  10.6     75
          13    Oklahoma Gas & Electric 10.7         73
          14    Wisconsin Energy        10.7         63
          15    Green Mountain Power    10.8         87
```

Interpretation of output

Output 3.2 lists the 15 stocks with the lowest PE ratios and their dividend pay-out ratio. These 15 stocks are used in later examples for cluster analysis, based on their average dividend yields over the previous five years (1986-1990).

Sorting by More Than One Variable

You can also use PROC SORT to sort stocks by more than one variable. For example, with a large number of stocks, you may want to sort first by price-earnings ratio (PE), then by dividend pay-out ratio (PR). You can perform this sort with the following PROC SORT statements. The output from these statements is not shown.

```
proc sort data=dcf9 out=dcf9a1;
   by pe pr;
run;
```

The previous statements sort first by price-earnings ratio (from low to high); then, the stocks within each level of price-earnings ratio are sorted by dividend pay-out ratio (from low to high). You may want to sort by price-earnings ratio (from low to high), then, within each level of price-earnings ratio, by dividend pay-out ratio (from high to low). You can perform a sort from the highest value to the lowest value with the DESCENDING option of the BY statement in PROC SORT.

The following PROC SORT statements sort first by PE (low to high), then within each PE level by PR (high to low). The output from these statements is not shown.

```
proc sort data=dcf9 out=dcf9a2;
   by pe descending pr;
run;
```

For more information on sorting data with PROC SORT, see the *SAS Procedures Guide, Version 6, Third Edition, SAS Language and Procedures, Usage, Version 6, First Edition*, and *SAS Language and Procedures, Usage 2, Version 6, First Edition.*

Clustering Stocks by Financial Characteristics

Intuitively, you can think of cluster analysis as an advanced form of sorting, and, like sorting, any measurable criteria of similarity can be utilized. The goal is to group similar stocks into clusters. This section uses the 15 stocks with the lower price-earnings ratios for cluster analysis based on dividend yields over the period 1986-1990. This section proceeds by

□ creating the DCF10 data set

□ plotting analysis with PROC PLOT

□ performing preliminary analysis with PROC CORR and the DATA step

□ performing cluster analysis with PROC CLUSTER.

After performing cluster analysis, you can use the SAS/STAT TREE procedure (and the output from PROC CLUSTER) to draw *tree diagrams* (also known as dendrograms) to graphically represent the distance between clusters.

Creating the DCF10 Data Set

You use a DATA step to create the DCF10 data set containing the average dividend yields over the period 1986-1990. The variable names are the NYSE symbols. The 15 stocks with the low PE ratios from Output 3.2 are included in the DCF10 data set. These statements produce no output.

```
data dcf10;
    input year cin txu dte oru ku kan uep d ayp mpl
          iwg ppl oge wse gmp;
    label cin='Cincinnati G&E'
          txu='Texas Utilities'
          dte='Detroit Edison'
          oru='Orange & Rockland Utilities'
          ku='Kentucky Utilities'
          kan='Kansas Power & Light'
          uep='Union Electric'
          d='Dominion Resources'
          ayp='Allegheny Power'
          mpl='Minnesota Power & Light'
          iwg='Iowa-Ill Gas & Electric'
          ppl='Pennsylvania Power & Light'
          oge='Oklahoma Gas & Electric'
          wse='Wisconsin Energy'
          gmp='Green Mountain Power';
    cards;
1986  8.4  7.9  9.7 6.5 6.5 5.9 7.1 6.7 6.7 5.6 7.1 7.2 6.1 5.1 7.1
1987  8.2  8.9 10.7 7.2 6.9 6.4 7.5 6.9 7.3 6.1 7.5 7.6 6.7 5.7 7.4
1988  8.4 10.4 11.4 7.3 7.0 6.9 8.4 7.0 7.8 7.2 8.5 7.7 7.4 6.0 7.8
1989  8.1  8.9  7.8 7.7 7.2 7.4 7.8 7.0 7.9 7.0 7.8 7.4 6.7 5.7 7.8
1990  8.0  8.3  6.5 7.9 7.5 8.0 7.7 7.4 8.3 7.5 8.0 7.1 6.8 5.9 8.3
;
```

For the purposes of the examples in this chapter, no additional sorting of the data is performed. For example, you may want to form a subset of the data containing only the 1990 values, sort the data by dividend yields in descending order, and then perform cluster analysis on the stocks with the highest dividend yields.

Plotting Analysis

Prior to performing cluster analysis, you may want to visually examine the data for clusters and patterns. For this example, you are searching for stocks whose dividend yields tend to move together over time. The following PROC PLOT statements plot the dividend yields over time (for the first five stocks), and the results are shown in Output 3.3.

```
proc plot data=dcf10 vpct=200;
    plot cin * year ='c'
         txu * year ='t'
         dte * year ='d'
         oru * year ='o'
         ku  * year ='k' / overlay;
    title2 'Plotting Dividend Yields 1986-1990';
run;
```

Output 3.3
Plotting Dividend
Yields Over Time

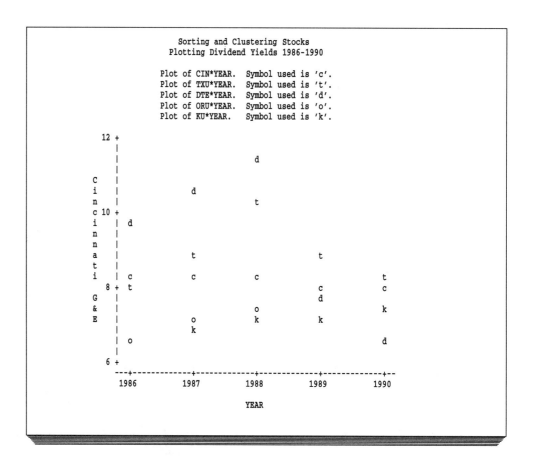

```
                            Sorting and Clustering Stocks
                          Plotting Dividend Yields 1986-1990

                    Plot of CIN*YEAR.   Symbol used is 'c'.
                    Plot of TXU*YEAR.   Symbol used is 't'.
                    Plot of DTE*YEAR.   Symbol used is 'd'.
                    Plot of ORU*YEAR.   Symbol used is 'o'.
                    Plot of KU*YEAR.    Symbol used is 'k'.

        12 +
           |
           |                           d
           |
    C      |
    i      |             d
    n      |                           t
    c  10 +
    i      | d
    n      |
    n      |
    a      |             t                        t
    t      |
    i      | c           c             c
        8 + t                                     c           t
    G      |                                      d
    &      |                           o                      k
    E      |             o             k          k
           |             k
           | o                                                d
           |
        6 +
           ---+-------------+-------------+-------------+-------------+--
           1986          1987          1988          1989          1990

                                    YEAR
```

Interpretation of output

Output 3.3 shows that the dividend yields for the stocks over the period 1986-1988 tend to rise (all except CIN). For the period 1989-1990, the output shows less dispersion but no clear pattern of increases and decreases emerges.

From a visual inspection of this plot, no obvious clusters of stocks appear. Note that all of these stocks are already similar in that they are all utility stocks and have lower price-earnings ratios. However, the correlations between the stock dividend yields can reveal which stocks are more similar (in terms of dividend yields), as shown in the next section.

Preliminary Analysis

Cluster analysis is based on the distance between the observations of the variables. Distance matrices are calculated by transforming correlation matrices or by some other method to generate decreasing scale Euclidean distance measures.

Prior to using PROC CLUSTER to perform cluster analysis, you need to either create a matrix of Euclidean coordinates or a matrix of distance dissimilarities as an input data set for PROC CLUSTER. This section takes you through the following steps to create one type of distance dissimilarity input data sets.

1. Use the CORR PROCEDURE to calculate the matrix of Pearson correlation coefficients for each pairwise combination of stocks.

2. Use a DATA step to tailor the matrix of correlation coefficients.

3. Use a DATA step to convert the tailored matrix of correlations to decreasing scale Euclidean distances (also called *dissimilarities*).

If you have already calculated a matrix of dissimilarities between the stock returns, you can proceed to the section, "Performing Cluster Analysis" and perform the cluster analysis using PROC CLUSTER.

Creating a Correlation Matrix

You use PROC CORR and the DCF10 data set to create a matrix of Pearson correlation coefficients. The Pearson correlation coefficient between the average dividend yields of stocks x and y (with means $\bar{x}$ and $\bar{y}$) is calculated in the following formula:

$$r_{xy} = \frac{\sum_{t=1}^{T} \left(x_t - \bar{x} \right) \left(y_t - \bar{y} \right)}{\sqrt{\sum_{t=1}^{T} \left(x_t - \bar{x} \right)^2 \sum_{t=1}^{T} \left(y_t - \bar{y} \right)^2}}$$

These PROC CORR statements calculate the pairwise correlations between the average dividend yields of the 15 stocks. In all, 225 (15 × 15) pairwise correlations are calculated.

Explanation of syntax

PROC CORR
 invokes the CORR PROCEDURE. The following options of the PROC CORR statement are specified:

DATA= specifies the input data set for analysis. In this example, the input data set is the DCF10 data set.

OUTP= creates an output data set containing the Pearson correlation coefficients. In this example, the output data set is DCF10A.

NOSIMPLE suppresses the printing of simple descriptive statistics for each variable used in the analysis.

VAR
 lists the variables for analysis.

Example code

```
proc corr data=dcf10 outp=dcf10a nosimple;
   var cin txu dte oru ku kan uep d ayp mpl
       iwg ppl oge wse gmp;
   title2 'Part of the Correlation Matrix';
run;
```

A partial listing of the results from these statements is shown in Output 3.4.

Output 3.4
Partial Listing of the
Pearson Correlation
Matrix

```
                        Sorting and Clustering Stocks
                        Part of the Correlation Matrix

                            Correlation Analysis

        Pearson Correlation Coefficients / Prob > |R| under Ho: Rho=0 / N = 5

                              CIN        TXU        DTE        ORU         KU

     CIN                   1.00000    0.32667    0.83588   -0.83278   -0.83822
     Cincinnati G&E           0.0     0.5916     0.0778     0.0800     0.0762

     TXU                    0.32667   1.00000    0.57160    0.21531    0.14366
     Texas Utilities        0.5916      0.0      0.3141     0.7280     0.8177

     DTE                    0.83588   0.57160    1.00000   -0.62067   -0.67396
     Detroit Edison         0.0778    0.3141       0.0      0.2639     0.2122

     ORU                   -0.83278   0.21531   -0.62067    1.00000    0.98495
     Orange & Rockland Utilities 0.0800 0.7280   0.2639       0.0      0.0022
```

Interpretation of output

Output 3.4 is a partial listing of the symmetric pairwise correlation matrix between the average dividend yields of the 15 firms. Correlation coefficients range from -1 to +1. The larger the correlations, the greater the tendency for the average dividend yields to move together over time.

For example, the average dividend yields of Cincinnati Gas & Electric (CIN) and Detroit Edison (DTE) have a correlation coefficent of .83588, which is higher than the correlation coefficient of .32667 between Cincinnati Gas and Electric and Texas Utilities (TXU). You can conclude that the average dividend yields of Cincinnati G&E and Detroit Edison move together more closely than the average dividend yields of Cincinnati Gas and Electric and Texas Utilities.

Note that PROC CORR also performs a test that shows the correlation coefficients are equal to 0. The *p*-value of the test (listed under the correlation coefficients) indicates the level of significance. The tests indicate that the correlation between CIN and TXU is not different from 0, while the correlation between CIN and DTE is different from 0 at the .10 level of significance.

Positively signed correlations indicate that the average dividend yields move in the same direction. Negatively signed correlations indicate that the average dividend yields move in opposite directions. Intuitively, you expect that stocks with negatively correlated average dividend yields are farther apart (in distance) than stocks with positively correlated average dividend yields.

Printing a PROC CORR Output Data Set

You use the following PROC PRINT statements to print the PROC CORR output data set DCF10A. Only the first ten observations of the _TYPE_, _NAME_, CIN, TXU, and DTE variables are shown in Output 3.5.

```
proc print data=dcf10a (obs=10) label;
   var _type_ _name_ cin txu dte;
   title2 'PROC CORR Output Data Set, DCF10A';
run;
```

Output 3.5
Partial Listing of the
PROC CORR
Output Data Set
DCF10A

```
                        Sorting and Clustering Stocks
                     PROC CORR Output Data Set, DCF10A

                                    Cincinnati    Texas      Detroit
          OBS    _TYPE_   _NAME_       G&E       Utilities    Edison

            1    MEAN                8.22000     8.88000     9.22000
            2    STD                 0.17889     0.94974     2.03642
            3    N                   5.00000     5.00000     5.00000
            4    CORR     CIN        1.00000     0.32667     0.83588
            5    CORR     TXU        0.32667     1.00000     0.57160
            6    CORR     DTE        0.83588     0.57160     1.00000
            7    CORR     ORU       -0.83278     0.21531    -0.62067
            8    CORR     KU        -0.83822     0.14366    -0.67396
            9    CORR     KAN       -0.80170     0.10941    -0.73438
           10    CORR     UEP        0.02946     0.91565     0.20705
```

Interpretation of output

The first three data set observations in Output 3.5 are the mean, the standard deviation, and the number of values used to calculate the listed statistics. The remaining observations are the Pearson correlations which can be used to create a distance matrix for PROC CLUSTER. The section "Creating a Distance Matrix for PROC CLUSTER" shows you how to tailor the PROC CORR output data set to create a distance matrix.

Sorting a PROC CORR Output Data Set

You can use the correlation coefficients as a measure of the "closeness" of one stock to another, as noted in the interpretation of Output 3.4. You may want to sort the PROC CORR output data set by a stock to discover with which stocks it is most and least correlated. You sort the DCF10A data set by the variable CIN and print the results with the following statements. Note that the DATA step deletes unneeded observations. The results are shown in Output 3.6.

```
      /* Deleting Unneeded Observations */
data dcf10b (drop=_type_);
   set dcf10a;
   if _type_='CORR';
run;

      /* Sorting by CIN */
proc sort data=dcf10b out=dcf10b1;
   by cin;
run;

      /* Printing Sorted Data Set */
proc print data=dcf10b1;
   var _name_ cin;
   title2 'Sorted Correlation Matrix';
run;
```

Output 3.6
Sorting the DCF10B
Data Set by the
Variable CIN

```
                    Sorting and Clustering Stocks
                      Sorted Correlation Matrix

            OBS      _NAME_      CIN

             1        KU       -0.83822
             2        ORU      -0.83278
             3        KAN      -0.80170
             4        D        -0.76743
             5        AYP      -0.70281
             6        GMP      -0.70035
             7        MPL      -0.53932
             8        WSE      -0.39211
             9        IWG      -0.10090
            10        OGE      -0.01211
            11        UEP       0.02946
            12        TXU       0.32667
            13        PPL       0.43853
            14        DTE       0.83588
            15        CIN       1.00000
```

Interpretation of output

The correlation coefficients of CIN are listed in ascending order in Output 3.6. The correlation coefficients corresponds to the "closeness" of dividend yield movements between CIN and the dividend yields of the other stocks. This order indicates that KU (Kentucky Utilities), ORU (Orange and Rockland Utilities), and KAN (Kansas Power and Light) are "farthest away from" CIN while DTE (Detroit Edison) and CIN, itself are "closest to" CIN.

The practical use for the information from this example output is that if you want to include a stock with similar dividend yields to CIN in your portfolio, select DTE. If you want to include a stock with dissimilar dividend yields to CIN in your portfolio, select KU, ORU, or KAN.

Creating a Distance Matrix for PROC CLUSTER

Although PROC CLUSTER can perform cluster analysis on coordinate data, for this example, it is more appropriate to create a distance matrix as input for PROC CLUSTER. The DCF10B data set (created in the code producing Output 3.6) can be transformed to a dissimilarities matrix in a DATA step by

Tasks performed by the program

1. converting the correlations (r) to dissimilarities (d) by computing the following (or by using some other decreasing function):

    $$d = 1 - r$$

    $$d = \sqrt{1 - r}$$

    $$d = 1 - r^2$$

    Note that your choice of conversion can affect the cluster analysis results. For this example, each correlation is transformed to a dissimilarity by the formula

    $$d = 1 - r \quad .$$

2. setting the data set TYPE= to DISTANCE.

Example code

```
/* Setting TYPE=DISTANCE and */
/* Converting Correlations to Dissimilarities */
data dist1(type=distance);
    set dcf10b;
    cin_d=1-cin;
    txu_d=1-txu;
    dte_d=1-dte;
    oru_d=1-oru;
    ku_d =1-ku;
    kan_d=1-kan;
    uep_d=1-uep;
    d_d  =1-d;
    ayp_d=1-ayp;
    mpl_d=1-mpl;
    iwg_d=1-iwg;
    ppl_d=1-ppl;
    oge_d=1-oge;
    wse_d=1-wse;
    gmp_d=1-gmp;
run;
```

You use PROC PRINT to print the dissimilarity matrix. Output 3.7 shows only the first eight variables of the first eight observations.

```
proc print data=dist1 (obs=8) label;
    title2 'Dissimilarity Distance Matrix';
run;
```

Output 3.7
Partial Listing of the
Dissimilarity
Distance Matrix

```
                        Sorting and Clustering Stocks
                        Dissimilarity Distance Matrix

  OBS   CIN_D    TXU_D    DTE_D    ORU_D    KU_D     KAN_D    UEP_D    D_D

   1   0.00000  0.67333  0.16412  1.83278  1.83822  1.80170  0.97054  1.76743
   2   0.67333  0.00000  0.42840  0.78469  0.85634  0.89059  0.08435  0.93805
   3   0.16412  0.42840  0.00000  1.62067  1.67396  1.73438  0.79295  1.66450
   4   1.83278  0.78469  1.62067  0.00000  0.01505  0.03962  0.47331  0.11082
   5   1.83822  0.85634  1.67396  0.01505  0.00000  0.01657  0.51586  0.04627
   6   1.80170  0.89059  1.73438  0.03962  0.01657  0.00000  0.51959  0.05851
   7   0.97054  0.08435  0.79295  0.47331  0.51586  0.51959  0.00000  0.58655
   8   1.76743  0.93805  1.66450  0.11082  0.04627  0.05851  0.58655  0.00000
```

Interpretation of output

Output 3.7 prints the dissimilarity matrix to be used as input for PROC CLUSTER. Note the following items about the dissimilarity matrix:

□   There are no negative values. This particular transformation has a range from 0 to 2.

□   The dissimilarity distance matrix is square and symmetric.

□   All elements of the main diagonal are 0. Intuitively, you expect a stock to have 0 distance from itself.

□ Elements that were negative in the correlation matrix are greater than 1 as transformed.

□ Correlations that were relatively larger positive values are transformed to relatively smaller dissimilarities.

These are general characteristics required of dissimilarity matrices of distances used as input for PROC CLUSTER. Note that these characteristics indicate a decreasing scale of dissimilarities. Intuitively, you expect stocks to be closest to other stocks with which they are highly positively correlated and farthest from other stocks with which they are highly negatively correlated.

Note: An excellent example of distance matrices can be found on most road maps, that is, the matrix of distances between cities.

After creating a dissimilarity distance matrix, you are ready to perform cluster analysis, as discussed in the following section.

Performing Cluster Analysis

You can perform clustering analyses with the following SAS/STAT procedures:

□ PROC CLUSTER performs hierarchical clustering using agglomerative methods for coordinate or distance data.

□ PROC FASTCLUS finds a specified number of disjoint clusters for coordinate data. PROC FASTCLUS is especially suitable for large data sets containing as many as 100,000 observations.

□ PROC VARCLUS finds both hierarchical and disjoint clustering of variables.

To illustrate cluster analysis, the examples in this chapter use PROC CLUSTER and distance data. The remainder of this section discusses some of the methods of cluster analysis available with PROC CLUSTER. Each method may produce different clusters. All methods are based on the standard agglomerative hierarchical clustering process. Each observation begins as a cluster by itself. The two closest clusters are merged to form a new cluster that replaces the two old clusters. Merging of the two closest clusters is repeated until only one cluster is left. The various clustering methods differ in how the distance between two clusters is computed.

In cluster analysis, distance is Euclidean length. For example, the Euclidean length of the vector **x** is the square root of the sum of the squares of the elements of **x**.

The following list describes some of the clustering methods available in PROC CLUSTER. Each is specified by the appropriate value for the METHOD= option in the PROC CLUSTER statement.

single linkage
    is obtained by specifying METHOD=SINGLE. The distance between two clusters is the minimum distance between an observation in one cluster and an observation in the other cluster. Single linkage has desirable theoretical properties, but it also has a notorious *chaining tendency* (tendency for observations to enter existing clusters rather than initiating new clusters).

average linkage
    is obtained by specifying METHOD=AVERAGE. The distance between two clusters is the average distance between pairs of observations, one in each cluster. By default, the average distance is squared unless you specify the NOSQUARE option.

centroid method linkage
> is obtained by specifying METHOD=CENTROID. The distance between two clusters is the squared Euclidean distance between the *centroids* (also known as means) of the clusters. This method is more robust to outliers than other methods.

complete linkage
> is obtained by specifying METHOD=COMPLETE. The distance between two clusters is the maximum distance between an observation in one cluster and an observation in the other cluster. Complete linkage is strongly biased toward producing clusters with roughly equal diameters and can be severely distorted by moderate outliers.

density linkage
> is obtained by specifying METHOD=DENSITY, which uses nonparametric probability density estimation. You must also specify one of the K=, R=, or HYBRID options to indicate the type of density estimation to be used.

K=	specifies the number of neighbors to use for the Kth-nearest-neighbor density estimation. The number of neighbors must be at least two but less than the number of observations.
R=	specifies the radius of the sphere of support for uniform-kernal density estimation. The value of R= must be greater than 0.
HYBRID	requests Wong's hybrid clustering method in which density estimates are computed from a preliminary cluster analysis using the K-means method. The DATA= data set must contain means, frequencies, and root-mean-square standard deviations of the preliminary clusters.

The remaining methods are EML method, flexible-beta method, McQuitty's similarity analysis, median method, two-stage density linkage, and Ward's minimum-variance method. Note that if you have no idea what kinds of clusters to expect, then select a relatively unbiased method, such as density linkage. For more information about these methods, see Chapter 6, "Introduction to Clustering Procedures," and Chapter 18, "The Cluster Procedure" in *SAS/STAT User's Guide, Version 6, Fourth Edition, Volume 1.*

The next section uses the SAS/STAT CLUSTER procedure to group stocks into clusters of similar stocks based on the distance data of the DIST1 data set.

K-Nearest-Neighbor Density-Linkage Cluster Analysis

The clustering analysis of this example uses the density-linkage method with the K= (Kth-nearest-neighbor method) option. In general, for this method, you decide the appropriate number of neighbors to initiate a cluster, perform the cluster analysis, and then examine the number of clusters and the stocks in each cluster.

The following PROC CLUSTER statements perform the Kth-nearest-neighbor density-linkage cluster analysis with K=2 for the DIST1 data set. The results are printed in Output 3.8.

Explanation of syntax

PROC CLUSTER
:   invokes the CLUSTER procedure. The following options of the PROC CLUSTER statement are specified.

DATA=
:   specifies the input data set containing observations to be clustered. Note that you cannot use a TYPE=CORR data set as input to PROC CLUSTER because PROC CLUSTER uses dissimilarities such as $1 - r$ or $1 - r^2$, where r is the correlation. You use a TYPE=DISTANCE input data set. For this example, the input data set is the DIST1 data set created for Output 3.7.

METHOD=
:   specifies the clustering method to be used by PROC CLUSTER. In this example METHOD=DENSITY. (With METHOD=DENSITY, you must also specify one of the following options: K=, R=, HYBRID.)

K=
:   specifies the number of neighbors to use for the K-nearest-neighbor density linkage cluster analysis. In this example, K=2.

OUTTREE=
:   creates an output data set that can be used by PROC TREE to draw a tree diagram. For this example, the OUTTREE= data set is the CLUST1 data set.

VAR
:   lists numeric variables to be used in the cluster analysis.

ID
:   identifies observations in the printed cluster history and in the OUTTREE= data set. If the ID statement is omitted, each observation is denoted by OBn, where n is the observation number.

Example code

```
proc cluster data=dist1 method=density k=2 outtree=clust1;
   var cin_d txu_d dte_d oru_d ku_d kan_d uep_d d_d
      ayp_d mpl_d iwg_d ppl_d oge_d wse_d gmp_d;
   id _name_ ;
   title 'Sorting and Clustering Stocks';
   title2 'Record of Clustering';
run;
```

Output 3.8
Cluster Record for
Kth-Nearest
Neighbor
Density-Linkage
Cluster Analysis for
K=2

```
                        Sorting and Clustering Stocks
                            Record of Clustering

                      Density Linkage Cluster Analysis

                                  K = 2

                                               Normalized
                                            Maximum Density
                                            in Each Cluster
     Number                    Frequency  Normalized
       of                       of New     Fusion
     Clusters  -Clusters Joined--  Cluster    Density    Lesser    Greater  Tie

       14     ORU    KU         2    100.0000   100.0000   100.0000
       13     CL14   KAN        3     95.1819    90.8068   100.0000
       12     AYP    GMP        2     77.2483    77.2483    77.2483
       11     CL12   MPL        3     68.6180    61.7223    77.2483
       10     CL11   D          4     60.6604    49.9371    77.2483
        9     UEP    IWG        2     52.5478    52.5478    52.5478
        8     CL9    OGE        3     51.9341    51.3346    52.5478
        7     CL8    WSE        4     27.8406    19.0995    52.5478
        6     CL7    TXU        5     26.6384    17.8414    52.5478
        5     CL6    PPL        6     13.2362    10.5207    52.5478
        4     CIN    DTE        2      9.1698     9.1698     9.1698

                    4 modal clusters have been formed.
```

Interpretation of output

Output 3.8 prints the cluster record of the Kth-nearest-neighbor density-linkage cluster analysis, where K=2, for the stocks in the DIST1 data set.

Initially, each of the 15 stocks is in a cluster by itself. The first two stocks to cluster were ORU and KU. This new cluster is designated CL14. After this clustering, only 14 clusters remain (1 consisting of ORU and KU, and 13 consisting of individual stocks).

The second clustering is between the CL14 and KAN. After the second clustering, 13 clusters remain (1 consisting of ORU, KU, and KAN, and 12 consisting of individual stocks).

The third clustering is a new cluster, initiated by the clustering of AYP (Allegheny Power) and GMP (Green Mountain Power), designated as CL12. Note that the fourth and fifth clusterings chain MPL (Minnesota Power and Light) and D (Dominion Resources) to the cluster with AYP and GMP, for a total of four stocks in this cluster.

The sixth clustering is a new cluster, initiated by the clustering of UEP (Union Electric) and IWG (Iowa-Illinois Gas and Electric), designated as CL9. The seventh through tenth clusterings chain OGE (Oklahoma Gas and Electric), WSE (Wisconsin Energy), TXU (Texas Utilities), and PPL (Pennsylvania Power and Light) to CL9.

The eleventh clustering is a new cluster, initiated by the clustering of CIN and DTE. After this clustering, four clusters remain:

□ ORU, KU, and KAN

□ AYP, GMP, MPL, and D

□ UEP, IWG, OGE, WSE, TXU, and PPL

□ CIN and DTE

If your research indicates that *K*th-nearest-neighbor density-linkage cluster analysis (where K=2) is appropriate, then you conclude that there are four clusters of stocks in the DIST1 data set. The stocks in each of the clusters are more similar to each other than to stocks in other clusters. In the section "Creating a Tree Diagram" later in this chapter, you use PROC TREE to create a tree diagram of the clusterings; that is, a visual representation of the clustering record.

The column titled "Frequency of New Cluster" contains the number of observations in the new cluster. The column titled "Normalized Fusion Density" contains the estimated density of the cluster. Consider a closed sphere centered at *x* with radius *r* (where *r* is the distance to the *K*th nearest neighbor). The estimated density at *x* is the proportion of the observations within the sphere divided by the volume of the sphere.

The column titled "Normalized Maximum Density in Each Cluster" lists the lesser (or minimum value) and the greater (or maximum values) of the two maximum-density values.

Additional *K*-Nearest-Neighbor Density-Linkage Cluster Analysis

Your research may indicate that K=3 density-linkage cluster analysis is appropriate. Specifying K=3 yields the following clusters.

□   KU, KAN, GMP, AYP, ORU, MPL, and D

□   UEP, IWG, OGE, TXU, WSE, PPL, DTE, and CIN

Specifying K=4 yields one cluster containing all of the stocks in the DIST1 data set. In general, the value you select for K depends on the number of stocks in your data set, the dissimilarity distance between them, and the magnitude of similarity appropriate for your analysis.

R-Radius Density-Linkage Cluster Analysis

The cluster analysis of this example uses the density-linkage method with the R= option (radius of the clustering sphere). The following PROC CLUSTER statements perform the *R*-radius density-linkage cluster analysis for R=.1. The results are printed in Output 3.9.

```
proc cluster data=dist1 method=density r=.1 outtree=clust2;
   var cin_d txu_d dte_d oru_d ku_d kan_d uep_d d_d
       ayp_d mpl_d iwg_d ppl_d oge_d wse_d gmp_d;
   id _name_ ;
run;
```

Output 3.9
Cluster Record
for R-Radius
Density-Linkage
Cluster Analysis for
R=.1

```
                         Sorting and Clustering Stocks
                              Record of Clustering

                         Density Linkage Cluster Analysis

                                    R = 0.1


                                                        Normalized
                                                     Maximum Density
                                                      in Each Cluster
        Number                    Frequency Normalized
          of                       of New    Fusion
        Clusters  -Clusters Joined--  Cluster   Density    Lesser   Greater  Tie

            14   KU       GMP         2     100.0000   100.0000  100.0000   T
            13   CL14     AYP         3     100.0000   100.0000  100.0000   T
            12   CL13     KAN         4     100.0000   100.0000  100.0000
            11   CL12     ORU         5      83.3333    71.4286  100.0000   T
            10   CL11     MPL         6      83.3333    71.4286  100.0000   T
             9   CL10     D           7      83.3333    71.4286  100.0000
             8   UEP      OGE         2      63.4921    57.1429   71.4286   T
             7   CL8      IWG         3      63.4921    57.1429   71.4286
             6   CL7      TXU         4      53.5714    42.8571   71.4286   T
             5   CL6      WSE         5      53.5714    42.8571   71.4286

                       5 modal clusters have been formed.
```

Interpretation of output

In Output 3.9, the first two stocks to cluster were KU and GMP. This new cluster is designated CL14. The next five clusterings chain AYP, KAN, ORU, MPL, and D to CL14.

Next, a second cluster is initiated consisting of UEP and OGE. This new cluster is designated CL8. The last three clusterings chain IWG, TXU, and WSE.

The remaining three stocks CIN, DTE, and PPL are farther than .1 away from these two clusters; therefore, these three stocks remain in clusters by themselves.

The five clusters are

□ KU, GMP, AYP, KAN, ORU, MPL, D

□ UEP, OGE, IWG, TXU, and WSE

□ PPL

□ CIN

□ DTE

Lastly, note that there are several ties in the cluster history. When there are ties, the cluster analysis results depend on the order of the observations in the input data set. In general, ties that occur early in the cluster history have little effect on the later clusterings. Ties that occur in the middle part of the cluster history are cause for further investigation. Ties late in the cluster history indicate important indeterminancies.

Additional *R*-Radius Density-Linkage Cluster Analysis

Your research may indicate that a different R= radius value is the appropriate criterion for your cluster analysis. In general, the smaller the specified R= value, the greater the number of clusters and the more similar the observations in each cluster.

The following table lists the R= radius values and the number of clusters that are formed for the 15 stocks in the DIST1 data set.

R= Radius Values	Number of Clusters
.025	10
.030	8
.035-.075	7
.080	6
.085-.130	5
.135-.140	4
.145-.160	3
.165-.195	2
.200	1

Additional Methods of Cluster Analysis

This section shows the results of using PROC CLUSTER with the following methods of cluster analysis:

□ single linkage

□ average linkage

□ centroid method

□ complete linkage

The following PROC CLUSTER statements perform the cluster analyses for the DIST1 data set. The only differences in the statements for each method are the specifications for the METHOD= option and the name of the OUTTREE= data set. The results are presented in Output 3.10.

```
/* Single Linkage Cluster Analysis */
proc cluster data=dist1 method=single outtree=clust3;
   var cin_d txu_d dte_d oru_d ku_d kan_d uep_d d_d
       ayp_d mpl_d iwg_d ppl_d oge_d wse_d gmp_d;
   id _name_ ;
run;

/* Average Linkage Cluster Analysis */
proc cluster data=dist1 method=average outtree=clust4;
   var cin_d txu_d dte_d oru_d ku_d kan_d uep_d d_d
       ayp_d mpl_d iwg_d ppl_d oge_d wse_d gmp_d;
   id _name_ ;
run;

/* Centroid Method of Cluster Analysis */
proc cluster data=dist1 method=centroid outtree=clust5;
   var cin_d txu_d dte_d oru_d ku_d kan_d uep_d d_d
       ayp_d mpl_d iwg_d ppl_d oge_d wse_d gmp_d;
   id _name_ ;
run;
```

```
                            /* Complete Linkage Cluster Analysis */
                       proc cluster data=dist1 method=complete outtree=clust6;
                          var cin_d txu_d dte_d oru_d ku_d kan_d uep_d d_d
                              ayp_d mpl_d iwg_d ppl_d oge_d wse_d gmp_d;
                          id _name_ ;
                       run;
```

Output 3.10
Clustering Records

```
                        Sorting and Clustering Stocks
                             Record of Clustering

                        Single Linkage Cluster Analysis

        Mean Distance Between Observations              =  0.58138

            Number                           Frequency    Normalized
              of                               of New      Minimum
            Clusters    --Clusters Joined--    Cluster     Distance      Tie

              14      ORU       KU                2       0.025885
              13      CL14      KAN               3       0.028506
              12      AYP       GMP               2       0.033509
              11      CL13      CL12              5       0.040670
              10      CL11      MPL               6       0.041938
               9      UEP       IWG               2       0.049261
               8      CL9       OGE               3       0.050425
               7      CL10      D                 7       0.051836
               6      CL8       WSE               4       0.135529
               5      TXU       CL6               5       0.145086
               4      CL5       CL7              12       0.226888
               3      CL4       PPL              13       0.246043
               2      CIN       DTE               2       0.282289
               1      CL2       CL3              15       0.336884
```

```
                        Sorting and Clustering Stocks
                             Record of Clustering

                        Average Linkage Cluster Analysis

        Root-Mean-Square Distance Between Observations   =  0.803778

            Number                           Frequency    Normalized
              of                               of New        RMS
            Clusters    --Clusters Joined--    Cluster     Distance      Tie

              14      ORU       KU                2       0.018723
              13      AYP       GMP               2       0.024238
              12      KAN       CL13              3       0.032916
              11      UEP       IWG               2       0.035631
              10      CL11      OGE               3       0.042714
               9      CL14      CL12              5       0.050223
               8      CL9       D                 6       0.087520
               7      CL8       MPL               7       0.106158
               6      CL10      WSE               4       0.132771
               5      TXU       PPL               2       0.177965
               4      CIN       DTE               2       0.204182
               3      CL5       CL6               6       0.460039
               2      CL3       CL7              13       0.806514
               1      CL4       CL2              15       1.706684
```

```
                        Sorting and Clustering Stocks
                           Record of Clustering

                      Centroid Hierarchical Cluster Analysis

        Root-Mean-Square Distance Between Observations   = 0.803778

             Number                          Frequency   Normalized
               of                             of New     Centroid
            Clusters    --Clusters Joined--   Cluster    Distance    Tie

               14      ORU        KU             2        0.018723
               13      AYP        GMP            2        0.024238
               12      KAN        CL13           3        0.030604
               11      UEP        IWG            2        0.035631
               10      CL11       OGE            3        0.038821
                9      CL14       CL12           5        0.046137
                8      CL9        D              6        0.083247
                7      CL8        MPL            7        0.098483
                6      CL10       WSE            4        0.130697
                5      TXU        PPL            2        0.177965
                4      CIN        DTE            2        0.204182
                3      CL5        CL6            6        0.447331
                2      CL3        CL7           13        0.773574
                1      CL4        CL2           15        1.652093
```

```
                        Sorting and Clustering Stocks
                           Record of Clustering

                       Complete Linkage Cluster Analysis

        Mean Distance Between Observations              = 0.58138

             Number                          Frequency   Normalized
               of                             of New     Maximum
            Clusters    --Clusters Joined--   Cluster    Distance    Tie

               14      ORU        KU             2        0.025885
               13      AYP        GMP            2        0.033509
               12      UEP        IWG            2        0.049261
               11      KAN        CL13           3        0.049878
               10      CL12       OGE            3        0.066572
                9      CL14       CL11           5        0.124908
                8      CL9        MPL            6        0.182588
                7      CL8        D              7        0.219629
                6      CL10       WSE            4        0.240652
                5      TXU        PPL            2        0.246043
                4      CIN        DTE            2        0.282289
                3      CL5        CL6            6        0.995718
                2      CL3        CL7           13        2.249289
                1      CL4        CL2           15        3.161819
```

Interpretation of output

Output 3.10 prints the cluster histories of the stock in the DIST1 data set for the single-linkage, average-linkage, centroid-method, and complete-linkage cluster analyses.

Note the following similarities among the methods:

□   ORU and KU are the first stocks to cluster.

□   CIN and DTE are the last stocks to join a cluster.

□   There are no ties.

Note the following differences among the methods:

□ The order of the stocks clustering differs among the methods for the intermediate clusterings.

□ The single-linkage approach initiates four clusters, while all other methods initiate five clusters.

□ The normalized distances of the single linkage, the average linkage, and the centroid method are derived from the squared input distances. The normalized distances of the complete method are derived from the values themselves. You use the NOSQUARE option in the PROC CLUSTER statement to prevent input values from being squared.

▶ *Caused* . . . . **Use Cluster Analysis with Care**

You are encouraged to perform cluster analysis with as many different methods as necessary until you are fully satisfied with your understanding of the results. Only when you are fully satisfied with your understanding of the results of your cluster analyses should you consider basing your investment strategies upon them. ▲

When you are fully satisfied with the results of your cluster analysis and you have selected a distance criteria, then you can select the stock clusters of interest for building your portfolio.

Additional Processing of Data Prior to Performing Cluster Analysis

For some data sets and for some purposes, you may find it useful to process the data prior to performing cluster analysis using some or all of the following procedures:

□ PROC ACECLUS (**A**pproximate **C**ovariance **E**stimation for **CLUS**tering) estimates the pooled within-cluster covariance matrix from coordinate data without knowledge of the clusters. If the clusters have equal and known within-cluster covariances, then the data can be transformed to make the clusters spherical so that any of the clustering methods can find the correct clusters. PROC ACECLUS outputs a data set containing the transformed variables as canonical scores to be used in the cluster analysis proper.

For example, the following PROC ACECLUS statements transform the variables X and Y into the canonical variables CAN1 and CAN2, which can be used by PROC CLUSTER for cluster analysis:

```
proc aceclus data=SASdataset1 out=SASdataset2 p=n;
   var x y;
run;

proc cluster data=SASdataset2 method=method;
   var can1 can2;
run;
```

□ PROC FACTOR calculates scoring coefficients and performs factor rotations. *Factor analysis* explains the correlations or covariances among a set of variables in terms of a limited number of unobservable latent variables (also known as scoring factors).

PROC FACTOR output data sets can be used as input for PROC VARCLUS. For example, the following PROC FACTOR statements specify a rotation, print the scoring factors, and create an output data set to be used as input for PROC VARCLUS.

```
proc factor data=SASdataset1 rotate=method score
          outstat=SASdataset2;
run;

proc varclus data=SASdataset2 initial=input;
run;
```

□ PROC PRINCOMP performs a principal component analysis and outputs principal component scores. *Principal component analysis* transforms a set of variables into a small number of linear combinations (new variables) that retain as much of the information as possible. If you have many different characteristics (variables) for each stock, you may want to perform principal component analysis to obtain a smaller set of characteristics for cluster analysis.

If your data are categorical (qualitative), use PROC CORRESP (instead of PROC PRINCOMP). If you want to find linear and nonlinear transformations of variables to optimize properties of the transformed variables' covariance or correlation matrix, you use PROC PRINQUAL.

□ PROC STANDARD standardizes variables to a specified mean and variance. With coordinate data, you can use the STANDARD option in the PROC CLUSTER statement to transform variables to a mean of 0 and standard deviation of 1. Note that outliers should be removed before standardization (unless the TRIM=n option is also specified in the PROC CLUSTER statement, which omits the specified percentage (n) of data points.)

Creating Tree Diagrams

You can use PROC TREE and the CLUST1 data set to create a tree diagram of the stages of the cluster analysis performed in Output 3.8. The following PROC TREE statements create the tree diagram.

Explanation of syntax

DATA= specifies the input data set defining the tree. For this example, the CLUST1 data set is specified.

HORIZONTAL orients the tree diagram with the height axis horizontal and the root at the left. If this option is not used, the height axis will be vertical, with the root at the top. For some tree diagrams, specifying the HORIZONTAL option can make the tree diagram considerably easier to read.

Example code

```
proc tree data=clust1 horizontal;
   title 'Sorting and Clustering Stocks';
   title2 'K-th Nearest Neighbor Clustering';
   title3 'Tree Diagram';
run;
```

Output 3.11
Tree Diagram for
Kth-Nearest-Neighbor
Cluster Analysis

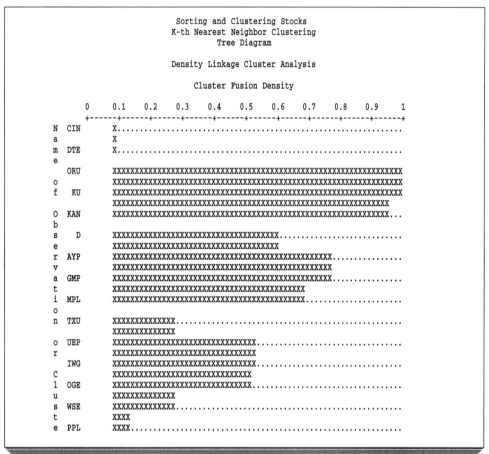

Interpretation of output

The tree diagram in Output 3.11 is a visual representation of the clustering history shown numerically in Output 3.8. In this horizontally oriented tree diagram, density is measured horizontally across the the tree diagram, with lower densities to the left. (Note that the right side of the diagram corresponds to closer *K*th nearest neighbors, while the left side corresponds to more distant *K*th nearest neighbors.) The root of the tree diagram is to the left, where the names of the variables are listed.

Each stock has two rows of Xs associated with it. The upper line of Xs indicates clustering with the stock above, while the lower line of Xs indicates the clustering with the stock below. (Note that the first stock joins only the cluster containing the second stock, while the last stock joins only the cluster containing the next to last stock.)

For example, the next-to-last stock, Wisconsin Energy (WSE), clusters with Oklahoma Gas and Electric (OGE) at a density of about .28, and it clusters with Pennsylvania Power and Light (PPL) at a density of about .13. You can conclude that WSE is more similar to

OGE than PPL, based on the criterion (dividend yield) used in this analysis. In general, the most similar stocks cluster first, while the least similar cluster last.

Additional Tree Diagrams

You can create tree diagrams for the clustering histories of Outputs 3.9 and 3.10 with the following PROC TREE statements. The MAXHEIGHT= and MINHEIGHT= options are used to specify the maximum and minimum values for some of the tree diagrams. The results are shown in Output 3.12.

```
proc tree data=clust2 horizontal;
    title2 'R-Radius Density Linkage Clustering';
    title3 'Tree Diagram';
run;

proc tree data=clust3 maxheight=.35 minheight=0 horizontal;
    title2 'Single Linkage Clustering Tree Diagram';
    title3';
run;

proc tree data=clust4 maxheight=1.8 minheight=0 horizontal;
    title2 'Average Linkage Clustering Tree Diagram';
run;

proc tree data=clust5 maxheight=1.8 minheight=.3 horizontal;
    title2 'Centroid Linkage Clustering Tree Diagram';
run;

proc tree data=clust6 maxheight=3.25 minheight=.3 horizontal;
    title2 'Complete Linkage Clustering Tree Diagram';
run;
```

Output 3.12
Tree Diagrams for
Cluster Analyses

```
                          Sorting and Clustering Stocks
                       R-Radius Density Linkage Clustering
                                 Tree Diagram

                        Density Linkage Cluster Analysis

                             Cluster Fusion Density

          0.5  0.55   0.6  0.65   0.7  0.75   0.8  0.85   0.9  0.95    1
          +-----+------+------+------+------+------+------+------+------+------+
   N  CIN    .
   a
   m  DTE    .
   e
      D    XXXXXXXXXXXXXXXXXXXXXXXXXXXXXXXXXXXXXXXX......................
   o       XXXXXXXXXXXXXXXXXXXXXXXXXXXXXXXXXXXXXXXX
   f  ORU  XXXXXXXXXXXXXXXXXXXXXXXXXXXXXXXXXXXXXX....................
           XXXXXXXXXXXXXXXXXXXXXXXXXXXXXXXXXXXXXX
   O  KU   XXXXXXXXXXXXXXXXXXXXXXXXXXXXXXXXXXXXXXXXXXXXXXXXXXXXXXXXXXXXX
   b       XXXXXXXXXXXXXXXXXXXXXXXXXXXXXXXXXXXXXXXXXXXXXXXXXXXXXXXXXXXXX
   s  GMP  XXXXXXXXXXXXXXXXXXXXXXXXXXXXXXXXXXXXXXXXXXXXXXXXXXXXXXXXXXXXX
   e       XXXXXXXXXXXXXXXXXXXXXXXXXXXXXXXXXXXXXXXXXXXXXXXXXXXXXXXXXXXXX
   r  AYP  XXXXXXXXXXXXXXXXXXXXXXXXXXXXXXXXXXXXXXXXXXXXXXXXXXXXXXXXXXXXX
   v       XXXXXXXXXXXXXXXXXXXXXXXXXXXXXXXXXXXXXXXXXXXXXXXXXXXXXXXXXXXXX
   a  KAN  XXXXXXXXXXXXXXXXXXXXXXXXXXXXXXXXXXXXXXXXXXXXXXXXXXXXXXXXXXXXX
   t       XXXXXXXXXXXXXXXXXXXXXXXXXXXXXXXXXXXXXXXXXX
   i  MPL  XXXXXXXXXXXXXXXXXXXXXXXXXXXXXXXXXXXXXXXX......................
   o
   n  PPL    .

   o  TXU  X...........................................................
   r       X
      UEP  XXXXXXXXXXXXXXX.............................................
   C       XXXXXXXXXXXXXXX
   l  OGE  XXXXXXXXXXXXXXX
   u       XXXXXXXXXXXXXXX
   s  IWG  XXXXXXXXXXXXXXX.............................................
   t       X
   e  WSE  X...........................................................
```

```
                              Single Linkage Clustering Tree Diagram

                                Single Linkage Cluster Analysis

                              Minimum Distance Between Clusters

                0.35      0.3      0.25      0.2      0.15      0.1      0.05       0
                +---------+---------+---------+---------+---------+---------+---------+
        N  CIN  XXXXXXXXXXX.......................................................
        a       XXXXXXXXXXX
        m  DTE  XXXXXXXXXXX........................................................
        e       X
           TXU  XXXXXXXXXXXXXXXXXXXXXXXXXXXXXXXXXXXXXXX.........................
        o       XXXXXXXXXXXXXXXXXXXXXXXXXXXXXXXXXXXXXXX
        f  UEP  XXXXXXXXXXXXXXXXXXXXXXXXXXXXXXXXXXXXXXXXXXXXXXXXXXXXXXX.........
                XXXXXXXXXXXXXXXXXXXXXXXXXXXXXXXXXXXXXXXXXXXXXXXXXXXXXXX
        O  IWG  XXXXXXXXXXXXXXXXXXXXXXXXXXXXXXXXXXXXXXXXXXXXXXXXXXXXXXXX.........
        b       XXXXXXXXXXXXXXXXXXXXXXXXXXXXXXXXXXXXXXXXXXXXXXXXXXXXXXXX
        s  OGE  XXXXXXXXXXXXXXXXXXXXXXXXXXXXXXXXXXXXXXXXXXXXXXXXXXXXX.........
        e       XXXXXXXXXXXXXXXXXXXXXXXXXXXXXXXXXXXXXXXXXXX
        r  WSE  XXXXXXXXXXXXXXXXXXXXXXXXXXXXXXXXXXXXXXXXXX.........................
        v       XXXXXXXXXXXXXXXXXXXXXXXXXX
        a  ORU  XXXXXXXXXXXXXXXXXXXXXXXXXXXXXXXXXXXXXXXXXXXXXXXXXXXXXXXXXXX.....
        t       XXXXXXXXXXXXXXXXXXXXXXXXXXXXXXXXXXXXXXXXXXXXXXXXXXXXXXXXXXX
        i  KU   XXXXXXXXXXXXXXXXXXXXXXXXXXXXXXXXXXXXXXXXXXXXXXXXXXXXXXXXXXX.....
        o       XXXXXXXXXXXXXXXXXXXXXXXXXXXXXXXXXXXXXXXXXXXXXXXXXXXXXXXXXXX
        n  KAN  XXXXXXXXXXXXXXXXXXXXXXXXXXXXXXXXXXXXXXXXXXXXXXXXXXXXXXXXXXX......
                XXXXXXXXXXXXXXXXXXXXXXXXXXXXXXXXXXXXXXXXXXXXXXXXXXXXXXXXXXXX
        o  AYP  XXXXXXXXXXXXXXXXXXXXXXXXXXXXXXXXXXXXXXXXXXXXXXXXXXXXXXXXXXX......
        r       XXXXXXXXXXXXXXXXXXXXXXXXXXXXXXXXXXXXXXXXXXXXXXXXXXXXXXXXXXX
           GMP  XXXXXXXXXXXXXXXXXXXXXXXXXXXXXXXXXXXXXXXXXXXXXXXXXXXXXXXXXXX......
        C       XXXXXXXXXXXXXXXXXXXXXXXXXXXXXXXXXXXXXXXXXXXXXXXXXXXXXXXXXXX
        l  MPL  XXXXXXXXXXXXXXXXXXXXXXXXXXXXXXXXXXXXXXXXXXXXXXXXXXXXXXXXXX.......
        u       XXXXXXXXXXXXXXXXXXXXXXXXXXXXXXXXXXXXXXXXXXXXXXXXXXXXXXXX
        s   D   XXXXXXXXXXXXXXXXXXXXXXXXXXXXXXXXXXXXXXXXXXXXXXXXXXXXXXX.........
        t       XXXXXXXXXXXXXXXXXXXX
        e  PPL  XXXXXXXXXXXXXXXXXXXX..............................................
```

```
                         Average Linkage Clustering Tree Diagram

                           Average Linkage Cluster Analysis

                           Average Distance Between Clusters

               1.8   1.6   1.4   1.2   1    0.8   0.6   0.4   0.2   0
               +-----+-----+-----+-----+-----+-----+-----+-----+-----+
      N  CIN   XXXXXXXXXXXXXXXXXXXXXXXXXXXXXXXXXXXXXXXXXXXXXXXX......
      a         XXXXXXXXXXXXXXXXXXXXXXXXXXXXXXXXXXXXXXXXXXXXXXX
      m  DTE   XXXXXXXXXXXXXXXXXXXXXXXXXXXXXXXXXXXXXXXXXXXXXXX......
      e         X
         TXU   XXXXXXXXXXXXXXXXXXXXXXXXXXXXXXXXXXXXXXXXXXXXXXX.....
      o         XXXXXXXXXXXXXXXXXXXXXXXXXXXXXXXXXXXXXXXXXXXXXX
      f  PPL   XXXXXXXXXXXXXXXXXXXXXXXXXXXXXXXXXXXXXXXXXXXXXXX.....
                XXXXXXXXXXXXXXXXXXXXXXXXXXXXXXXXXXXXXXXXXX
      O  UEP   XXXXXXXXXXXXXXXXXXXXXXXXXXXXXXXXXXXXXXXXXXXXXXXXXX.
      b         XXXXXXXXXXXXXXXXXXXXXXXXXXXXXXXXXXXXXXXXXXXXXXXXXX
      s  IWG   XXXXXXXXXXXXXXXXXXXXXXXXXXXXXXXXXXXXXXXXXXXXXXXXXX.
      e         XXXXXXXXXXXXXXXXXXXXXXXXXXXXXXXXXXXXXXXXXXXXXXXXXX
      r  OGE   XXXXXXXXXXXXXXXXXXXXXXXXXXXXXXXXXXXXXXXXXXXXXXXXXX.
      v         XXXXXXXXXXXXXXXXXXXXXXXXXXXXXXXXXXXXXXXXXXXXXXXX
      a  WSE   XXXXXXXXXXXXXXXXXXXXXXXXXXXXXXXXXXXXXXXXXXXXXXX.....
      t         XXXXXXXXXXXXXXXXXXXXXXXXXXXXXXXX
      i  ORU   XXXXXXXXXXXXXXXXXXXXXXXXXXXXXXXXXXXXXXXXXXXXXXXXXX.
      o         XXXXXXXXXXXXXXXXXXXXXXXXXXXXXXXXXXXXXXXXXXXXXXXXXX
      n  KU    XXXXXXXXXXXXXXXXXXXXXXXXXXXXXXXXXXXXXXXXXXXXXXXXXX.
                XXXXXXXXXXXXXXXXXXXXXXXXXXXXXXXXXXXXXXXXXXXXXXXXXX
      o  KAN   XXXXXXXXXXXXXXXXXXXXXXXXXXXXXXXXXXXXXXXXXXXXXXXXXX.
      r         XXXXXXXXXXXXXXXXXXXXXXXXXXXXXXXXXXXXXXXXXXXXXXXXXX
         AYP   XXXXXXXXXXXXXXXXXXXXXXXXXXXXXXXXXXXXXXXXXXXXXXXXXX.
      C         XXXXXXXXXXXXXXXXXXXXXXXXXXXXXXXXXXXXXXXXXXXXXXXXXX
      l  GMP   XXXXXXXXXXXXXXXXXXXXXXXXXXXXXXXXXXXXXXXXXXXXXXXXXX.
      u         XXXXXXXXXXXXXXXXXXXXXXXXXXXXXXXXXXXXXXXXXXXXXXXX
      s  D     XXXXXXXXXXXXXXXXXXXXXXXXXXXXXXXXXXXXXXXXXXXXXXXX...
      t         XXXXXXXXXXXXXXXXXXXXXXXXXXXXXXXXXXXXXXXXXXXXXXXX
      e  MPL   XXXXXXXXXXXXXXXXXXXXXXXXXXXXXXXXXXXXXXXXXXXXXXXXX....
```

```
                         Centroid Linkage Clustering Tree Diagram

                         Centroid Hierarchical Cluster Analysis

                          Distance Between Cluster Centroids

              1.8    1.6    1.4    1.2     1     0.8    0.6    0.4    0.2     0
              +------+------+------+------+------+------+------+------+------+
     N  CIN   XXXXXXXXXXXXXXXXXXXXXXXXXXXXXXXXXXXXXXXXXXXXXXXX......
     a         XXXXXXXXXXXXXXXXXXXXXXXXXXXXXXXXXXXXXXXXXXXXX
     m  DTE   XXXXXXXXXXXXXXXXXXXXXXXXXXXXXXXXXXXXXXXXXXXXXXX......
     e         X
        TXU   XXXXXXXXXXXXXXXXXXXXXXXXXXXXXXXXXXXXXXXXXXXXXXXX.....
     o         XXXXXXXXXXXXXXXXXXXXXXXXXXXXXXXXXXXXXXXXXXXXXXXX
     f  PPL   XXXXXXXXXXXXXXXXXXXXXXXXXXXXXXXXXXXXXXXXXXXXXXXX.....
              XXXXXXXXXXXXXXXXXXXXXXXXXXXXXXXXXXXXXXXXXX
     O  UEP   XXXXXXXXXXXXXXXXXXXXXXXXXXXXXXXXXXXXXXXXXXXXXXXXXXXXX.
     b         XXXXXXXXXXXXXXXXXXXXXXXXXXXXXXXXXXXXXXXXXXXXXXXXXXXX
     s  IWG   XXXXXXXXXXXXXXXXXXXXXXXXXXXXXXXXXXXXXXXXXXXXXXXXXXXXX.
     e         XXXXXXXXXXXXXXXXXXXXXXXXXXXXXXXXXXXXXXXXXXXXXXXXXXXXX
     r  OGE   XXXXXXXXXXXXXXXXXXXXXXXXXXXXXXXXXXXXXXXXXXXXXXXXXXXXX.
     v         XXXXXXXXXXXXXXXXXXXXXXXXXXXXXXXXXXXXXXXXXXXXXXXXXXXX
     a  WSE   XXXXXXXXXXXXXXXXXXXXXXXXXXXXXXXXXXXXXXXXXXXXXXXXXXX.....
     t         XXXXXXXXXXXXXXXXXXXXXXXXXXXXXXXXXXXX
     i  ORU   XXXXXXXXXXXXXXXXXXXXXXXXXXXXXXXXXXXXXXXXXXXXXXXXXXXXX.
     o         XXXXXXXXXXXXXXXXXXXXXXXXXXXXXXXXXXXXXXXXXXXXXXXXXXXXX
     n  KU    XXXXXXXXXXXXXXXXXXXXXXXXXXXXXXXXXXXXXXXXXXXXXXXXXXXXX.
              XXXXXXXXXXXXXXXXXXXXXXXXXXXXXXXXXXXXXXXXXXXXXXXXXXXXX
     o  KAN   XXXXXXXXXXXXXXXXXXXXXXXXXXXXXXXXXXXXXXXXXXXXXXXXXXXXX.
     r         XXXXXXXXXXXXXXXXXXXXXXXXXXXXXXXXXXXXXXXXXXXXXXXXXXXX
        AYP   XXXXXXXXXXXXXXXXXXXXXXXXXXXXXXXXXXXXXXXXXXXXXXXXXXXXX.
     C         XXXXXXXXXXXXXXXXXXXXXXXXXXXXXXXXXXXXXXXXXXXXXXXXXXXX
     l  GMP   XXXXXXXXXXXXXXXXXXXXXXXXXXXXXXXXXXXXXXXXXXXXXXXXXXXXX.
     u         XXXXXXXXXXXXXXXXXXXXXXXXXXXXXXXXXXXXXXXXXXXXXXXXXXX
     s  D     XXXXXXXXXXXXXXXXXXXXXXXXXXXXXXXXXXXXXXXXXXXXXXXXXXX...
     t         XXXXXXXXXXXXXXXXXXXXXXXXXXXXXXXXXXXXXXXXXXXXXXXXXXX
     e  MPL   XXXXXXXXXXXXXXXXXXXXXXXXXXXXXXXXXXXXXXXXXXXXXXXXXXXXX...
```

```
                    Complete Linkage Clustering Tree Diagram

                       Complete Linkage Cluster Analysis

                       Maximum Distance Between Clusters

          3.25 3  2.75 2.5 2.25  2  1.75 1.5 1.25  1  0.75  0.5 0.25  0
          +----+----+----+----+----+----+----+----+----+----+----+----+
    N  CIN XXXXXXXXXXXXXXXXXXXXXXXXXXXXXXXXXXXXXXXXXXXXXXXXXXXXXXXX......
    a      XXXXXXXXXXXXXXXXXXXXXXXXXXXXXXXXXXXXXXXXXXXXXXXXXXXXXX
    m  DTE XXXXXXXXXXXXXXXXXXXXXXXXXXXXXXXXXXXXXXXXXXXXXXXXXXXXXXXX......
    e      X
       TXU XXXXXXXXXXXXXXXXXXXXXXXXXXXXXXXXXXXXXXXXXXXXXXXXXXXXXXXXX.....
    o      XXXXXXXXXXXXXXXXXXXXXXXXXXXXXXXXXXXXXXXXXXXXXXXXXXXXXXX
    f  PPL XXXXXXXXXXXXXXXXXXXXXXXXXXXXXXXXXXXXXXXXXXXXXXXXXXXXXXXX.....
           XXXXXXXXXXXXXXXXXXXXXXXXXXXXXXXXXXXXXXXXXX
    O  UEP XXXXXXXXXXXXXXXXXXXXXXXXXXXXXXXXXXXXXXXXXXXXXXXXXXXXXXXXXXX.
    b      XXXXXXXXXXXXXXXXXXXXXXXXXXXXXXXXXXXXXXXXXXXXXXXXXXXXXXXXXXX
    s  IWG XXXXXXXXXXXXXXXXXXXXXXXXXXXXXXXXXXXXXXXXXXXXXXXXXXXXXXXXXXX.
    e      XXXXXXXXXXXXXXXXXXXXXXXXXXXXXXXXXXXXXXXXXXXXXXXXXXXXXXXXXXX
    r  OGE XXXXXXXXXXXXXXXXXXXXXXXXXXXXXXXXXXXXXXXXXXXXXXXXXXXXXXXXXXX.
    v      XXXXXXXXXXXXXXXXXXXXXXXXXXXXXXXXXXXXXXXXXXXXXXXXXXXXXXXX
    a  WSE XXXXXXXXXXXXXXXXXXXXXXXXXXXXXXXXXXXXXXXXXXXXXXXXXXXXX.....
    t      XXXXXXXXXXXXXXXXXXX
    i  ORU XXXXXXXXXXXXXXXXXXXXXXXXXXXXXXXXXXXXXXXXXXXXXXXXXXXXXXXXXXX.
    o      XXXXXXXXXXXXXXXXXXXXXXXXXXXXXXXXXXXXXXXXXXXXXXXXXXXXXXXXXXX
    n  KU  XXXXXXXXXXXXXXXXXXXXXXXXXXXXXXXXXXXXXXXXXXXXXXXXXXXXXXXXXXX.
           XXXXXXXXXXXXXXXXXXXXXXXXXXXXXXXXXXXXXXXXXXXXXXXXXXXXXXXXXXX
    o  KAN XXXXXXXXXXXXXXXXXXXXXXXXXXXXXXXXXXXXXXXXXXXXXXXXXXXXXXXXXXX.
    r      XXXXXXXXXXXXXXXXXXXXXXXXXXXXXXXXXXXXXXXXXXXXXXXXXXXXXXXXXXX
       AYP XXXXXXXXXXXXXXXXXXXXXXXXXXXXXXXXXXXXXXXXXXXXXXXXXXXXXXXXXXX.
    C      XXXXXXXXXXXXXXXXXXXXXXXXXXXXXXXXXXXXXXXXXXXXXXXXXXXXXXXXXXX
    l  GMP XXXXXXXXXXXXXXXXXXXXXXXXXXXXXXXXXXXXXXXXXXXXXXXXXXXXXXXXXXX.
    u      XXXXXXXXXXXXXXXXXXXXXXXXXXXXXXXXXXXXXXXXXXXXXXXXXXXXXX
    s  MPL XXXXXXXXXXXXXXXXXXXXXXXXXXXXXXXXXXXXXXXXXXXXXXXXXXXXXXXX....
    t      XXXXXXXXXXXXXXXXXXXXXXXXXXXXXXXXXXXXXXXXXXXXXXXXXXXXX
    e  D   XXXXXXXXXXXXXXXXXXXXXXXXXXXXXXXXXXXXXXXXXXXXXXXXXXXXXXX....
```

Printing A Specified Number of Clusters

You can use the NCLUSTERS= option in the PROC TREE statement to specify the number of clusters in the OUT= data set. Then, you can print out the clusters using PROC PRINT. In the following PROC TREE statement, the NCLUSTERS= option specifies that the output data set contains three clusters, the OUT= option creates the output data set CLUST3A, and the NOPRINT option suppresses the printed output.

```
proc tree data=clust3 nclusters=3 out=clust3a noprint;
run;
```

The following PRINT procedure prints the output data set CLUST3A, created by the previous TREE procedure. The results are shown in Output 3.13.

```
proc print data=clust3a;
   title2 'Three Clusters of the';
   title3 'Single Linkage Clustering';
run;
```

Output 3.13
Printing a Specified
Number of Clusters
in the Output Data
Set CLUST3A

```
                      Sorting and Clustering Stocks
                           Three Clusters of the
                         Single Linkage Clustering

              OBS    _NAME_    CLUSTER    CLUSNAME

               1      ORU         1         CL3
               2      KU          1         CL3
               3      KAN         1         CL3
               4      AYP         1         CL3
               5      GMP         1         CL3
               6      MPL         1         CL3
               7      UEP         1         CL3
               8      IWG         1         CL3
               9      OGE         1         CL3
              10      D           1         CL3
              11      WSE         1         CL3
              12      TXU         1         CL3
              13      PPL         1         CL3
              14      CIN         2         CIN
              15      DTE         3         DTE
```

Interpretation of output

Output 3.13 lists the three clusters of the CLUST3A data set. The variable labeled
CLUSTER contains the cluster number, while the variable CLUSNAME contains the cluster
name.

The first cluster consists of the first 13 observations. The second cluster consists of
CIN, while the third cluster consists of DTE. For cluster analyses of large numbers of
variables, the NCLUSTERS= option in the PROC TREE statement can be particularly
useful in analyzing which stocks join which clusters.

Learning More

□ For more information on the DATA step, see *SAS Language, Reference, Version 6,
First Edition* and *SAS Language and Procedures, Usage 2, Version 6, First Edition.*

□ For more information on PROC ACECLUS, PROC CLUSTER, PROC CORRESP,
PROC FACTOR, PROC FASTCLUS, PROC PRINCOMP, PROC PRINQUAL, PROC
TREE, and PROC VARCLUS, see *SAS/STAT User's Guide, Version 6, Fourth Edition,
Volume 1* and *Volume 2.*

□ For more information on PROC CORR, PROC PLOT, PROC PRINT, PROC SORT,
and PROC STANDARD, see *SAS Procedures Guide, Version 6, Third Edition* and *SAS
Language and Procedures, Usage 2, Version 6, First Edition.*

References

Basu, S. (1977), "Investment Performance of Common Stocks in Relation to Their
Price-Earnings Ratios: A Test of the Efficient Market Hypothesis," *Journal of Finance*,
Vol. 32, No. 2, pp. 663-682.

Basu, S. (1983), "The Relationship between Earnings' Yield, Market Value and Return for
NYSE Common Stocks: Further Evidence," *Journal of Financial Economics*, Vol. 12,
pp. 129-156.

Elton, E. and Gruber, M. (1987), *Modern Portfolio Theory and Investment Analysis,
Third Edition*, New York: John Wiley & Sons, Inc.

Hagin, R. (1979), *Modern Portfolio Theory*, Homewood, Illinois: Dow Jones-Irwin.

Jones, C. (1991), *Investments: Analysis and Management, Third Edition*, New York: John Wiley & Sons, Inc.

Chapter **4** The Capital Asset Pricing Model (CAPM)

Introduction

The Capital Asset Pricing Model (CAPM) is used to predict the return on assets. The CAPM relates the returns of an asset to the returns of the market portfolio. Thus, by using the CAPM, you can predict returns on assets, given returns on the market portfolio. In this chapter, the asset is limited to one or more common stocks, but in general, the asset may be any financial instrument or capital asset that offers returns.

The CAPM was pioneered by the modern portfolio work of Harry Markowitz (1952 and 1959) and was formulated independently by Sharpe, Linter, and Mossin (see Sharpe, 1985). This chapter shows you how to fit, test, interpret, and use CAPM equations with the SAS System.

The CAPM in Risk Premium Form

The basic time series CAPM equation developed in risk premium form by Black, Jensen, and Scholes (1972) is

$$R_{i,t} - R_{f,t} = \alpha_i + \beta_i \times \left(R_{M,t} - R_{f,t} \right) + \epsilon_{i,t} \quad .$$

The parameters and variables of the CAPM equation are defined as follows:

α_i the intercept parameter to be estimated, often called Alpha, and on average α_i is expected to be 0.

β_i the slope parameter to be estimated, often called Beta. β is a relative measure of systematic, nondiversifiable risk. Ranking stocks by (the absolute value of) β is the same as ranking them by systematic risk.

β_i is a proportionality factor of asset i's dependence on the market's rate of return. The market β is 1.0. The returns of a stock with a β of .5 change 50 percent as much as market returns change (on average). The returns of a stock with a β of 1.5 change 150 percent as much as market returns change (on average). The returns of a stock with a β of -.5 change 50 percent as much as market returns change (on average) but in the opposite direction.

$\epsilon_{i,t}$ the random error term for the ith asset in the tth period, interpreted as nonsystematic (diversifiable) risk; holding additional assets can eliminate this risk.

$R_{i,t}$ the return on asset i in the tth period,

$$R_{i,t} = \frac{P_{i,t} - P_{i,t-1} + D_{i,t}}{P_{i,t-1}} \quad .$$

In this equation, $P_{i,t}$ is the price of the ith asset at the end of the tth time period; $D_{i,t}$ are the dividends (if any) of the ith asset paid during the tth period; and $P_{i,t-1}$ is the price of the i-th asset at the end of the t-1th time period.

$R_{f,t}$ the return on a risk-free asset for the tth period. The return on 30-day U.S. Treasury bills is often used in empirical work.

$R_{M,t}$ the return on the market portfolio (all assets) for the tth period. The Center for Research on Securities Prices (CRSP) at the University of Chicago provides an R_M based on the value-weighted transactions of all stocks listed on the New York and American Stock exchanges.

The differences on each side of the CAPM equation are the risk premiums. $R_{i,t} - R_{f,t}$ is the risk premium of asset i in the tth period (that is, the excess return over the risk-free rate that investors require to compensate them for the additional risk of investing in asset i over the tth period), and $R_{M,t} - R_{f,t}$ is the overall market's risk premium for the tth period.

The CAPM is based on the following assumptions:

□ Investors make buying/selling/holding decisions based on the expected values and standard deviations of the returns of their portfolios. The latter is a quantifiable measure of portfolio risk suggested by Markowitz (1952).

□ Investors are indifferent between capital gains and dividends.

□ There is perfect competition in the stock market; that is, there are many buyers and sellers, and an individual investor cannot affect the price of a stock by an individual action.

There are other assumptions that simplify the derivation of the CAPM but are not required. Some of these assumptions are that

□ assets are infinitely divisible

□ there are no transaction costs

□ all assets are marketable

□ investors can borrow and lend at the risk-free rate.

For more information about the CAPM, see Markowitz (1959), Sharpe (1985), and Black, Jensen, and Scholes (1972).

Preliminary Analysis

Before fitting the CAPM regression, you need to perform the following tasks:

1. Use the DATA step to create a data set named RETURN1, which contains

   □ returns of the Gerber Corporation's common stock (GERBER)

   □ market returns (R_M)

   □ risk-free asset returns (R_F)

   □ newly created variables representing the risk premiums of Gerber and the market (R_GERBER and R_MKT, respectively)

   □ date values created by the INTNX function.

2. Use PROC PRINT to print the first five observations of the RETURN1 data set.

3. Use PROC PLOT to plot the risk premiums of GERBER versus the risk premiums of the market.

Creating the RETURN1 Data Set

The following statements create the RETURN1 data set and print the first five observations. The results are shown in Output 4.1.

```
data return1;
   input r_m r_f gerber @@;
   retain date '01dec77'd;
   date=intnx('month',date,1);
   format date monyy.;

      /* Creating of New Variables */
   r_gerber = gerber - r_f;
   r_mkt = r_m - r_f;
```

```
                 /* Labeling Variables */
        label r_m='Market Rate of Return'
          r_f='Risk-Free Rate of Return'
          gerber='Rate of Return for Gerber Corporation'
          r_gerber='Risk Premium for Gerber Corporation'
          r_mkt='Risk Premium for Market';
    cards;
    -.045 .00487 -.048    .010 .00494  .160    .050 .00526 -.036
     .063 .00491  .004    .067 .00513  .046    .007 .00527  .028
     .071 .00528 -.012    .079 .00607 -.079    .002 .00645  .104
    -.189 .00685 -.138    .084 .00719  .078    .015 .00690 -.086
     .058 .00761  .042    .011 .00761 -.023    .123 .00769  .065
     .026 .00764 -.088    .014 .00772 -.023    .075 .00715  .095
    -.013 .00728 -.096    .095 .00789  .148    .039 .00802 -.009
    -.097 .00913 -.090    .116 .00819 -.014    .086 .00747 -.036
     .124 .00883  .048    .112 .01073 -.004   -.243 .01181 -.237
     .080 .00753  .027    .062 .00630  .233    .086 .00503  .011
     .065 .00602  .005    .025 .00731 -.008    .015 .00860  .066
     .006 .00895  .026    .092 .01137  .023   -.056 .00977  .070
    -.014 .01092  .056   -.009 .01096 -.020    .067 .01025  .023
    -.008 .01084  .031    .064 .01255  .008   -.003 .01128  .066
    -.033 .01154  .021   -.031 .01169  .031   -.164 .01054  .000
     .062 .01003 -.012    .069 .00816  .011   -.039 .00740 -.077
    -.079 .00949 -.004   -.101 .00946 -.111   -.028 .01067  .136
     .041 .00972  .044    .003 .00908  .043   -.078 .00914 -.033
    -.006 .00714  .019    .122 .00503  .130    .008 .00563  .209
     .136 .00620 -.009    .049 .00614 -.072    .014 .00648  .015
     .065 .00646  .015    .028 .00599  .024    .043 .00686  .084
     .097 .00652  .119    .080 .00649  .016    .048 .00673  .114
    -.017 .00714 -.007   -.034 .00668  .062    .000 .00702  .049
    -.082 .00678  .000    .066 .00683  .077   -.012 .00693  .063
    -.029 .00712  .065   -.030 .00672 -.091    .003 .00763 -.003
    -.003 .00741 -.025   -.058 .00627 -.087    .005 .00748  .105
    -.058 .00771 -.112    .146 .00852  .018    .000 .00830  .165
    -.035 .00688 -.160   -.019 .00602  .094   -.001 .00612 -.005
     .097 .00606  .091    .012 .00586  .006    .008 .00650  .013
    -.010 .00601 -.037    .019 .00512  .234   -.003 .00536 -.031
     .012 .00562 -.036    .005 .00545  .025   -.055 .00571 -.048
     .026 .00577  .097    .059 .00540  .137    .013 .00479  .063
    -.009 .00548 -.088    .049 .00523  .034    .048 .00508  .174
    -.009 .00444  .113    .049 .00469 -.040    .004 .00478 -.038
    -.076 .00458 -.105    .049 .00343  .111   -.047 .00416  .037
     .018 .00418 -.069    .000 .00420 -.020   -.005 .00382 -.060
    ;

        /* Printing the First Five Observations */
    proc print data=return1 (obs=5) label;
      var date r_gerber r_mkt r_m r_f gerber;
        title 'CAPM Analysis';
        title2 'Returns and Risk Premiums';
    run;
```

Output 4.1
*Creating the
RETURN1 Data Set*

```
                                  CAPM Analysis
                             Returns and Risk Premiums


                                                                    Rate of
                        Risk Premium      Risk       Market   Risk-Free  Return for
                         for Gerber     Premium     Rate of   Rate of     Gerber
          OBS   DATE    Corporation    for Market    Return    Return   Corporation

           1   JAN78     -0.05287      -0.04987      -0.045    .00487     -0.048
           2   FEB78      0.15506       0.00506       0.010    .00494      0.160
           3   MAR78     -0.04126       0.04474       0.050    .00526     -0.036
           4   APR78     -0.00091       0.05809       0.063    .00491      0.004
           5   MAY78      0.04087       0.06187       0.067    .00513      0.046
```

Plotting Risk Premiums

The following PROC PLOT statements plot the risk premiums (return in excess of the
risk-free rate) of Gerber Corporation common stock versus the risk premiums of the market.

The HREF= option draws a reference line perpendicular to the specified values on the
horizontal axis. In this example, a reference line is drawn at the value of 0.

The results of the statements are shown in Output 4.2.

```
     /* Plotting Gerber Returns versus the Market Returns */
  proc plot data=return1 vpct=125;
     plot r_gerber*r_mkt = '*' / href=0;
     title2 'Gerber Corporation Stock Premiums';
     title3 'Versus Market Premiums';
  run;
```

Output 4.2
*Scatter Plot of Risk
Premiums*

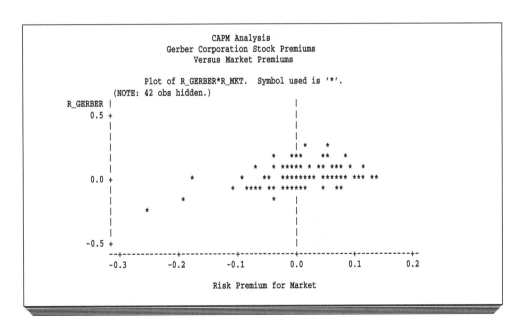

Interpretation of output

Output 4.2 provides visual evidence of the relationship between the risk premiums of Gerber Corporation and the risk premiums of the market. For any given level of market risk premium, there is a corresponding range of Gerber risk premiums. For example, in the scatter plot, the reference line for market risk premiums of 0 indicates the range of observed risk premiums of Gerber common stock. For a market risk premium of 0, the observed range of Gerber risk premiums is about -.20 to .25. This range is typical for common stock risk premiums.

The range of risk premiums is a visual representation of the risk associated with holding stock. That is, you may receive returns at the upper end of the range, or you may receive returns at the lower end of the range. By holding more than one stock in your portfolio, you can reduce risk.

Additional Plots

Because the RETURN1 data set contains time series data, you may also want to visually examine the fluctuations of Gerber (returns and risk premiums), the market (returns and risk premiums), and the risk-free returns over time. By examining the plots of the data versus time, you may discover visual evidence of trends or patterns for later analysis. This section shows you how to use the PLOT and TIMEPLOT procedures to create these plots.

Using PROC PLOT to plot data versus time

You can create two sets of three scatter plots with the following PROC PLOT statements. The first PLOT statement creates the first set of scatter plots: R_GERBER versus DATE, R_MKT versus DATE, and R_F versus DATE. The second PLOT statement creates the second set of scatter plots: GERBER versus DATE, R_M versus DATE, and R_F versus DATE.

```
proc plot data=return1 vpct=125;
    /* Plotting Risk Premiums and Risk-Free Returns versus Time */
  plot (r_gerber r_mkt r_f)*date;
    /* Plotting Returns versus Time */
  plot (gerber r_m r_f)*date;
run;
```

The results from these statements are not shown.

You can create two overlaid scatter plots with the following PROC PLOT statements. The first PLOT statement creates the first overlaid scatter plot: R_GERBER versus DATE, R_MKT versus DATE, and R_F versus DATE, plotted with the symbols G, M, and F, respectively. The second PLOT statement creates the second overlaid scatter plot: GERBER versus DATE, R_M versus DATE, and R_F versus DATE, plotted with the symbols G, M, and F, respectively.

```
proc plot data=return1 vpct=125;
    /* Overlay Plot of Risk Premiums and Risk-Free Returns */
  plot r_gerber*date='G'
     r_mkt*date='M'
     r_f*date='F' / overlay;
    /* Overlay Plot of Returns */
  plot gerber*date='G'
     r_m*date='M'
     r_f*date='F' / overlay;
run;
```

The results from these statements are not shown.

Using PROC TIMEPLOT to plot data versus time

You can also create plots of data versus time with PROC TIMEPLOT. PROC TIMEPLOT has several distinctive features, including the following:

□ The vertical axis of PROC TIMEPLOT plots always represents time.

□ Each observation appears sequentially on a separate line of the plot. No observations are hidden, as can occur with PROC PLOT.

□ Each observation in the plot is accompanied by a printing of the values plotted.

You create two sets of three time plots with the following PROC TIMEPLOT statements. The first PLOT statement creates the first set of time plots: R_GERBER, R_MKT, and R_F, plotted with the symbols G, M, and F, respectively. The second PLOT statement creates the second set of time plots: GERBER, R_M, and R_F, plotted with the symbols G, M, and F, respectively. The REF= option in the PLOT statement draws lines on the plot perpendicular to the specified values on the horizontal axis. For this example, a reference line is drawn at 0.

The MAXDEC= option in the PROC TIMEPLOT statement specifies the maximum number of decimal positions to print. The default is MAXDEC=2. The ID statement prints the values of the ID variable in the listing but does not plot them.

```
proc timeplot data=return1 maxdec=5;
     /* Plotting Risk Premiums and Risk-Free Returns versus Time */
   plot r_gerber='G' r_mkt='M' r_f='F' / ref=0;
     /* Plotting Returns versus Time */
   plot gerber='G' r_m='M' r_f='F' / ref=0;
   id date;
run;
```

The results from these statements are not shown.

You can create two overlaid time plots with the following PROC TIMEPLOT statements. The first PLOT statement creates the first overlaid time plot: R_GERBER, R_MKT, and R_F, plotted with the symbols G, M, and F, respectively. The second PLOT statement creates the second overlaid time plot: GERBER, R_M, and R_F, plotted with the symbols G, M, and F, respectively.

```
proc timeplot data=return1 maxdec=5;
     /* Plotting Risk Premiums and Risk-Free Returns versus Time */
   plot r_gerber='G' r_mkt='M' r_f='F' / overlay;
     /* Plotting Gerber, Market, and Risk-Free Returns vs Time */
   plot gerber='G' r_m='M' r_f='F' / overlay;
   id date;
   title2 'Time Plot';
   title3 'Gerber, Market, and Risk Free';
run;
```

The first twelve observations of the first overlaid timeplot are shown in Output 4.3.

Output 4.3
Plotting Risk
Premiums and the
Risk-Free Return
Using PROC
TIMEPLOT

```
                                    CAPM Analysis
                                      Time Plot
                             Gerber, Market, and Risk Free

          DATE    Risk Premium       Risk      Risk-Free    min                   max
                   for Gerber       Premium      Rate of    -0.29158        0.22888
                   Corporation    for Market     Return     *-------------------*
          JAN78      -0.05287       -0.04987     0.00487    |          @ F         |
          FEB78       0.15506        0.00506     0.00494    |            @      G  |
          MAR78      -0.04126        0.04474     0.00526    |          GF M        |
          APR78      -0.00091        0.05809     0.00491    |          @ M         |
          MAY78       0.04087        0.06187     0.00513    |           F GM       |
          JUN78       0.02273        0.00173     0.00527    |          @G          |
          JUL78      -0.01728        0.06572     0.00528    |          @  M        |
          AUG78      -0.08507        0.07293     0.00607    |        G F  M        |
          SEP78       0.09755       -0.00445     0.00645    |          @  G        |
          OCT78      -0.14485       -0.19585     0.00685    |    M G    F          |
          NOV78       0.07081        0.07681     0.00719    |           F @        |
          DEC78      -0.09290        0.00810     0.00690    |        G  FM         |
```

Interpretation of output

In Output 4.3, the vertical axis represents time, and the symbols G, M, and F represent Gerber risk premiums, the market risk premiums, and the risk-free returns, respectively. The @ symbol indicates that multiple variables have approximately the same value. For example, in January 1978 the risk premium for Gerber and the risk premium of the market are approximately -.05.

For complete documentation on PROC TIMEPLOT, see *SAS Procedures Guide, Version 6, Third Edition* and *SAS Language and Procedures, Usage 2, Version 6, First Edition.*

Fitting a CAPM Regression

CAPM regressions can be fit and tested using the SAS/STAT REG procedure. To analyze the RETURN1 data set, you need to perform the following tasks:

□ Fit the CAPM to the risk premiums of the Gerber Corporation's common stock over the period January 1978-December 1986.

□ Perform individual *t*-tests on the estimated parameters.

□ Calculate the Durbin-Watson D statistic.

□ Test for *heteroskedasticity*, the lack of constancy of the residual variance.

□ Create an output data set containing the predicted and residual values.

The results for the following example are shown in Output 4.4.

Explanation of syntax

PROC REG
> invokes the REG procedure. The DATA= option specifies the RETURN1 data set.

MODEL
> specifies the regression model to be fit. In this example, R_GERBER is the dependent variable and R_MKT is the independent variable. The following options of the MODEL statement are specified:

> DW   specifies the Durbin-Watson D statistic and that the first-order autocorrelation coefficient be printed.

> SPEC   specifies a test for heteroskedasticity.

OUTPUT
> creates an output data set containing the requested variables and diagnostic statistics of the fitted model. The following options of the OUTPUT statement are specified.

> OUT=   names the output data set. For this example, the output data set is named R_OUT1.

> RESIDUAL=   specifies that the residual values be included in the output data set in the specified variable. For this example, the residuals are named GERBER_R. You may also specify this option using the alias R=.

> PREDICTED=   specifies that the predicted values be included in the output data set in the specified variable. For this example, the predicted values are named P1. You may also specify this option using the alias P=.

> L95=   specifies that the lower 95 percent confidence limit values for an individual prediction be included in the output data set in the specified variable. For this example, the lower 95 percent confidence limit values are named L.

> U95=   specifies that the upper 95 percent confidence limit values for an individual prediction be included in the output data set in the specified variable. For this example, the upper 95 percent confidence limit values are named U.

TEST
> tests linear hypotheses about the parameters estimated in the preceding MODEL statement. For this example, an *F*-test is used to test if the slope parameter equals 1.0. The *F*-test is labeled SLOPE.

Example code

```
proc reg data=return1;
   model r_gerber = r_mkt / dw spec;
   output out=r_out1 r=gerber_r p=p1 l95=l u95=u;
   slope: test r_mkt=1;
   title2 'Gerber Corporation Common Stock';
   title3;
run;
```

Output 4.4
CAPM Fit to
Returns from
Common Stock of
the Gerber
Corporation

```
                              CAPM Analysis
                     Gerber Corporation Common Stock

        Model: MODEL1
        Dependent Variable: R_GERBER   Risk Premium for Gerber Corporation

                            Analysis of Variance

                                 Sum of        Mean
              Source       DF    Squares       Square     F Value    Prob>F

              Model         1    0.12676       0.12676     23.101    0.0001
              Error       106    0.58166       0.00549
              C Total     107    0.70843
                                                  ❶
                 Root MSE      0.07408    R-square      0.1789
                 Dep Mean      0.01043    Adj R-sq      0.1712
                 C.V.        710.15401


                            Parameter Estimates

                         Parameter      Standard    T for H0:
              Variable DF  Estimate        Error   Parameter=0   Prob > |T|
                            ❷                         ❸
              INTERCEP  1  0.006299    0.00717972       0.877      0.3823
              R_MKT     1  0.530929    0.11046401       4.806      0.0001


                             Variable
              Variable  DF   Label

              INTERCEP   1   Intercept
              R_MKT      1   Risk Premium for Market
```

```
                              CAPM Analysis
                     Gerber Corporation Common Stock

        Dependent Variable: R_GERBER
                  ❹  Test of First and Second Moment Specification
              DF:  2   Chisq Value:       0.3299   Prob>Chisq:   0.8480

        Durbin-Watson D              2.250  ❺
        (For Number of Obs.)           108
        1st Order Autocorrelation   -0.129


        Dependent Variable: R_GERBER                              ❻
        Test: SLOPE   Numerator:      0.0989  DF:   1  F value:  18.0316
                      Denominator:    0.005487 DF: 106  Prob>F:    0.0001
```

Interpretation of output

The fitted CAPM for the Gerber Corporation is

$$R\_GERBER = .006299 + .530929 \times R\_MKT \qquad .$$

The following list interprets items of interest from Output 4.4. The numbers of the list correspond to the callout numbers in the output.

❶   The R-square for the model is .1789, and the Adjusted R-square is .1712. R-square shows the portion of the dependent variable's variance that is accounted for by the model. Regressing the risk premium of Gerber stock on the risk premium of the market accounts for 17.89 percent of the observed variation in the risk premium of Gerber's stock. (R-squares for CAPM regressions are often low; this is a typical value.)

For CAPM regressions, R-square can be interpreted as the portion of risk premium movements accounted for by the movements of the market. R-square measures the systematic (nondiversifiable) risk of the risk premiums. An R-square of 1.0 indicates that market movements account for all of the movements in the risk premium; that is, all risk is systematic and cannot be diversified away by investing in other stocks. An R-square of 0 indicates that market movements account for none of the movements in the risk premium; that is, all risk is nonsystematic and can be diversified away by investing in other stocks. An R-square between 0 and 1 indicates that some risk is systematic and cannot be diversified away, while some risk is nonsystematic and can be diversified away. For the Gerber stock, the R-square of .1789 indicates that about 18 percent of the risk of holding Gerber stock is related to market movements and cannot be diversified away, and that about 82 percent of the risk of holding Gerber stock is not related to market movements and can be diversified away.

❷ The estimated intercept α is .006299. A value of α greater than 0 would indicate that this stock systematically returns more than is expected for any level of market returns. A value of α less than 0 would indicate the stock systematically returns less than is expected for any level of market returns.

The estimated slope parameter β is .530929. This value implies that if the market risk premium rose by 1 percent, then the risk premium of stock issued by the Gerber Corporation would rise by about .53 percent. The risk premiums of Gerber stock move with the market risk premiums and are less volatile than the market.

Note that the estimates of α and β have been calculated with historical data. There are no guarantees that in the future these estimates will be accurate.

❸ The t-test that α is not different from 0 yields a t-statistic of .877 and a p-value of .3823. This test implies that at significance levels less than the p-value, the intercept is not different from 0. Typical levels of significance for empirical research are .05 and .10.

The t-test that β is not different from 0 yields a t-statistic of 4.806 with a p-value of .0001. You can conclude that the estimated slope parameter differs from 0 and that the risk premiums of the Gerber common stock are related to the risk premiums of the market. This conclusion enables you to use the estimated CAPM equation to predict the risk premium of Gerber common stock given the risk premium of the market.

❹ The White test for heteroskedasticity, nonconstancy of the residual variance, labeled Test of First and Second Moment Specification, yields a chi-square value of .3299 with a p-value of .8480. At the .05 level of significance, you conclude that the residuals have constant variance (*homoskedasticity*).

❺ The Durbin-Watson D statistic is 2.250. Although they are not shown in this output, the D_l and D_u limits are approximately 2.31 and 2.35, respectively, for the .05 level of significance. If the D statistic is used as a test for first-order autocorrelation, then you would conclude that these residuals are not first-order autocorrelated at the .05 level of significance. You may want to use the SAS/ETS ARIMA or AUTOREG procedures for further investigation.

❻ The F-test that β is not different from 1 (the market β) yields an F-statistic of 18.0316 with a p-value of .0001. You conclude that the estimated slope parameter differs from 1.0. If a stock has a β greater than 0 and less than 1, the returns of that stock move with the market and, on average, are less volatile than the market.

For additional information on the test for heteroskedasticity, see White (1980) and *SAS/ETS Software: Applications Guide 2*. For additional information on the Durbin-Watson D statistic and its interpretation as a test for autocorrelation, see Durbin and Watson (1951), Durbin (1960), and *SAS/ETS Software: Applications Guide 2*.

Plotting Residuals

Residual values generated from CAPM regressions contain important financial and statistical information. By definition, the residuals are the difference between the actual and predicted values. In terms of the CAPM, the residuals represent the random component of the stock returns – a portion of the returns that are not associated with market movements.

Residual values are important in a statistical sense in that they can be used to test the statistical assumptions of the linear regression model. In Output 4.3, the Durbin-Watson D statistic and the White test are used to formally test for autocorrelation and heteroskedasticity, respectively.

In many cases, it is useful to plot the residuals and visually examine the distribution. By plotting the residuals versus time, you can visually check for autocorrelation. By plotting the residuals versus the independent variable, you can visually check for outliers and constancy of residual variance (homoskedasticity).

Residuals versus Time

You can use PROC PRINT to print the actual, predicted, and residual values as well as the upper and lower 95 percent confidence limits. Only the first five observations are printed in Output 4.5.

You can use the following PLOT procedure statements to plot the CAPM regression residuals (GERBER_R) versus time (DATE) and the independent variable. The scatter plot produced by these statements is shown in Output 4.5.

Explanation of syntax

VREF=   draws reference lines on the plot perpendicular to the specified values on the vertical axis. In the following example, a reference line is drawn at 0.

VAXIS= specifies values for tick marks on the vertical axis. In the following example, the tick marks run from -.25 to .25 at intervals of .1.

HAXIS= specifies values for tick marks on the horizontal axis. In the following example, the tick marks run from December 1977 to December 1986 at yearly intervals. Note that dates are put in single quotes and followed by a "d."

Example code

```
    /* Printing First Five Observations */
proc print data=r_out1 (obs=5);
   var date r_gerber u p1 l gerber_r;
   title2 'Actual, Predicted, and Residual Values';
   title3 'with Upper and Lower Confidence Limits';
run;
```

```
                    /* Plotting Residuals versus Time */
            proc plot data=r_out1 vpct=125;
                plot gerber_r*date='*' / vref=0 vaxis=-.25 to .25 by .1
                                haxis='01dec77'd to '31dec86'd by year;
                title2 'Gerber Residuals versus Date';
                title3;
            run;
```

Output 4.5
First Five CAPM
Residual Values and
Residuals Plotted
versus Time and the
Market Risk
Premiums

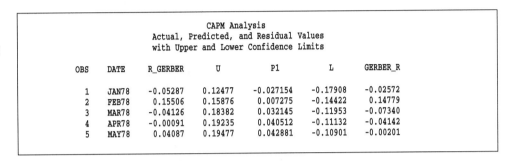

```
                              CAPM Analysis
                  Actual, Predicted, and Residual Values
                    with Upper and Lower Confidence Limits

        OBS    DATE    R_GERBER      U         P1         L       GERBER_R

         1     JAN78   -0.05287   0.12477   -0.027154  -0.17908   -0.02572
         2     FEB78    0.15506   0.15876    0.007275  -0.14422    0.14779
         3     MAR78   -0.04126   0.18382    0.032145  -0.11953   -0.07340
         4     APR78   -0.00091   0.19235    0.040512  -0.11132   -0.04142
         5     MAY78    0.04087   0.19477    0.042881  -0.10901   -0.00201
```

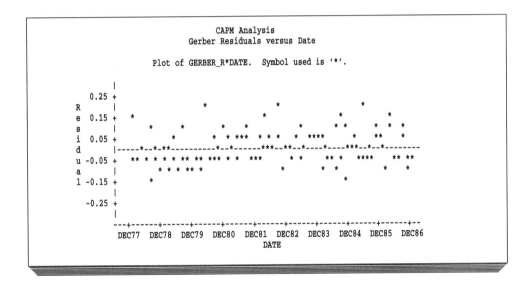

Interpretation of output

Output 4.5 shows the actual, predicted, and residual values contained in the variables R_GERBER, P1, and GERBER_R, respectively. The upper and lower 95 percent confidence limits are contained in the variables U and L.

The scatter plot is a plot of the Gerber CAPM regression residuals versus time. Using this plot, you can visually check for patterns in the residuals versus time.

When using time series data, you should visually check for and formally test for autocorrelation. An often used test for autocorrelation is performed with the Durbin-Watson D statistic. Visual patterns include

□   alternating residual signs, which are a symptom of negative autocorrelation.

□   sequences of like-signed residuals, which are a symptom of positive autocorrelation.

□   extreme values for a sequence of residuals or extreme values that occur on a regular basis, which are symptoms of systematic factors affecting the estimated CAPM regression. You may want to examine these values to determine their cause and respecify the CAPM regression with one or more additional variables.

A statistical consequence of an autocorrelated error structure is that the tests of significance for the CAPM regression parameters are inaccurate. A financial consequence of a truly autocorrelated error structure is that you may have discovered a systematic effect that can be exploited for additional profit. For example, if you conclude that the CAPM residuals display positive autocorrelation, this implies that sequences of same sign residuals are likely. In more practical terms, this period's overpriced stock may still be overpriced next period. If you conclude that the CAPM residuals display negative autocorrelation, then this period's overpriced stock is more likely to be next period's underpriced stock, and vice versa.

Residuals versus the Independent Variable

You can use PROC PLOT to plot the CAPM regression residuals versus the independent variable. The following statements plot the residuals (GERBER_R) versus the market risk premiums (R_MKT).

```
proc plot data=r_out1 vpct=125;
    plot gerber_r*r_mkt='*' / vref=0 vaxis=-.25 to .25 by .1;
    title2 'Gerber Residuals versus R_MKT';
    title3;
run;
```

Output 4.6
CAPM Residuals
Plotted versus the
Market Risk
Premiums

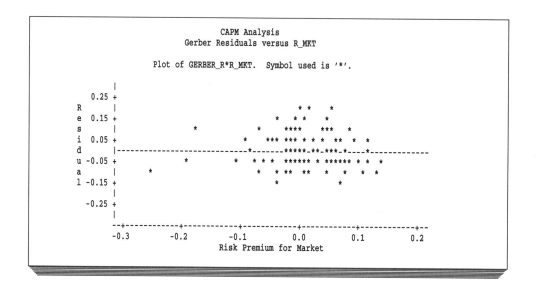

Interpretation of output

In Output 4.6 the scatter plot is a plot of the Gerber CAPM regression residuals versus the independent variable, R_MKT, in the CAPM regression.

You can visually check for constancy of the residual variance using this scatter plot. Consistent residual variance implies the range or distribution of the residuals is approximately the same width for all levels of market risk premiums. The residuals for the Gerber CAPM appear to have a relatively consistent variance, which corroborates the conclusion from the White test of the first and second moments of the residual distribution with the SPEC option in PROC REG, as shown in Output 4.3.

Visual and statistical evidence of nonconstancy of residual variance may indicate heteroskedasticity or possibly a misspecification of the estimated model. A statistical consequence of heteroskedastic residuals is that the tests of significance of the CAPM regression parameters are inaccurate. A financial consequence is that for some range of market returns, the stock returns have a wider distribution; that is, the forecast for returns are less precise, implying greater risk.

Plotting Predicted and Actual Values

Each predicted value represents the expected value of the stock's risk premium for a given level of market risk premiums. On average, the predicted values are accurate. However, there are no guarantees that any particular predicted value will be accurate.

You can use the SAS/GRAPH GPLOT procedure to plot the actual and predicted values and 95 percent confidence limits. The GPLOT procedure enables you to create high-resolution graphics and to connect data points as well as to perform many other plotting tasks.

You should be aware that PROC GPLOT does have system-specific characteristics, and it requires that you specify a device driver and possibly additional options for some systems. You can specify a device driver to run SAS/GRAPH software (including PROC GPLOT) with the following GOPTIONS statement:

GOPTIONS DEVICE=*device-driver-name*;

For more information on specifying device drivers, see *SAS/GRAPH Software: Reference, Version 6, First Edition, Volume 1* and *Volume 2.*

The PROC GPLOT example in this book is run with the following graphics options. To make sure that your graphs look as much like this example, submit the following program:

```
goptions reset=global gunit=pct cback=white border
         htitle=6 htext=3 ftext=swissb colors=(black);
```

When you want to create a series of graphs using PROC GPLOT and you want to use a variety of symbols, precede the PROC GPLOT statements with this GOPTIONS statement:

```
goptions reset=symbol;
```

This statement resets the symbols for each plot. After ending your SAS/GRAPH session, the graphics options are reset to the default values.

You may want a legend in your PROC GPLOT plot. You can create a legend by using PROC SORT to sort the data and by using array processing in a DATA step to assign labels to the variables. The following statements perform these tasks and produce no output:

```
   /* Sorting the R_OUT1 Data Set */
proc sort data=r_out1;
   by r_mkt;
run;

   /* Assigning Labels to Variables for PROC GPLOT Legend */
data regdata (keep=y_value pt_type r_mkt);
   set r_out1;
   label pt_type='Observation Type';
   array regvar(4) r_gerber p1 l u;
   array varlabel(4) $12 _temporary_
```

```
                  ('Actual' 'Predicted' 'Lower Limits' 'Upper Limits');
        do i=1 to 4;
           y_value=regvar(i);
           pt_type=varlabel(i);
        output;
        end;
     run;
```

Explanation of syntax

PROC GLOT
> invokes the GPLOT procedure. The DATA= option specifies that the REGDATA data set is to be used.

PLOT
> specifies the vertical axis variable (listed first) to be plotted versus the horizontal axis variable (listed second). The following options of the PLOT statement are specified:

HAXIS=	specifies the horizontal axis for the plot.
VAXIS=	specifies the vertical axis for the plot.
HMINOR=	specifies the number of minor tick marks between each major tick mark on the horizontal axis.
VMINOR=	specifies the number of minor tick marks between each major tick mark on the vertical axis.

SYMBOL
> defines the characteristics of the lines and symbols displayed in the plot. The following options of the SYMBOL statement are specified:

V=	specifies a plot symbol for the data points.
H=	specifies the height of plot symbols.
I=	specifies interpolation between each point.
FONT=	specifies a font.
L=	specifies the type of interpolation line between points.
COLOR=	specifies the symbol color.

AXIS
> specifies the axes of the plot. The following options of the AXIS statement are specified:

LABEL=	labels the axes.
ANGLE=	specifies the angle of the axes labels, where 0 implies horizontal and 90 implies vertical.
ORDER=	specifies the range and order of major tick marks on the axes.

TITLE
> titles the plot.

QUIT
> ends the interactive PROC GPLOT session.

The graph produced by these statements is presented in Display 4.1.

Example code

```
proc gplot data=regdata;
    plot y_value*r_mkt=pt_type / haxis=axis1 vaxis=axis2
                                 hminor=4 vminor=4;
    symbol1 v=* h=3.5 pct font=swissb color=black;
    symbol2 i=join font=swissb l=2 color=blue;
    symbol3 i=join font=swissb l=1 color=green;
    symbol4 i=join font=swissb l=2 color=red;
    axis1 order=(-.3 to .15 by .05);
    axis2 label=(angle=90 'Gerber Stock Risk Premium')
        order=(-.5 to .5 by .25);
    title1 'Actual and Predicted Values';
    title2 'with Upper and Lower Confidence Limits';
run;
quit;
```

Display 4.1
Actual and Predicted Values with 95 Percent Confidence Limits

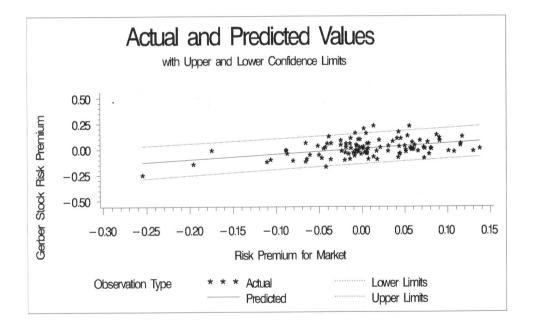

Interpretation of output

The scatter plot in Display 4.1 shows the actual and predicted risk premiums and the upper and lower 95 percent confidence limits. As you may expect, most of the actual values are within the confidence limits and are centered about the predicted values.

In the plot, the confidence limits provide visual evidence of the expected range of the risk premiums. On average, you would expect the actual values to lie between the upper and lower 95 percent confidence limits 95 percent of the time. The closer the confidence limits are to the predicted values, the more precise are forecasts of Gerber returns based on market returns.

The predicted values are the best point estimate of stock risk premiums, given market risk premiums. The predicted values reflect the part of the risk premiums associated with market movements, that is, the systematic (nondiversifiable) risk of holding the stock. The residual values (as shown in Output 4.6) are the difference between the stock's expected risk premiums and the actual risk premiums. The residual values reflect the part of the risk premiums that are not associated with market movements, that is, the nonsystematic (diversifiable) risk of holding the stock.

Applying the CAPM to Additional Stocks

This section shows you how to apply the CAPM to additional stocks. The CAPM regressions you fit to these stocks give you more examples of the magnitude of the estimated parameters and the goodness of fit for typical CAPM regressions. The results of these regressions are also used in later examples.

In this section, you proceed as follows:

1. Use a DATA step to create a data set named RETURN2, which contains returns for additional common stocks.

2. Use a DATA step to merge the RETURN1 and RETURN2 data sets and to create a new data set, RETURN3, containing the risk premium values of the stocks.

3. Use PROC PRINT to print the first ten observations of selected variables.

4. Use PROC REG to fit the CAPM regressions.

The RETURN2 data set contains monthly returns on common stocks from January 1978 through December 1986 for the following firms:

□ Tandy Corporation (TANDY)

□ General Mills (GENMIL)

□ Consolidated Edison (CONED)

□ Weyerhauser (WEYER)

□ International Business Machines (IBM)

□ Digital Equipment Corporation (DEC)

□ Mobil Corporation (MOBIL)

□ Texaco Corporation (TEX)

□ Carolina Power and Light (CPL)

Tasks performed by the program

These tasks are performed by the following example:

□ The first DATA step creates the RETURN2 data set.

□ The second DATA step merges the RETURN1 and RETURN2 data sets.

□ PROC PRINT prints the first ten observations of the risk premiums of the Tandy Corporation contained in the variable R_TANDY. These values are printed in Output 4.7.

Example code

```
      /* Creating the RETURN2 Data Set */
      /* Containing Common Stock Returns */
data return2;
   input tandy genmil coned weyer ibm dec mobil tex cpl @@;
   retain date '01dec77'd;
   date=intnx('month',date,1);
   format date monyy.;
   label tandy='Rate of Return for Tandy Corporation'
      genmil='Rate of Return for General Mills'
      coned='Rate of Return for Con Edison'
      weyer='Rate of Return for Weyerhauser'
      ibm='Rate of Return for IBM'
      dec='Rate of Return for DEC'
      mobil='Rate of Return for Mobil Corporation'
      tex='Rate of Return for Texaco'
      cpl='Rate of Return for CPL';
   cards;
-.075 -.099 -.079 -.116 -.029 -.100 -.046 -.054 -.069
-.004  .018 -.003 -.135 -.043 -.063 -.017 -.010  .006
 .124 -.023  .022  .084 -.063  .010  .049  .015  .017
 .055  .046 -.005  .144  .130  .165  .077  .000 -.063
 .176  .063 -.014 -.031 -.018  .038 -.011 -.029  .091
-.014  .008  .034  .005 -.004 -.021 -.043 -.025  .021
 .194  .075  .011  .164  .092  .107  .028  .042  .034
 .222 -.051  .024  .039  .049 -.017  .056  .000 -.011
-.100 -.012  .048 -.021 -.051 -.037  .064  .010  .033
-.206 -.032 -.067 -.090 -.046 -.077 -.069 -.066 -.117
 .086  .009  .035 -.033  .031  .064  .037  .055  .067
 .085  .022  .005 -.034  .108  .117  .041  .000  .011
-.046 -.032  .076  .203  .034 -.012  .061  .037  .029
-.135 -.079 -.011 -.038 -.017 -.066 -.002 -.010 -.028
 .122 -.043  .000  .097  .052  .088  .029  .068  .006
-.094  .022 -.057 -.069 -.004  .005  .079  .059 -.099
-.148  .035  .032 -.013 -.022 -.028 -.086 -.040  .059
 .096 -.043  .066  .053 -.035  .059  .088  .083  .069
 .006 -.013  .015  .000 -.049  .009  .018  .032 -.042
 .250  .138 -.021  .165  .016  .140  .111  .041  .025
-.005 -.032  .000 -.015 -.032 -.027  .180  .030  .006
-.037 -.067 -.049 -.083 -.079 -.010 -.031 -.053 -.083
 .170  .005  .109 -.065  .060  .095  .051  .067  .041
 .037  .005  .005  .104 -.013  .018  .063 -.029 -.006
 .032  .003 -.039  .069  .066  .058  .075  .229 -.071
 .143 -.096 -.061  .033 -.062  .034  .366  .161 -.072
-.105  .011  .006 -.129 -.122 -.182 -.176 -.179  .047
-.038  .059  .140  .027 -.016  .047  .119  .082  .188
 .256  .018  .043  .089  .025  .016  .003  .007  .006
 .041 -.013  .040 -.026  .061  .021 -.024  .032  .103
 .446  .012 -.027  .140  .111  .183  .054  .003 -.032
 .167  .018 -.005 -.041  .017  .081 -.059  .031 -.025
 .157 -.013 -.010 -.064 -.021  .045  .007 -.037 -.025
-.015 -.073 -.021  .017  .039 -.028  .059  .087 -.075
```

```
 .212 -.030 -.035  .015  .035  .056  .193  .399  .000
 .022  .102  .131  .007 -.004  .035 -.081 -.109  .051
-.139  .079 -.015  .028 -.052 -.089 -.082 -.145  .010
 .082  .013 -.021  .025  .011  .006 -.067 -.012 -.035
 .299  .146  .151  .088 -.029  .075 -.042 -.063  .066
 .092  .019  .061 -.050 -.060  .075 -.025 -.003  .017
 .136  .030  .017 -.031  .017  .107 -.092 -.055  .049
-.167  .094  .022  .021 -.015 -.112  .053  .025  .026
 .032 -.045  .026 -.081 -.030 -.014  .021  .045 -.003
-.063 -.031  .021 -.061 -.002 -.065 -.057  .003  .027
-.008  .036 -.013 -.113 -.018 -.019 -.106 -.093 -.006
 .241  .067  .112 -.020 -.048  .102  .025  .008  .031
-.037 -.030  .038  .179  .075 -.065  .038  .065  .065
-.046 -.024 -.008 -.072  .044 -.060 -.090 -.047 -.006
 .059 -.030  .042 -.079  .119  .027 -.016 -.045  .054
-.101  .098  .036  .014 -.014 -.049 -.016 -.004  .012
-.051  .020  .022 -.009 -.034 -.104 -.038 -.029  .054
 .053  .076  .050  .059  .075  .054 -.011 -.008  .016
-.163 -.027  .016 -.086 -.029 -.056  .092  .034 -.023
 .023  .050 -.024 -.015 -.014 -.073 -.038 -.017 -.047
 .050  .038 -.032 -.012  .082 -.055 -.073 -.060 -.007
 .017  .032  .133  .221  .087  .273  .157  .056  .108
-.026  .000  .039 -.029  .041 -.061  .043  .027 -.098
 .454  .160 -.050  .150  .089  .133  .020  .056  .056
 .273 -.025 -.011  .141  .094  .175 -.040  .012  .025
-.042 -.020  .123 -.040  .113 -.052  .069  .029  .042
 .091 -.039 -.012  .023  .027  .225  .055  .036  .080
 .032  .067  .060  .065  .010 -.010  .009  .008 -.006
-.004  .061  .048 -.023  .028  .034  .095  .039  .006
 .084  .066  .045  .091  .150 -.060  .091  .098 -.007
-.010  .023 -.012 -.067 -.041 -.052 -.052 -.038  .023
-.168 -.026  .000 -.013  .081  .075  .077  .018  .000
-.123 -.072  .017 -.071  .001 -.142 -.060  .036 -.007
-.048 -.010 -.023 -.011  .001  .007  .118  .059  .006
-.083 -.037  .087 -.033  .062 -.005 -.050 -.037  .069
-.058  .116  .101 -.046 -.001 -.364 -.032 -.014  .065
 .082 -.014 -.025  .151 -.066  .065 -.033  .011 -.005
 .095 -.009  .005 -.069  .039  .034  .009  .021 -.057
-.190 -.009  .005 -.039 -.065  .208  .084  .108  .023
-.100 -.073 -.069 -.093 -.026 -.024  .024  .151 -.061
-.008 -.018  .055  .094  .034  .057 -.028 -.122  .024
 .120  .065  .031 -.088 -.002  .053  .029  .022 -.029
-.231  .018  .021 -.087 -.044 -.071 -.146 -.105 -.006
-.037  .055  .020  .019 -.019 -.043  .010 -.046  .019
 .029 -.018  .054  .036  .047 -.009 -.092 -.044  .006
 .079  .061  .029  .055  .127  .159  .261  .140  .099
-.100  .011  .051 -.069  .004 -.025  .013  .045  .045
-.096 -.010  .019  .035  .012  .093  .014 -.080  .060
 .027 -.072  .004  .032 -.023  .006 -.042  .007  .058
 .005  .017  .084  .026  .011  .070 -.052  .000  .005
 .170  .095 -.021  .084  .108  .084  .053  .044  .040
 .119  .000  .034 -.016 -.009 -.067  .071  .022 -.019
 .094  .054  .057 -.081 -.052 -.071  .000  .014  .069
```

```
         -.133 -.083  .019  .003 -.004 -.050  .027  .111  .047
          .091  .137  .098  .031  .025  .057  .029 -.065  .023
          .087  .060  .046 -.004 -.038 -.101 -.032  .031  .066
         -.119 -.099 -.084  .020  .062  .080  .002 -.030 -.095
          .063  .002  .043 -.013 -.028  .032 -.013  .021  .014
         -.011  .081 -.032 -.074 -.022  .036  .004 -.007 -.046
          .098  .013  .066  .008  .048  .040  .100  .099  .098
          .021  .114  .032  .171  .085  .073 -.008 -.175  .045
          .098  .027  .082 -.004  .113  .095 -.040 -.077  .043
         -.040  .019  .022  .072 -.026  .162 -.021 -.038  .047
          .096  .121  .048  .123  .003  .093 -.003  .071  .069
         -.047  .072  .021  .051  .004 -.063 -.026 -.004  .080
         -.058 -.051 -.006 -.037  .031  .119  .042  .050 -.065
          .094  .109  .042  .010 -.018  .037  .082  .069  .000
         -.092  .071  .017 -.061 -.039 -.063  .012 -.042  .046
         -.078  .049  .125 -.048 -.096  .066 -.022 -.036  .130
          .018  .003  .061  .122  .055  .105  .173  .135  .112
         -.108 -.088 -.139 -.058 -.031 -.110  .053  .026 -.077
          .242  .123  .045  .135 -.081  .103  .020  .043  .040
          .094  .011  .070  .006  .037  .048  .044 -.028  .006
         -.023 -.034 -.046 -.041 -.056  .008  .019  .047 -.034
         ;

             /* Merging RETURN1 and RETURN2 Data Sets */
             /* Merging Stock Returns with Market and Risk Free Returns */
         data return3;
             merge return1 return2;
             by date;

                 /* Creating New Variables */
             r_tandy = tandy - r_f;
             r_genmil = genmil - r_f;
             r_coned = coned - r_f;
             r_weyer = weyer - r_f;
             r_ibm=ibm - r_f;
             r_dec=dec - r_f;
             r_mobil = mobil - r_f;
             r_tex=tex - r_f;
             r_cpl=cpl - r_f;

                 /* Labeling Variables */
             label r_tandy='Risk Premium for Tandy Corporation'
                 r_genmil='Risk Premium for General Mills'
                 coned='Risk Premium for Con Edison'
                 weyer='Risk Premium for Weyerhauser'
                 ibm='Risk Premium for IBM'
                 dec='Risk Premium for DEC'
                 mobil='Risk Premium for Mobil Corporation'
                 tex='Risk Premium for Texaco'
                 cpl='Risk Premium for Carolina Power & Light';
         run;
```

```
                        /* Printing First 10 Observations */
                   proc print data=return3 (obs=10) label;
                      var date r_tandy;
                      title2 'Risk Premiums for Tandy Corporation';
                   run;
```

Output 4.7
First Ten
Observations of
R_TANDY in
RETURN3 Data Set

```
                              CAPM Analysis
                   Risk Premiums for Tandy Corporation

                                     Risk Premium
                                       for Tandy
                      OBS    DATE     Corporation

                       1     JAN78     -0.07987
                       2     FEB78     -0.00894
                       3     MAR78      0.11874
                       4     APR78      0.05009
                       5     MAY78      0.17087
                       6     JUN78     -0.01927
                       7     JUL78      0.18872
                       8     AUG78      0.21593
                       9     SEP78     -0.10645
                      10     OCT78     -0.21285
```

Fitting Additional CAPM Regressions

You can use one invocation of PROC REG to fit many CAPM regression models. The
following statements fit CAPM regressions to the risk premiums of nine new firms in the
RETURN3 data set. The DW option specifies the calculation of the Durbin-Watson D
statistic. The SPEC option performs the White test of the first and second moments of the
residual distributions, that is, a test for heteroskedasticity. The output from these statements
is not shown.

```
          proc reg data=return3;
             model r_tandy = r_mkt / dw spec;
             model r_genmil = r_mkt / dw spec;
             model r_coned = r_mkt / dw spec;
             model r_weyer = r_mkt / dw spec;
             model r_ibm = r_mkt / dw spec;
             model r_dec = r_mkt / dw spec;
             model r_mobil = r_mkt / dw spec;
             model r_tex = r_mkt / dw spec;
             model r_cpl = r_mkt / dw spec;
          run;
```

The slope parameter associated with R_MKT in each equation is the CAPM β for that
stock. These βs are used in Chapter 5, "Portfolio Creation with Linear Programming."

For this example, TEST statements are included for each CAPM regression. The TEST
statements, labeled SLOPE, enable you to test if the estimated CAPM slope parameter is
different from unity.

Lastly, the OUTEST= option in the PROC REG statement creates an output data set containing the parameter estimates and optional statistics. In this example, the OUTEST= data set is named CAPMEST1.

```
proc reg data=return3 outest=capmest1;
    model r_tandy = r_mkt / dw spec;
    slope: test r_mkt=1;

    model r_genmil = r_mkt / dw spec;
    slope: test r_mkt=1;

    model r_coned = r_mkt / dw spec;
    slope: test r_mkt=1;

    model r_weyer = r_mkt / dw spec;
    slope: test r_mkt=1;

    model r_ibm = r_mkt / dw spec;
    slope: test r_mkt=1;

    model r_dec = r_mkt / dw spec;
    slope: test r_mkt=1;

    model r_mobil = r_mkt / dw spec;
    slope: test r_mkt=1;

    model r_tex = r_mkt / dw spec;
    slope: test r_mkt=1;

    model r_cpl = r_mkt / dw spec;
    slope: test r_mkt=1;
run;
```

The results from these statements are not shown, but selected statistics are shown in the following table. Each row contains a fitted CAPM regression for the specified company. Also included in the table are selected statistics from the CAPM regression for the Gerber Corporation fit in Output 4.4.

Table 4.1 *CAPM Regressions*

Company	Intercept (*t*-statistic)	Slope (*t*-statistic)	*F*-statistic slope=1.0 (*p*-value)	R-Sq.	D.W.	White Test (*p*-value)
Gerber	.006299 (0.877)	.530929 (4.806)	18.0316 (.0001)	.1789	2.250	.3299 (.8480)
Tandy	.013467 (1.286)	1.048230 (6.504)	.0896 (.7653)	.2852	1.901	2.0226 (.3637)

(continued)

Table 4.1 (continued)

Company	Intercept (*t*-statistic)	Slope (*t*-statistic)	F-statistic slope=1.0 (*p*-value)	R-Sq.	D.W.	White Test (*p*-value)
General Mills	.006604 (1.174)	.138337 (1.598)	99.1320 (.0001)	.0235	2.022	.4547 (.7967)
Con Ed	.013044 (2.649)	.102044 (1.347)	140.4491 (.0001)	.0168	2.136	.0835 (.6691)
Weyer	− .003558 (− .574)	.723119 (7.578)	8.4187 (.0045)	.3514	2.325	10.1817 (.0062)
IBM	.000095 (0.020)	.395362 (5.298)	65.6575 (.0001)	.2094	1.915	1.1133 (.5731)
DEC	.005509 (0.724)	.715704 (6.114)	5.8982 (.0168)	.2607	2.149	.6732 (.7142)
Mobil	.004688 (0.752)	.685563 (7.148)	10.7477 (.0014)	.3252	2.047	3.4948 (.1742)
Texaco	.000391 (0.061)	.578628 (5.876)	18.3080 (.0001)	.2457	2.011	2.2995 (.3167)
CP&L	.005803 (1.145)	.206764 (2.652)	103.5415 (.0001)	.0622	1.879	3.5000 (.1738)

The columns of the table contain the following information:

◻ The first column contains the firm names.

◻ The second column contains the estimated intercepts: α_i and the *t*-statistics for the test if α equals 0. Only the intercept for the Consolidated Edison (CONED) CAPM regression is different from 0 at the .05 level. (Note the critical *t*-value is about 1.98 for the .05 level of significance.)

◻ The third column contains the estimated slope parameters: β_i and the *t*-statistics for the test if β equals 0. All of the slope parameters are different from 0 at the .05 level, except for General Mills and Consolidated Edison. (Note the critical *t*-value is about 1.98 for the .05 level of significance.)

◻ The fourth column contains the *F*-statistic and *p*-value (in parenthesis) for the test if the estimated slope parameter equals unity. For the larger *F*-statistics, the *p*-values may be smaller than .0001.

◻ The fifth column contains the R-squares for the CAPM regressions. Note that CONED, GENMIL (General Mills) and CPL have the lowest R-squares and low βs (relative to this sample), implying that the returns of their stocks are less correlated with the market than other stocks in the sample.

◻ The sixth column contains the Durbin-Watson D statistics. When used as a test statistic in tests for first-order autocorrelation, the Durbin-Watson D lower and upper limits, D_l and D_u at the .05 level, are approximately 2.31 and 2.35, respectively, for the upper end of the distribution and approximately 1.65 and 1.69 for the lower end of the distribution.

These limits are appropriate for regression models with 1 independent variable and 108 observations. The limits vary for different levels of significance, different numbers of independent variables, and different numbers of observations.

The D-statistic value for Weyerhauser (WEYER) is 2.325, which is in the inconclusive region. None of the remaining D values are significant at the .05 level. For practical purposes, you conclude that there is little evidence of a problem with autocorrelated residuals for these regression models.

□ The seventh column contains the chi-square statistics and *p*-values for the White test for heteroskedasticity. There is little evidence of problems with heteroskedasticity except for the WEYER CAPM regression. You may want to perform further analysis on this equation.

When using the CAPM regressions to predict stock risk premiums, be aware that the predicted values are more accurate for models with R-squares closer to 1 because R-squares closer to 1 imply

□ higher correlations of stock risk premiums with market risk premiums

□ smaller parameter standard errors, hence, smaller confidence intervals for parameters (for a given level of significance)

□ smaller confidence intervals for predicted values (for a given level of significance).

Further Analysis

You may want to continue the analysis of these stocks. You may find items of statistical, economic, or financial interest that suggest further analysis. Areas of further analysis discussed in this section are heteroskedastic residuals, adding more regressors to CAPM regressions, and joint estimation of seemingly unrelated CAPM regressions.

Heteroskedastic Residuals

One example of further statistical analysis is correcting the CAPM regression of the Weyerhauser Corporation for heteroskedastic residuals.

If you conclude that the residuals of the Weyerhauser CAPM regression are heteroskedastic and the heteroskedasticity is of the form that the residual variance is proportional to the market risk premiums, then you want to fit a weighted least-squares CAPM regression to mitigate the effects of the heteroskedasticity.

To estimate weighted least-squares CAPM regressions, use a DATA step to create the new variables weighted by R_MKT, then use PROC REG. The following statements create the weighted variables to fit a CAPM regression model corrected for heteroskedasticity:

```
data return4;
   set return3;
   r_weyerw=r_weyer/r_mkt;
   r_mkt_w=1/r_mkt;
run;

proc reg data=return4;
   model r_weyerw = r_mkt_w / dw spec;
   B_ne_1: test intercept=1;
run;
```

The fitted model is of the following form:

$$R\_WEYERW = \alpha \times \frac{1}{R\_MKT} + \beta$$

The intercept and slope parameters have exchanged roles. The TEST statement labeled B_NE_1 tests if the CAPM β differs from unity.

For more information on heteroskedasticity, see *SAS/ETS Software: Applications Guide 2* and Pindyck and Rubinfeld (1991), *Econometric Models and Economic Forecasts, Third Edition.*

Testing the Residual Distributions for Normality

Another example of further analysis you may want to perform is testing the CAPM regression residual distributions for normality. An assumption of ordinary least-squares (OLS) regression is that the residuals are distributed normally. This assumption enables you to use standard F and t distributions to test the estimated parameters.

You can test the CAPM regression residual distributions for normality by first creating output data sets (in PROC REG with OUTPUT statements) containing the residuals from each CAPM regression merging the output data sets in a DATA step, and then using the NORMAL option in the UNIVARIATE procedure. The PROC REG statements to fit the CAPM regressions and create output data sets containing the residuals are as follows:

```
proc reg data=return3;
    model r_tandy = r_mkt;
    output out=r_out2 r=tandy_r;

    model r_genmil = r_mkt / dw spec;
    output out=r_out3 r=g_mils_r;



    model r_cpl = r_mkt / dw spec;
    output out=r_out10 r=cpl_r;
run;
```

The NORMAL option in the PROC UNIVARIATE statement specifies the calculation of the Shapiro-Wilk statistic (for a sample size less than 2000) or the Kolmogorov statistic (for a sample size greater than 2000). The p-values are also calculated for the null hypothesis that the input data are a random sample from a normal distribution.

The PLOT option in the PROC UNIVARIATE statement specifies the plotting of three descriptive plots as follows.

□ a stem-and-leaf plot (if no more than 48 observations fall into a single interval) or a horizonal bar chart (if more than 48 observations fall into a single interval).

□ a box plot (also known as a schematic plot) with top and bottom edges at the 25th and 75th percentiles, a center horizontal line drawn at the sample median, and a central plus sign (+) at the sample mean. Additionally, central vertical lines, called *whiskers*, extend from the box as far as the data extend; extreme values are marked with an asterisk (*).

□   a normal probability plot, which plots the sample quantiles against the quantiles of a standard normal distribution. Asterisks mark the data values. If the data are from a normal distribution, the asterisks tend to fall along the reference line.

An excellent description and interpretation of these plots is provided in *SAS System for Elementary Statistical Analysis.*

The following DATA step merges the output data sets by the variable DATE and the PROC UNIVARIATE statements test the normality of the residuals. The results of these statements are not shown.

```
     /* Merging Output Data Sets */
data out_r;
   merge return3 r_out1 r_out2 r_out3 r_out4 r_out5
         r_out6 r_out7 r_out8 r_out9 r_out10;
   by date;
run;


     /* Testing for Normality of Residuals */
proc univariate data=out_r normal plot;
   var gerber_r tandy_r g_mils_r con_ed_r weyer_r ibm_r
       dec_r mobil_r texaco_r cpl_r;
run;
```

Regression models that generate non-normal residual distributions may suggest further analysis. Neter, Wasserman, and Kutner (1985) assert that small departures from normality do not create any serious problems. Large departures from normality, that is, small *p*-values for the Shapiro-Wilk or Kolmogorov statistics, indicate that you should consider remedial measures. For example, the departure from normality may be caused by autocorrelation or heteroskedasticity, and the model can be refit to account for the non-normality. If necessary, Monte Carlo studies can be performed to find the actual critical values of the distribution. Alternatively, you may want to respecify the equation by adding more regressors, as discussed in the next section, and testing the resulting residuals.

Adding Additional Regressors to CAPM Regressions

The CAPM presented in this chapter is a single index model; that is, it employs only one independent variable, the market risk premium (R_MKT). As shown in previous examples, CAPM regressions for individual stocks typically explain less than half of the variation in the risk premiums (R_i), as indicated by the low R-square values of the CAPM regressions.

In theory, the CAPM can be extended to explain more of the variation in the risk premiums of an individual company's common stock by adding more independent variables to the CAPM regression equation. (See Cohen and Pogue, 1967; Elton and Gruber, 1973; and King, 1966). Because additional independent variables display a wide range of explanatory power in CAPM regressions of individual stocks, investors typically explore many additional independent variables and then fine-tune the CAPM regressions on a stock-by-stock basis.

Variables you may want to consider adding to CAPM regressions include

□   real GNP (Gross National Product), that is, GNP deflated by the consumer price index (the CPI), or Real GDP (Gross Domestic Product)

□   inflation rate as measured by the CPI or some other index

- □   measures of the real money supply

- □   interest rates

- □   bond yields

- □   industrial indices of performance

- □   any other variables you believe are correlated with the returns on stocks.

The variables can be included in level form, as percentage growth, as a rational expectation (a forecast from a mathematical model), or as the unexpected level or growth amount (deviations from the amount forecasted by a mathematical model).

If additional variables can be found that account for the variance of stock returns, the forecasted returns of your model may be much more accurate and precise.

Seemingly Unrelated CAPM Regressions

One last example of further analysis you may consider performing is to use the statistical method of *seemingly unrelated regression* (SUR), also known as joint generalized least squares (JGLS), to simultaneously estimate the parameters of many CAPM regressions. Often with separate regression models that appear unrelated, the cross-equation error correlations are nonzero and can be used to simultaneously and more efficiently estimate the regression models. However, when the independent variables are exactly the same in each equation, SUR estimation is equivalent to equation-by-equation ordinary least-squares estimates, and there is no efficiency gain from SUR estimation. Note that efficiency is measured by magnitude of estimated parameter standard errors. (See Pindyck and Rubinfeld, 1991, for details.)

If you are estimating multiple CAPM regressions with different independent variables, you can use the SAS/ETS MODEL and SYSLIN procedures to simultaneously fit and test the estimated models. For more information on PROC MODEL and PROC SYSLIN, see *SAS/ETS User's Guide, Version 6, Second Edition.*

Arbitrage Pricing Model

Steven Ross (1976) hypothesized that stock returns depend partially on macroeconomic variables and partially on events that are unique to that company. The returns are expected to be linearly related to the factors, as follows:

$$\text{R}_i = a + b_1\left(r_{factor\,1}\right) + b_2\left(r_{factor\,2}\right) + \ldots + error$$

The factors can be any variables, including interest rates, energy prices, bond rates, and so on. Chen, Roll, and Ross (1986) suggest including the level of industrial activity, the inflation rate, the difference between short-term and long-term interest rates, and the difference between low-risk and high-risk corporate bond yields. The return on the market portfolio might or might not be included as a factor.

The returns of some stocks will be more responsive to one factor than the returns of other stocks. Thus, there may be a unique set of factors in the expected risk premium equation for stock. The risk premium equations are of the form

$$\text{R}_i - \text{R}_f = b_1\left(r_{factor\,1} - r_f\right) + b_2\left(r_{factor\,2} - r_f\right) + \ldots + b_n\left(r_{factor\,n} - r_f\right) \quad .$$

A well-diversified portfolio is expected to be insensitive to macroeconomic factors and is essentially risk free; therefore, it is expected to yield the risk-free rate of return. If the well-diversified portfolio were priced so that it returned a greater amount than the risk-free return, then investors would borrow to purchase the portfolio and arbitrage away the difference. If the risk-free return is greater, then investors would sell the well-diversified portfolio and invest in U.S. Treasury bills (the risk-free asset) to arbitrage away the difference.

A diversified portfolio's risk premiums vary in direct proportion to the variation of the factors (as measured by the parameters b_1, b_2, ..., b_n). If two portfolios are equivalent in all ways except that the first is twice as sensitive to the variations of factor 1 as the second, then the first portfolio is expected to offer risk premiums that reflect that difference. If this relationship between the two portfolios did not hold, then investors would buy and sell the portfolios (as was appropriate) to arbitrage away the difference.

To implement the arbitrage pricing model, you follow these steps:

1. Identify the macroeconomic factors.

2. Estimate the risk premium required by investors for bearing risk of the macroeconomic factors. One approach to estimating these risk premiums is to construct portfolios that reflect the underlying macroeconomic structures and measure the historical risk premium, that is, the difference between the portfolio returns and U.S. Treasury bills (the risk-free asset).

3. Estimate the factor sensitivities; that is, estimate the parameters b_1, b_2, through b_n. One approach is to estimate CAPM-like regressions for the returns of the portfolio constructed in the previous step.

4. Calculate the expected values for the risk premiums and the stock returns by using the factor sensitivities, the expectations of macroeconomic risk premiums, and the arbitrage pricing equation.

The details of this approach are beyond the scope of this book; however, you can modify the examples shown in this chapter to implement the arbitrage pricing model.

Using the CAPM Regressions to Predict Stock Risk Premiums

The estimated CAPM regressions shown in the previous table can be used to predict stock risk premiums. In this section, you print the CAPMEST1 data set containing the fitted CAPM regressions, and you use a DATA step to calculate point estimates of stock risk premiums and returns for various market risk premiums and a given risk-free return.

Printing the Estimated CAPM Regression Parameters

You use PROC PRINT to print the CAPMEST1 data set:

```
proc print data=capmest1;
   var _depvar_ intercep r_mkt;
   title2 'Estimated CAPM Regression Parameters';
run;
```

Output 4.8
Estimated CAPM
Regression
Parameters

```
                              CAPM Analysis
                   Estimated CAPM Regression Parameters


           OBS    _DEPVAR_      INTERCEP      R_MKT

            1     R_TANDY       0.013467     1.04823
            2     R_GENMIL      0.006604     0.13834
            3     R_CONED       0.013044     0.10204
            4     R_WEYER      -0.003558     0.72312
            5     R_IBM         0.000095     0.39536
            6     R_DEC         0.005509     0.71570
            7     R_MOBIL       0.004688     0.68556
            8     R_TEX         0.000391     0.57863
            9     R_CPL         0.005803     0.20676
```

Interpretation of output

In Output 4.8, the column labeled _DEPVAR_ lists the dependent variables; the column labeled INTERCEP lists the CAPM αs; and the column labeled R_MKT lists the CAPM βs.

Predicting Stock Risk Premiums and Returns

You can use the CAPMEST1 data set and an iterative DO LOOP in a DATA step to calculate point estimates of stock risk premiums and returns, given market risk premiums and the risk-free return. In this example, future market risk premiums (F_R_MKT) range from -.02 to .07, and the risk-free return is assumed to be .03. Note that the CAPM slope parameters (the βs) are labeled R_MKT; the future market risk premiums are labeled F_R_MKT; and the future risk-free return is labeled RISK_FRE.

The following statements calculate and print the first ten point estimates of stock risk premiums and returns:

```
data forecast;
   set capmest1;
   do f_r_mkt = -.02 to .07 by .01;
      pred=intercep + f_r_mkt * r_mkt;
      risk_fre=.03;
      return = pred + risk_fre;
      output;
   end;
   label _depvar_='Stock'
         f_r_mkt='Future Market Risk Premium'
         pred='Predicted Stock Risk Premium'
         return='Predicted Future Stock Return';
run;

proc print data=forecast (obs=10) label;
   var _depvar_ f_r_mkt pred;
   title2 'Point Estimates of';
   title3 'Stock Risk Premiums and Returns';
run;
```

Output 4.9
Point Estimates of
Stock Risk
Premiums and
Returns

```
                                CAPM Analysis
                               Point Estimates of
                           Stock Risk Premiums and Returns

                        Future
                        Market      Predicted       Predicted
                         Risk      Stock Risk     Future Stock
           OBS   Stock  Premium      Premium          Return

            1   R_TANDY  -0.02      -0.007497        0.02250
            2   R_TANDY  -0.01       0.002985        0.03298
            3   R_TANDY   0.00       0.013467        0.04347
            4   R_TANDY   0.01       0.023950        0.05395
            5   R_TANDY   0.02       0.034432        0.06443
            6   R_TANDY   0.03       0.044914        0.07491
            7   R_TANDY   0.04       0.055396        0.08540
            8   R_TANDY   0.05       0.065879        0.09588
            9   R_TANDY   0.06       0.076361        0.10636
           10   R_TANDY   0.07       0.086843        0.11684
```

Interpretation of output

Output 4.9 lists the predicted stock risk premiums and returns for the Tandy Corporation. Note that these are point estimates for the given future market risk premium and the risk-free return. Prior to using the predictions in your investment decisions, you should continue to explore point estimates and confidence limits for the stock risk premiums and returns until you are fully satisfied with your analysis.

Using the CAPM βs and the Security Market Line

The security market line states that the expected return of an asset is linearly related to its β value. Moreover, in equilibrium, all assets and portfolios are expected to plot on the security market line:

$$R_i = a + b\beta_i$$

A line is determined by identifying two points. One point on the security market line is the risk-free asset with a β of 0 (or alternatively, you can use the return of a portfolio with β of 0):

$$R_f = a$$

A second point is the market portfolio with β of 1, so that

$$R_M = a + b$$

$$R_M - a = b \quad .$$

The security market line can be restated by substitution for its parameters a and b as

$$R_i = R_f + \beta_i\left(R_M - R_f\right) \quad .$$

This equation matches the intuitive expectation that the higher the β, the higher the expected return; and the lower the β, the lower the expected return. The security market line shows the equilibrium relationships.

Note that systematic risk (of which β is an index) is the factor determining expected returns. Also note that nonsystematic (or diversifiable) risk plays no role; that is, investors receive no reward for bearing diversifiable risk.

The security market line can be stated in risk premium form as

$$ R_i - R_f = \beta_i\left(R_M - R_f\right) \quad . $$

Thus, the security market line is, first, an intuitive approach to deriving the CAPM, and, second, a statement as to the expected return of stocks (given their βs, the expected return of the market, and the expected risk-free return). (For details, see Elton and Gruber, 1987.)

Individual factors affecting the return of a particular stock and differing expectations of investors imply that the risk premium and β of a stock may deviate temporarily from the security market line. If a stock's expected risk premium deviates from the security market line, then its price will be adjusted by the actions of buyers and sellers until the stock's expected risk premium is on the security market line. That is, deviations from the security market line will be arbitraged away because investors are actively searching these stocks. For example, a stock with a risk premium greater than expected (for its β value) will be sought after by investors, who bid up the stock's price until its risk premium falls to the appropriate level. A stock with a risk premium less than expected (for its β value) will be shunned or sold short by investors until its risk premium rises to the appropriate level.

Given estimates of the expected returns on the risk-free asset, the market portfolio, and the CAPM regression parameters, you can search for assets, stocks, and portfolios whose β and expected risk premiums deviate from the security market line.

You implement this strategy by

□   estimating the CAPM regressions for each stock.

□   calculating or estimating the expected returns for each stock, the market portfolio, and the risk-free rate.

□   calculating the security market line and predicting each stock's expected risk premium (SML).

□   calculating each stock's risk premium based on its CAPM regression (CAPM).

□   comparing the predicted risk premium values of CAPM and SML. As a general strategy, you want to buy stocks whose CAPM predicted risk premium values are greater than their SML predicted risk premium values, and you want to sell stocks whose CAPM predicted risk premium values are less than their SML predicted risk premium values.

Calculating Expected Returns

There are many approaches you can pursue to estimate the level of expected returns as discussed in Chapter 1, "Background Topics." For this example, you use the RETURN3 data set and the MEANS procedure to calculate the average, monthly common stock risk premiums (that is, $R_i - R_f$) for the ten stocks in the RETURN3 data set.

This approach is appropriate if you believe that the future performance of stock risk premiums will be similar to past performance and if you plan to buy and hold the stocks. This approach may be inappropriate if you believe that stock risk premiums will display major differences in performance in the future from their past performance or if you plan to pursue different investment strategies.

You can calculate and print the average monthly risk premiums with the following statements.

Explanation of syntax

PROC MEANS
> invokes the MEANS procedure. The following options of the PROC MEANS statement are specified:

> DATA=   specifies the data set to be used in the analysis.

> NOPRINT   suppresses the printed output.

VAR
> specifies the variables to be used in the analysis. In this example, the ten common stock returns used in the CAPM regressions are specified as variables for analysis.

OUTPUT
> specifies that the output statistics be stored in the data set created by the OUT= option. The following options of the OUTPUT statement are specified:

> OUT=   specifies the name of the output data set. In this example, the output data set is named M_OUT1.

> MEAN=   specifies that the mean of the variables listed in the VAR statement be calculated and stored in the output data set. In this example, the ten mean values are stored in the variables named M1 through M10.

Example code

```
    /* Calculating Average Monthly Returns */
proc means data=return3 noprint;
    var r_gerber r_tandy r_genmil r_coned r_weyer r_ibm
        r_dec r_mobil r_tex r_cpl;
    output out=m_out1 mean=m1-m10;
run;
```

You use PROC TRANSPOSE to transpose the M_OUT1 data set for ease in merging in a later example with the PROC REG OUTEST= data set CAPMEST1 (containing the estimated CAPM regression parameters).

```
proc transpose data=m_out1 out=m_out2(rename=(col1=mean));
    var m1-m10;
run;
```

Next, you use PROC PRINT to print the average risk premiums. The results are shown in Output 4.10.

```
    /* Printing the Average Monthly Returns */
proc print data=m_out2;
    title2 'Average Monthly Stock Returns';
run;
```

```
                            CAPM Analysis
                     Average Monthly Stock Returns

              OBS      _NAME_      MEAN

                1       M1       0.010431
                2       M2       0.021626
                3       M3       0.007681
                4       M4       0.013839
                5       M5       0.002070
                6       M6       0.003172
                7       M7       0.011079
                8       M8       0.010024
                9       M9       0.004894
               10       M10      0.007413
```

Interpretation of output

Output 4.10 shows values that represent the average monthly risk premiums over the nine-year period, 1978-1986. The observations are ordered (first to last) identically to the ordering (left to right) of the stocks included in the VAR statement of PROC MEANS.

Using DCF Analysis as a Check on Expected CAPM Returns

Note that you can use the discounted cash flow (DCF) analysis discussed in Chapter 2, "Discounted Cash Flow (DCF) Analysis," as a useful check on the expected returns. For stocks with constant dividend growth, the general DCF equation becomes

$$V = \frac{D_1}{K - G} \quad .$$

This DCF equation states that the current value of the stock (V) is the expected dividend in the next period (D_1) divided by the difference in the discount rate (K) and the growth rate of the constant growth rate of the dividends (G). The DCF equation can be rewritten as follows:

$$K = \frac{D_1}{V} + G$$

In this form, the rate of discounting the stock (K) equals the expected dividend yield (D_1 / V) plus the constant dividend growth rate. In this form, you expect K and R (expected returns) to be close in magnitude (as long as the constant dividend growth form of the DCF equation is appropriate). If K and R differ greatly, then you want to further analyze the stock's value and the appropriateness of the models.

Using the Security Market Line

You can use a DATA step to calculate stock risk premiums predicted by the CAPM (CAPM), stock risk premiums calculated by the security market line (SML), and deviations from the security market line.

Tasks performed by the program
In the following DATA step you

□ merge the CAPMEST1 data set, which contains the estimated CAPM regression parameters (created in the section "Fitting Additional CAPM Regressions"), and the M_OUT2 data set, which contains the expected risk premiums (created in the code that produces Output 4.10).

□ calculate the predicted equilibrium risk premiums from the security market line (SML) and the individual risk premiums, as predicted from the CAPM regressions (CAPM).

□ calculate the deviations (DEVIA) between the SML and CAPM predictions.

□ generate Actions to Consider with IF-THEN-ELSE statements. Stocks that offer greater predicted CAPM risk premiums than SML risk premiums should be considered as opportunities to buy. This example includes a safety factor of .01 (or 1 percent); that is, the deviation must be at least .01 or no action to buy is generated. Stocks that offer smaller predicted CAPM risk premiums than SML risk premiums should be considered as opportunities to sell (if owned), or they should be shunned or sold short (if not owned). This example includes a safety factor of .005 (or .5 percent); that is, the deviation must be at least .005 or no action to sell is generated. Lastly, stocks that offer risk premiums close to the security market line expected values are to be held (if owned).

Note that you should develop buy-sell-hold criteria that best suits your investing needs.

Example code

```
data out_m3;

    /* Merging Data Sets */
merge capmest1(rename=(r_mkt=beta)) m_out2;

    /* Expected Market Portfolio Risk Premium */
m_mkt=.007783;

    /* Security Market Line Risk Premiums */
sml=beta*(m_mkt);
    /* CAPM Risk Premiums */
capm=intercep+beta*(mean);

    /* Deviations from the Security Market Line */
devia=capm-sml;

    /* Actions to Consider */
if devia >= .01 then action='buy ';
else if devia <= -.005 then action='sell';
else action='hold';
run;
```

You print the risk premiums, their deviations, and actions generated with the following PROC PRINT statements. The results are shown in Output 4.11.

```
proc print data=out_m3;
    var capm sml devia action;
    title2 'Expected Risk Premiums';
    title3 'and Actions to Consider';
run;
```

Output 4.11
Expected Risk
Premiums and
Actions to Consider

```
                          CAPM Analysis
                      Expected Risk Premiums
                       and Actions to Consider

        OBS      CAPM       SML       DEVIA      ACTION

         1     0.011837   .0041322    0.007705    hold
         2     0.036136   .0081584    0.027977    buy
         3     0.007667   .0010767    0.006590    hold
         4     0.014456   .0007942    0.013662    buy
         5    -0.002061   .0056280   -0.007689    sell
         6     0.001349   .0030771   -0.001728    hold
         7     0.013438   .0055703    0.007868    hold
         8     0.011560   .0053357    0.006224    hold
         9     0.003222   .0045035   -0.001281    hold
        10     0.007336   .0016092    0.005727    hold
```

Interpretation of output

Output 4.11 lists the risk premiums (CAPM and SML, respectively), the deviations (DEVIA), and the actions (ACTION) suggested by the criteria of this example.

For this example, there are two stocks that meet the "buy" criterion (observations 2 and 4, corresponding to stocks TANDY and CONED) and one stock that meets the "sell" criterion (observation 5, corresponding to the WEYER stock); the remaining stocks meet neither criteria.

Chapter Summary

This chapter introduces the Capital Asset Pricing Model (CAPM) and presents examples of basic CAPM regressions in risk premium form for individual firms. The CAPM regression parameters were tested individually for difference from 0, and the slope parameters were also tested for difference from 1.

The CAPM regression residuals were plotted versus time to visually assess their independence. The residuals were also plotted versus the market risk premium (the independent variable in the CAPM regression) to visually assess the constancy of the residual variance. The Durbin-Watson D statistic was calculated to formally test residual independence across time, and the White Test was used to formally test residual variance constancy (homoskedasticity).

Then, the estimated CAPM regressions were used to predict point estimates of the stock risk premiums and returns for given values of the market risk premiums and the risk-free return.

Lastly, the security market line was derived and used (along with the CAPM regressions) to identify stocks to buy, sell, or hold.

Learning More

- [ ] For more information on the DATA step, see *SAS Language; Reference, Version 6, First Edition*; *SAS Language and Procedures: Usage, Version 6, First Edition*; and *SAS Language and Procedures, Usage 2, Version 6, First Edition.*

- [ ] For more information on PROC REG, see *SAS/STAT User's Guide, Version 6, Fourth Edition, Volume 1* and *Volume 2.*

- [ ] For more information on PROC PLOT, PROC PRINT, PROC SORT, PROC TIMEPLOT, and PROC UNIVARIATE, see *SAS Procedures Guide, Version 6, Third Edition* and *SAS Language and Procedures: Usage 2.*

- [ ] For more information on the PROC UNIVARIATE plots produced by the PLOT option in the PROC UNIVARIATE statement, see *SAS System for Elementary Statistical Analysis.*

- [ ] For more information on ordinary least-squares (OLS) regression and autocorrelated and heteroskedastic regression models, see *SAS/ETS Software: Applications Guide 2, Econometric Modeling, Simulation, and Forecasting, Version 6, First Edition*, and Pindyck and Rubinfeld (1991), *Econometric Models and Economic Forecasts, Third Edition.*

- [ ] For more information on SAS/ETS ARIMA, AUTOREG, MODEL, and SYSLIN procedures, see *SAS/ETS Software: User's Guide, Version 6, Second Edition.*

References

Black, F.; Jensen, M.; and Scholes, M. (1972), "The Capital Asset Pricing Model: Some Empirical Tests," ed., Michael Jensen, *Studies in the Theory of Capital Markets*, New York: Praeger, pp. 79-121.

Brealey, R. and Myers, S. (1991), *Principles of Corporate Finance, Fourth Edition*, New York: McGraw-Hill, Inc.

Chen, N-F.; Roll, R.; and Ross, S. (1986), "Economic Forces and the Stock Market," *Journal of Business*, Vol. 59, pp. 383-403.

Cohen, K. and Pogue, J. (1967); "An Empirical Evaluation of Alternative Portfolio Selection Models," *Journal of Business*, Vol. 46, pp. 166-193.

Durbin, J., and Watson, G.S. (1951), "Testing for Serial Correlation in Least Squares Regression," *Biometrika*, Vol. 38, pp. 159-178.

Durbin, J. (1960), "Estimation of Parameters in Time-Series Regression Models," *Journal of the Royal Statistical Society, Series B*, Vol. 22, pp. 139-153.

Elton, E. and Gruber, M. (1973), "Estimating the Dependence Structure of Share Prices - Implications for Portfolio Selection," *Journal of Finance*, Vol. 8, No. 5, pp. 1203-1232.

King, B. (1966), "Market and Industry Factors in Stock Price Behavior," *Journal of Business*, Vol. 39, pp. 139-140.

Markowitz, H. (1952), "Portfolio Selection," *Journal of Finance*, Vol. 7, pp. 77-91.

Markowitz, H. (1991), *Portfolio Selection: Efficient Diversification of Investments, Second Edition*, Cambridge, MA: Blackwell, Inc.

Neter J.; Wasserman W.; and Kutner M; (1985), *Applied Linear Statistical Models*, Homewood, Illinois: Richard Irwin, Inc.

Pindyck, R. and Rubinfeld, D. (1991), *Econometric Models and Economic Forecasts, Third Edition*, New York: McGraw-Hill, Inc.

Ross, S.A. (1976), "The Arbitrage Theory of Capital Asset Pricing," *Journal of Economic Theory*, Vol. 13, pp. 341-360.

Sharpe, W.F. (1985), *Investments, Third Edition*, Englewood Cliffs, N.J.: Prentice-Hall.

White, H. (1980), "A Heteroskedasticity-Consistent Covariance Matrix Estimator and a Direct Test for Heteroskedasticity," *Econometrica*, Vol. 48, 817-838.

Chapter 5 Portfolio Creation with Linear Programming

Introduction

After performing preliminary analyses to select stocks of interest, investors often want to find the optimal investment for each of these stocks, that is, what fraction of the portfolio should be invested in each stock. Typically, investors desire to maximize returns subject to a maximum acceptable level of risk and a variety of other constraints. After suitable measures of expected return and risk are obtained, portfolio selection problems can be expressed and solved through the linear programming techniques available in the SAS/OR LP procedure.
    This chapter describes linear programming and shows you how to

☐ use PROC LP to calculate optimal portfolio weights for a variety of linear programming problems, including integer programming

☐ use the DATA step to create input data sets for PROC LP, to calculate the dollar amounts to invest in each stock from the PROC LP solution weights, and to calculate comparable measures of portfolio risk and return for integer programming problems.

Portfolio Creation Using Linear Programming

In this section, you solve for optimal portfolio weights using linear programming, as outlined in the following steps:

1. Calculate the stock returns using the MEANS procedure.

2. Use a DATA step to create the input data set for PROC LP.

3. Use PROC LP to solve for the optimal portfolio weights.

4. Use PROC LP to perform sensitivity analyses.

5. Use a DATA step, the optimal weights, and the portfolio size to calculate the amounts to invest in each stock.

Calculating Expected Returns

Before you can use PROC LP to solve linear programming problems, you first estimate the level of expected returns. You should use the method you deem most appropriate for the calculation of expected future returns. (Methods of calculating and estimating expected returns are discussed in Chapter 1, "Background Topics.") For illustrative purposes, the examples of this chapter use the average return of past periods as a measure of expected returns.

You use the following PROC MEANS statements to calculate the stock returns. The results are printed with PROC PRINT and are shown in Output 5.1.

```
proc means data=return3 noprint;
    var gerber tandy genmil coned weyer ibm dec mobil tex cpl;
output out=m_out1a mean=m1-m10;
run;

proc print data=m_out1a;
    var m1-m10;
    title 'Linear Programming';
    title2 'Average Monthly Stock Returns';
run;
```

Output 5.1
Average Monthly
Returns

```
                          Linear Programming
                     Average Monthly Stock Returns

   OBS     M1         M2         M3        M4       M5        M6

    1    0.017593   0.028787   0.014843   0.021   .0092315  0.010333

   OBS     M7         M8         M9        M10

    1    0.018241   0.017185   0.012056   0.014574
```

Selecting a Risk Measure

Prior to using linear programming techniques, suitable measures of risk for an asset should be considered. Of the many risk measures you may consider, this section considers two: the first is standard deviation of individual stock returns, σ_i; the second is Capital Asset Pricing Model (CAPM) βs. If you have already selected a measure of risk, then you can proceed to the next section.

Using the Standard Deviation of Stock Returns

Standard deviation is a statistical measure of dispersion, and dispersion of stock returns is wherein lies the risk of holding stocks. The standard deviation of stock returns measures total risk that includes both systematic (or nondiversifiable) risk and nonsystematic (or diversifiable) risk. The greater the diversification of the portfolio, the more nonsystematic risk is diversified away. The risk level of well-diversified portfolios approaches that of the market.

You can use the total risk of each stock to create portfolios; however, it may be difficult to compare the riskiness of the resulting portfolios because reduction of the nonsystematic risk through diversification may not be accounted for. Moreover, the security market line, developed in Chapter 4, "The Capital Asset Pricing Model (CAPM)," indicates that investors are not rewarded for bearing nonsystematic risk.

If your research indicates that the standard deviation of stock returns is the appropriate risk measure, you can use PROC MEANS to calculate them. The following PROC MEANS statements calculate the standard deviations, store them in a data set named M_OUT1B, and name the standard deviations STD1-STD10. You can use PROC PRINT to print the standard deviations.

```
proc means data=return3 noprint;
    var gerber tandy genmil coned weyer ibm dec mobil tex cpl;
output out=m_out1b std=std1-std10;
run;
```

Using the CAPM βs

An alternative risk measure to consider is the CAPM β, which is an index of systematic risk. The remainder of this section shows that for well-diversified portfolios, the CAPM βs can be used as a measure of risk for linear programming techniques of portfolio selection.

A CAPM β is the slope parameter of a CAPM regression. Recall from Chapter 4 that a CAPM regression relates the expected returns of asset *i* to the expected returns of the market, as follows:

$$E(R_i) = \alpha_i + \beta_i E(R_M)$$

For portfolio p, the CAPM becomes

$$E(R_p) = \alpha_p + \beta_p E(R_M)$$

For portfolio weights X_i, the parameters α_p and β_p can be expressed as a linear combination of the individual stock α_i and β_i:

$$\alpha_p = \sum_{i=1}^{N} X_i \alpha_i$$

$$\beta_p = \sum_{i=1}^{N} X_i \beta_i$$

As noted previous, *total risk* is defined as the standard deviation of returns. For asset i, the variance of returns (the square of the standard deviation) in terms of the CAPM is

$$\sigma_i^2 = \beta_i^2 \sigma_M^2 + \sigma_i^2 \quad .$$

For portfolio p, the variance of returns becomes

$$\sigma_p^2 = \beta_p^2 \sigma_M^2 + \sum_{i=1}^{N} X_i^2 \sigma_i^2 \quad .$$

As the portfolio is diversified, the second term diminishes, and for well-diversified portfolios, it approaches 0. Evans and Archer (1968) found that the total risk of a 15-stock portfolio was approximately the same as that of the market portfolio. Thus, for well-diversified portfolios, the variance of portfolio returns approaches

$$\sigma_p^2 = \beta_p^2 \sigma_M^2 \quad .$$

The square root of the variance of portfolio returns (σ_p^2) is the standard deviation (σ_p) of portfolio returns:

$$\sigma_p = \beta_p \sigma_M$$

$$\sigma_p = \sigma_M \sum_{i=1}^{N} X_i \beta_i$$

The standard deviation of market returns is a common factor to all stocks. Minimizing the linear combination of the individual stock βs is the same as minimizing the monotonic transformation of σ_M times the linear combination of the βs. In this form, each stock is contributing only a monotonic transformation of its systematic risk to the portfolio risk; there is no overcounting of nonsystematic risk (which has been diversified away). Moreover, minimizing the linear combination of the CAPM βs also has the advantage that risk measures among well-diversified portfolios are directly comparable.

Thus, for creation of well-diversified portfolios, you may want to minimize the linear combination of the individual stock CAPM βs. Note that the better the diversification, the better is this approach. The CAPM βs are the risk measure used in examples for this chapter.

Calculating Optimal Portfolio Weights

After you have estimated (or calculated) future stock returns and risk levels, you can use PROC LP to find the optimal portfolio weights to maximize returns, subject to a maximum acceptable level of risk. The linear programming problem is of the following form:

maximize : $c'\mathbf{x}$
subject to : $\mathbf{Ax} \leq \mathbf{b}$
where : $l_i \leq x_i \leq u_i$

The terms are defined as follows:

A   is an $m \times n$ matrix of technological coefficients. In this example, **A** is a 2×10 matrix, where the first row represents the CAPM βs, and the second row ensures the weights sum to unity (or 100 percent of the portfolio).

b   is an $m \times 1$ vector of right-hand-side (rhs) constants. In this example, **b** is a 2×1 vector, where the first row represents the maximum acceptable risk level, and the second row ensures the weights sum to unity (or 100 percent). Note that the risk of the portfolio is the linear combination of the individual stock βs.

c   is an $n \times 1$ vector of price coefficients. In this example, **c** is a 10×1 vector, and the c_i represent the average annual returns. The portfolio return is the sum of the weights times the individual stock returns. The weights are to be calculated to maximize the portfolio return.

x   is an $n \times 1$ vector of structural variables. In this example, **x** represents the optimal portfolio weights.

l_i is a lower bound on x_i. In this example, the lower bounds are minimum portfolio weights. For example, following a buy-and-hold strategy, portfolio weights are non-negative; the lower bound on each X_i is 0. Alternatively, if you want to sell a stock short, then the weight would be negative. If no lower bound is given, the default lower bound in PROC LP is 0.

u_i is an upper bound on x_i. In this example, the upper bounds are maximum portfolio weights. For example, the maximum portfolio weight for each stock is unity or 100 percent and, for an optimal solution weight of unity, the entire portfolio amount would be invested in a single stock.

This example uses PROC LP to solve for the portfolio weights (x_i) that maximize the objective function

$$x_1 \times .0176 + x_2 \times .0288 + \ldots + x_{10} \times .0146 \quad .$$

The objective function is subject to the following constraints:

□   the portfolio risk is .7. That is, the portfolio weights are chosen so that the sum of the products of the weights times the individual stock βs is .7.

$$x_1 \times .5309 + x_2 \times 1.048 + \ldots + x_{10} \times .2068 = .7$$

□   the weights sum to unity,

$$x_1 \times 1 + x_2 \times 1 + \ldots + x_{10} \times 1 = 1 \quad .$$

□   the upper bound on the portfolio weights is 1. That is, no more than 100 percent of the portfolio may be in any one stock.

□   the lower bound on the portfolio weights is 0. That is, no less than 0 percent of the portfolio may be in any one stock.

The following DATA step defines a data set named WEIGHT that contains the linear programming problem in dense form for PROC LP.

Explanation of syntax

DATA
    begins a DATA step and provides names for any output SAS data sets. In this example, the SAS data set WEIGHT1 is created.

INPUT
    describes the arrangement of values in observations and assigns input values to the corresponding SAS variables. In this example, the input variables are GERBER, TANDY, and so on through CPL. The variables _ID_, _TYPE_, and _RHS_ create special variables for PROC LP.

        _ID_   contains an identifying name for the objective function and constraints. In this example, the objective function is named EXP_RETURN, and the constraints are named BETA (the risk constraint), SUM_WTS (that the weights sum to unity), and AVAILABLE (upper and lower bound constraints on the weights).

        TYPE   defines a character variable that specifies how PROC LP is to interpret the observation. For this example, the objective function has a _TYPE_ variable of MAX (the equation is to be maximized). The constraints BETA and SUM_WTS have _TYPE_ variables of EQ (an equality constraint). The AVAILABLE constraints have _TYPE_ variables of UPPERBD and LOWERBD (upper and lower bounds).

        RHS   identifies the variable in the problem data set that contains the right-hand-side (numeric) constants of the linear program. In this example, only the constraints BETA and SUM_WTS have right-hand-side constants. Note that the objective function is to be maximized (no constant value is given), while a right-hand-side constant for the upper and lower bound constraints is unnecessary.

CARDS
    indicates that data lines follow. The five lines that follow the CARDS statement contain the following information:

    1.   Average monthly returns from Output 5.1. The _TYPE_ of MAX indicates that this is the objective function to be maximized, that is, find solution values for the portfolio weights that maximize the expected portfolio returns. No right-hand-side constant is given because the objective is to maximize the portfolio return.

2. The CAPM βs estimated by the CAPM regression in Chapter 4. The weights are to be calculated so that the portfolio β is .7.

3. The constraint that the weights must sum to unity. That is, the sum of the products of the weights times 1 is unity.

4. The upper bound restriction that the weights have a maximum value of 1.

5. The lower bound restriction that the weights have a minimum value of 0.

```
data weight1;
   input _id_ $10. gerber tandy genmil coned weyer ibm dec mobil tex
      cpl _type_ $ _rhs_;
   cards;
exp_return .0176 .0288 .0148 .021 .0092 .0103 .0182 .0172 .0121 .0146 max      .
beta       .5309 1.048 .1383 .102 .7231 .3954 .7157 .6856 .5786 .2068 eq      .7
sum_wts    1.0   1.0   1.0   1.0  1.0   1.0   1.0   1.0   1.0   1.0   eq     1.0
available  1     1     1     1    1     1     1     1     1     1     upperbd  .
available  0     0     0     0    0     0     0     0     0     0     lowerbd  .
;
```

The following PROC LP statements calculate the optimal portfolio weights for the given constraints. The PROC LP statement invokes the LP procedure, the DATA= option specifies the WEIGHT data set, and the PRIMALOUT= option specifies that the solution values be stored in an output data set named LP_OUT1. The QUIT statement ends the interactive PROC LP session. The results from these statements are shown in Output 5.2.

```
proc lp data=weight1 primalout=lp_out1;
   title2 'Optimal Portfolio Weights';
run;
quit;
```

Output 5.2
PROC LP Output,
Including Optimal
Portfolio Weights

```
                         Linear Programming
                      Optimal Portfolio Weights

          L I N E A R   P R O G R A M M I N G   P R O C E D U R E

                     ❶   PROBLEM   SUMMARY

          Max exp_return              Objective Function
          _RHS_                             Rhs Variable
          _TYPE_                           Type Variable
          Problem Density                             1

          Variable Type                          Number

          Upper and Lower Bounded                     10

          Total                                       10
```

```
                      Linear Programming
                   Optimal Portfolio Weights

      L I N E A R   P R O G R A M M I N G   P R O C E D U R E

                      PROBLEM  SUMMARY

        Constraint Type                    Number

        EQ                                    2
        Objective                             1

        Total                                 3
```

```
                      Linear Programming
                   Optimal Portfolio Weights

      L I N E A R   P R O G R A M M I N G   P R O C E D U R E

                   ❷    SOLUTION  SUMMARY

                   Terminated Successfully

        Objective value                   0.025931

        Phase 1 iterations                    2
        Phase 2 iterations                    1
        Phase 3 iterations                    0
        Integer iterations                    0
        Integer solutions                     0
        Initial basic feasible variables      2
        Time used (secs)                      0
        Number of inversions                  3
```

```
                      Linear Programming
                   Optimal Portfolio Weights

      L I N E A R   P R O G R A M M I N G   P R O C E D U R E

                      SOLUTION  SUMMARY

        Machine epsilon                      1E-8
        Machine infinity          1.7976931349E308
        Maximum phase 1 iterations            100
        Maximum phase 2 iterations            100
        Maximum phase 3 iterations       99999999
        Maximum integer iterations            100
        Time limit (secs)                     120
```

```
                      Linear Programming
                   Optimal Portfolio Weights

      L I N E A R   P R O G R A M M I N G   P R O C E D U R E

                   ❸    VARIABLE  SUMMARY

        Variable                                        Reduced
    Col Name       Status   Type     Price   Activity      Cost

     1 GERBER              UPLOWBD   0.0176  0.000000  -0.006936
     2 TANDY       BASIC   UPLOWBD   0.0288  0.632135   0.000000
     3 GENMIL              UPLOWBD   0.0148  0.000000  -0.006499
     4 CONED       BASIC   UPLOWBD   0.021   0.367865   0.000000
     5 WEYER               UPLOWBD   0.0092  0.000000  -0.016921
     6 IBM                 UPLOWBD   0.0103  0.000000  -0.013119
```

```
      7 DEC          UPLOWBD   0.0182   0.000000   -0.007860
      8 MOBIL        UPLOWBD   0.0172   0.000000   -0.008612
      9 TEX          UPLOWBD   0.0121   0.000000   -0.012830
     10 CPL          UPLOWBD   0.0146   0.000000   -0.007264
```

```
                          Linear Programming
                      Optimal Portfolio Weights

              LINEAR  PROGRAMMING  PROCEDURE

                   ❹    CONSTRAINT  SUMMARY

      Constraint              S/S                          Dual
      Row Name       Type     Col      Rhs    Activity    Activity

        1 exp_return  OBJECT                   0.025931       .
        2 beta        EQ                0.7    0.700000    0.008245
        3 sum_wts     EQ                  1    1.000000    0.020159
```

Interpretation of output

The following list interprets items of interest from PROC LP in Output 5.2. The numbers of the list correspond to the callout numbers in the output.

❶ Problem summary including the number of equations in the linear program (objective function, linear constraints, and upper and lower bounds).

❷ Solution summary, including the following:

□ A message stating **Terminated Successfully**. If the linear program is infeasible, then you receive an error message (**Infeasible Problem**) and a note to check the boundary constraints.

□ Objective value of the objective function. In this example, the next month's expected portfolio return is .025931, or about 2.59%.

□ Also printed are the iterations, the maximum number of iterations, machine constraints on epsilon and infinity, and the time allowed and time used.

❸ Variable Summary, including the following items:

□ The list of variables, their status, type, price (expected return), activity level (solution weight), and the reduced cost.

□ The variables TANDY and CONED have activity levels of .632135 and .367865, respectively. The activity levels are the solution values for the portfolio weights. For this example, you would invest 63.21 percent of your funds in TANDY and 36.79 percent in CONED.

Note that both TANDY and CONED have reduced costs of 0. This implies that neither an increase nor a decrease in the solution values will increase the portfolio return.

Also note that TANDY and CONED have status of basic. That is, they are in the basis of the linear program, having solution values between the upper and lower bounds.

□ The variable GERBER has an activity level of 0, the lower bound, and a reduced cost (sometimes called a *shadow price*) of -.006936. These values imply the lower bound constraint is active and binding for this variable. If the solution weight for this stock could be further reduced, other weights could adjust to generate a greater return and still satisfy the remaining linear programming constraints. The values for the variables GENMIL, WEYER, IBM, DEC, MOBIL, TEX, and CPL can be interpreted similarly.

❹ Constraint Summary lists the objective function, the constraints, their _TYPE_, their right-hand-side constants, the activity levels (including the optimal solution level for the objective function), and their dual activity levels (shadow prices).

For further information on interpreting specific items in the PROC LP output data sets, setting options, and using the PROC LP, see Chapters 3 and 7 ("Introduction to Mathematical Programming Using SAS/OR Software" and "The LP Procedure," respectively) in *SAS/OR User's Guide, Version 6, First Edition*.

Including More Restrictive Bounds on Portfolio Weights

You may want to restrict the portfolio weights to a more narrow range than the 0-to-1 range used in the example code that produces Output 5.2. For example, you may want to include the upper bound restriction that the weights have a maximum value of .3333 and the lower bound restriction that the weights have a minimum value of .05. These upper and lower bound constraints can be used to ensure some diversification in the portfolio because no stock could be greater than 33.33 percent of the portfolio or less than 5 percent.

The following DATA step creates the WEIGHT2 data set. The code is very similar to that producing the WEIGHT1 data set; only the upper and lower bounds have been changed.

```
data weight2;
   input _id_ $10. gerber tandy genmil coned weyer ibm dec mobil tex
      cpl _type_ $ _rhs_;
   cards;
exp_return .0176 .0288 .0148 .021 .0092 .0103 .0182 .0172 .0121 .0146 max      .
beta       .5309 1.048 .1383 .102 .7231 .3954 .7157 .6856 .5786 .2068 eq       .7
sum_wts    1.0   1.0   1.0   1.0  1.0   1.0   1.0   1.0   1.0   1.0   eq      1.0
available  .3333 .3333 .3333 .333 .3333 .3333 .3333 .3333 .3333 .3333 upperbd  .
available  .05   .05   .05   .05  .05   .05   .05   .05   .05   .05   lowerbd  .
;
```

The following PROC LP statement solves this linear programming problem for the portfolio weights. Part of the output generated by these statements is shown in Output 5.3. Only the solution portion is shown.

```
proc lp data=weight2 primalout=lp_out2;
   title2 'More Restricted Portfolio Weights';
run;
quit;
```

Output 5.3
More Restricted
Portfolio Weights

```
                         Linear Programming
                   More Restricted Portfolio Weights

           L I N E A R   P R O G R A M M I N G   P R O C E D U R E

                          VARIABLE  SUMMARY

         Variable                                        Reduced
    Col  Name      Status   Type     Price    Activity    Cost

      1  GERBER            UPLOWBD   0.0176   0.050000  -0.001443
      2  TANDY             UPLOWBD   0.0288   0.333300   0.012116
      3  GENMIL            UPLOWBD   0.0148   0.050000  -0.006034
      4  CONED    BASIC    UPLOWBD   0.021    0.063379   0.000000
      5  WEYER             UPLOWBD   0.0092   0.050000  -0.008966
      6  IBM               UPLOWBD   0.0103   0.050000  -0.009361
      7  DEC      BASIC    UPLOWBD   0.0182   0.253321   0.000000
      8  MOBIL             UPLOWBD   0.0172   0.050000  -0.001137
      9  TEX               UPLOWBD   0.0121   0.050000  -0.006726
     10  CPL               UPLOWBD   0.0146   0.050000  -0.005922
```

```
                         Linear Programming
                   More Restricted Portfolio Weights

           L I N E A R   P R O G R A M M I N G   P R O C E D U R E

                         CONSTRAINT  SUMMARY

    Constraint           S/S                             Dual
    Row  Name     Type   Col    Rhs     Activity      Activity

      1  exp_return OBJECT              0.020330          .
      2  beta       EQ     0.7          0.700000     -0.004562
      3  sum_wts    EQ     1            1.000000      0.021465
```

Interpretation of output

In Output 5.3, the objective function value (labeled EXP_RETURN) is 0.020330 or 2.03 percent.

The activity levels (shown in the Variable Summary) are the solution values for the portfolio weights. For this example, you would invest 33.33 percent of your portfolio in TANDY, 25.33 percent in DEC, 5 percent in each of GERBER, GENMIL, WEYER, IBM, MOBIL, TEX, and CPL, and 6.34 percent in CONED.

Note the following items of interest:

□ The variable GERBER has an activity level of .05, the lower bound, and a reduced cost (shadow price) of -.001443. These values imply the lower bound constraint is active and binding. If the solution weight could be further reduced, the value of the objective function could be increased. The values for the variables GENMIL, WEYER, IBM, TEX, and CPL can be interpreted similarly.

□ The variable TANDY has an activity level of .3333, the upper bound, and a reduced cost of .012116. These values imply the upper bound constraint is active and binding. If the solution weight could be further increased, the other weights could adjust to generate a greater return and still satisfy the remaining linear programming constraints.

□ The variables CONED and DEC have a status of basic. That is, they are in the basis of the linear program, having solution values between the upper and lower bounds.

Sparse Data Form

For linear programming problems with many variables, you may prefer to create the input data set in the sparse data format. Often in linear programming, few of the coefficients in the constraint matrix are nonzero. In the sparse format, only the nonzero coefficients need to be specified.

Although this particular example is not very sparse, the PROC LP output shown in Output 5.3 can be generated with data in the sparse data format shown in the following example.

In this example, only the first and last stocks are included. You need to include all of the stocks to create an input data set for PROC LP. Also, the PROC LP statement requires the SPARSEDATA option when the input data set is in the sparse data format. The output from this example code is not printed.

```
            /* Creating the Sparse Input Data Set, WT_SPARS */
        data wt_spars;
           input _type_ $ @10 _col_ $13. @24 _row_ $16. _coef_;
           cards;
max          .              exp_return          .
eq           .              beta                .
upperbd      .             upper                .
lowerbd      .             lower                .
eq           .              sum_wts             .
             gerber        exp_return          .0176
             gerber        beta                .5309
             gerber        upper               .3333
             gerber        lower               .05
             gerber        sum_wts             1.0


                              .
                              .
                              .


             more lines of data, for all ten stocks


                              .
                              .
                              .


      .      cpl             exp_return          .146
      .      cpl             beta                .2068
      .      cpl             upper               .3333
      .      cpl             lower               .05
      .      cpl             sum_wts             1.0
      .      _rhs_           exp_return          0
      .      _rhs_           beta                .7
      .      _rhs_           sum_wts             1.0
      ;

            /* Solving for the LP Problem Using the WT_SPARS Data Set */
        proc lp sparsedata data=wt_spars primalout=sp_out;
        run;
        quit;
```

Sensitivity Analyses

As the values of the expected returns, the risk measures, and the constraint values change, so do the solution values for the portfolio weights. If a relatively small change in the return, risk, and constraint values generates relatively large changes in the portfolio weights, you conclude that the portfolio weights are sensitive to the market conditions. If relatively large changes in the return, risk, and constraint values generate relatively small (or no) changes in the portfolio weights, you conclude that the portfolio weights are robust to the market conditions.

You can assess the stability of the portfolio weights (the *primal solution values* of the linear programming problem) by performing sensitivity analyses. You can perform sensitivity analyses on the *price vector* (the average annual returns) or on the *right-hand-side vector* (the weights summing to unity and the portfolio β equaling .7). Sensitivity analyses show you the range over which the price vector or the right-hand-side vector can vary and the primal solution portfolio weights are still optimal.

You can perform these sensitivity analyses on the linear programming problem solved in Output 5.3 with the following statements. The sensitivity analyses are printed in Output 5.4.

Explanation of syntax

DATA=   specifies the data set to be used for analysis.

PRIMALIN= specifies the data set containing the solution for analysis.

RANGEPRICE specifies that range analysis is to be performed on the price coefficients.

RANGERHS   specifies that range analysis is to be performed on the right-hand-side vector.

Example code

```
proc lp data=weight2 primalin=lp_out2 rangeprice rangerhs;
   title2 'Sensitivity Analyses';
run;
quit;
```

Output 5.4
Sensitivity Analyses
of the Optimal
Portfolio Weights

```
                               Linear Programming
                               Sensitivity Analyses

              L I N E A R   P R O G R A M M I N G   P R O C E D U R E

                              RHS RANGE SUMMARY

                    ---------- Min Phi ----------  ---------- Max Phi ----------
           Row          Rhs Leaving   Objective      Rhs Leaving   Objective

           beta       0.575222 DEC    0.020900     0.708211 CONED   0.020293
           sum_wts    0.988528 CONED  0.020084     1.231195 CONED   0.025293
```

```
                              Linear Programming
                              Sensitivity Analyses

              L I N E A R   P R O G R A M M I N G   P R O C E D U R E

                             PRICE RANGE SUMMARY

          Variable    ---------- Min Phi ----------  ---------- Max Phi ----------
    Col   Name        Price Entering   Objective     Price Entering   Objective

      1   GERBER       -INF .              -INF     0.019043 GERBER     0.020403
      2   TANDY    0.016684 TANDY      0.016292         +INF .              +INF
      3   GENMIL       -INF .              -INF     0.020834 GENMIL     0.020632
      4   CONED    0.016207 GERBER     0.020027     0.764592 WEYER      0.067458
      5   WEYER        -INF .              -INF     0.018166 WEYER      0.020779
      6   IBM          -INF .              -INF     0.019661 IBM        0.020799
      7   DEC      0.017004 MOBIL      0.020027     0.026060 TANDY      0.022322
      8   MOBIL        -INF .              -INF     0.018337 MOBIL      0.020387
      9   TEX          -INF .              -INF     0.018826 TEX        0.020667
     10   CPL          -INF .              -INF     0.020522 CPL        0.020627
```

Interpretation of output

Output 5.4 displays the sensitivity analyses of the linear programming problem solved in Output 5.3.

The right-hand-side sensitivity analysis shows you

□ the name of the variables that leave the optimal primal solution. DEC leaves when the portfolio β constraint BETA is reduced to .575222, while CONED leaves when the BETA constraint is increased to .708211. CONED leaves when the SUM_WTS constraint is reduced to .988528, and CONED leaves when the SUM_WTS constraint is increased to 1.231195.

□ the value of the optimal objective function in the modified problems. In this example, the level of expected returns is shown for each case.

□ the optimal solution of the modified problem.

The price-range sensitivity analysis shows you

□ the name of the entering variables

□ the range of prices (or for this problem, the range of expected returns) at which a variable is in the basis of the linear programming problem. Prices (expected returns) outside of this range generate different solution values for the portfolio weights.

□ minimum and maximum price coefficients (expected returns) in the modified problems

□ the resulting value of the optimal objective function in the modified problems.

By examining the sensitivity analyses, you can judge how robust the optimal primal solution weights are. For example, you may want to compare the robustness of the solution weights for several portfolios. The more the right-hand-side coefficients and the prices (expected returns) can vary (with the solution weights still remaining optimal), the more robust the solution weights are.

Suppose you were performing sensitivity analysis on the expected returns, and slight changes in the expected returns caused large changes in the solution weights. You would conclude that the solution weights for that particular linear programming problem are not robust.

▶ *Caution* . . . . *Use Solution Weights with Care*

Only when you are fully satisfied with your assumptions about the future, your expectations of future stock returns and risks, and your linear programming analysis should you consider basing your investment strategies upon them. ▲

Setting Maximum Portfolio Risk Level while Calculating Portfolio Weights

You may want to examine the optimal portfolio weights calculated when the risk constraint is an inequality, that is, when the portfolio β can be less than or equal to a maximum acceptable value.

For example, you may want to explore how the primal solution changes in the previous problem if the portfolio β is allowed to be equal to or less than .7.

You can perform this task with a DATA step and PROC LP, as shown in the following statements. Part of the output generated by these statements is shown in Output 5.5. Only the solution portion is shown.

```
data weight3;
   set weight2;
   if _id_ = 'beta' then _type_ = 'le';
run;

proc lp data=weight3 primalout=lp_out3;
run;
quit;
```

Output 5.5
Optimal Portfolio
Weights when
Portfolio Risk Level
(Beta) is Equal to or
Less than .7.

```
          L I N E A R   P R O G R A M M I N G   P R O C E D U R E

                          VARIABLE   SUMMARY

        Variable                                              Reduced
    Col Name      Status    Type      Price    Activity         Cost

      1 GERBER            UPLOWBD     0.0176   0.050000     -0.003400
      2 TANDY             UPLOWBD     0.0288   0.333300      0.007800
      3 GENMIL            UPLOWBD     0.0148   0.050000     -0.006200
      4 CONED     BASIC   UPLOWBD     0.021    0.266700      0.000000
      5 WEYER             UPLOWBD     0.0092   0.050000     -0.011800
      6 IBM               UPLOWBD     0.0103   0.050000     -0.010700
      7 DEC               UPLOWBD     0.0182   0.050000     -0.002800
      8 MOBIL             UPLOWBD     0.0172   0.050000     -0.003800
      9 TEX               UPLOWBD     0.0121   0.050000     -0.008900
     10 CPL               UPLOWBD     0.0146   0.050000     -0.006400
     11 beta      BASIC   SLACK                0.124778      0.000000
```

```
          L I N E A R   P R O G R A M M I N G   P R O C E D U R E

                          CONSTRAINT   SUMMARY

        Constraint              S/S                               Dual
    Row Name        Type        Col      Rhs     Activity      Activity

      1 exp_return  OBJECT                        0.020900         .
      2 beta        LE          11       0.7      0.575222      0.000000
      3 sum_wts     EQ                   1        1.000000      0.021000
```

Interpretation of output

Output 5.5 includes the optimal solution weights and the constraint summary for the modified problem introduced and solved in Output 5.3.

Note in observation 11 (beta) that the TYPE variable is SLACK. This variable accounts for the excess of the right-hand side of the BETA inequality constraint over the left-hand side. (That is, the SLACK variable is a linear programming variable added by PROC LP to simplify the inequality BETA constraint to an equivalent equality constraint and, thereby, to simplify the mathematical analysis.)

The following table shows only the optimal portfolio weights *that changed*, the resulting objective function and portfolio β values as the equality BETA constraint (in Output 5.3) is modified to an inequality constraint (in Output 5.5):

Variables and Functions	Value from Output 5.3	Value from Output 5.5
CONED	.063379	.266700
DEC	.253321	.050000
Portfolio Return	.020330	.020900
Portfolio Risk	.700000	.575222

The inequality BETA constraint of Output 5.5 is less restrictive than the equality BETA constraint of Output 5.3. In the less restrictive problem, the objective function (portfolio return) increases, while the BETA constraint (risk measure) decreases. The higher return and lower risk indicate that the portfolio in Output 5.5 is superior to the portfolio of Output 5.3.

Calculating Dollar Amounts to Invest

For the dollar value of your portfolio, you can use a DATA step and the optimal portfolio weights to calculate the dollar amounts to invest in each stock. For example, suppose you wanted to invest $100,000 in the portfolio of stocks used in the analysis of this chapter. The following statements use the optimal weights from Output 5.5 to perform this task:

```
data lp_out3a;
    set lp_out3;
    if _n_ > 10 then delete;
    amount=_value_*100000;
    rename _var_ = asset;
run;

proc print data=lp_out3a;
    var asset amount;
    title 'Linear Programming';
    title2 'Amount to Invest in Each Asset';
run;
```

Output 5.6
Optimal Amounts to
Invest in Each Stock

```
                    Linear Programming
                Amount to Invest in Each Asset

           OBS    ASSET    AMOUNT

            1     GERBER     5000
            2     TANDY     33330
            3     GENMIL     5000
            4     CONED     26670
            5     WEYER      5000
            6     IBM        5000
            7     DEC        5000
            8     MOBIL      5000
            9     TEX        5000
           10     CPL        5000
```

Interpretation of output
The amounts shown in Output 5.6 are the optimal amounts to invest in these stocks to maximize returns, given the constraints listed previously (in the code producing Output 5.5).

This linear programming approach is most appropriate if you can purchase any number of common stock shares (including fractional amounts). Typically, mutual funds allow purchases of any number of shares (above a minimum investment level).

Typically, individually listed stocks are traded in lots of 100 shares. Trading in lots other than 100 shares is known as *odd-lot trading*. Finding the optimal number of 100-share lots to purchase involves solving integer programs. The next section presents integer programming examples that incorporate the constraint of trading in 100-share lots.

Portfolio Creation Using Integer Programming

Typically, for portfolio creation, you want to purchase individual stocks in lots of 100 shares. Finding the maximum expected return, subject to the constraint of purchasing 100-share lots, is an integer programming problem.

In this section, you

□   use PROC LP to solve integer programming problems

□   use PROC PRINT to print the primal and dual solution data sets

□   use the DATA step and PROC TRANSPOSE to calculate the expected portfolio return and the portfolio β.

Solving an Integer Programming Problem

You use PROC LP to solve integer programming problems. For this example, the expected returns calculated in Output 5.1 and the CAPM βs calculated in Chapter 4 are used. Because the expected returns and CAPM βs are calculated as of the end of 1986, the closing stock prices as of December 31 1986 (times 100) are used as the cost of 100-share lots of the stocks.

In the example that follows, the PROC LP statements

□   maximize the expected portfolio return, subject to the listed constraints. This is the first observation in the WEIGHT4 data set.

□   constrain the summation of the products of each individual stock β and the corresponding number of 100-share lots purchased to 10 or less. This is the second observation in the WEIGHT4 data set. Note that this risk measure is not comparable to the portfolio β constraint of previous examples in this chapter.

□   constrain the summation of the products of each 100-share lot cost times the number of lots purchased to be less than or equal to $100,000. This is the third observation in the WEIGHT4 data set. Note that for integer programming problems, inequality constraints are advised; otherwise, you may create infeasible problems.

□   set upper bounds of either four or seven 100-share lots for each stock. Stocks selling for over $100 per share are limited to four 100-share lots, while stocks selling for less than $100 per share are limited to seven 100-share lots. This is the fourth observation in the WEIGHT4 data set. The upper bounds ensure that the portfolio will not be concentrated into only one or two stocks.

□   set lower bounds of one 100-share lot for each stock. For this example, at least 100 shares of each stock in the portfolio are purchased. This constraint ensures diversification. This is the fifth observation in the WEIGHT4 data set.

□   specify integer programming with the _TYPE_ variable of INTEGER. Note that the coefficients in the integer constraint specify the order in which the stocks are included in the PROC LP iterations. In this example, the stocks are included in the order in which they are listed. This is the sixth observation in the WEIGHT4 data set.

With integer programming problems, you may want to increase the maximum limit of iterations above the default limit of 100 iterations. The PROC LP IMAXIT= option enables you to set the maximum number of iterations.

You can store the primal and dual solutions from this integer programming problem in output data sets with the PRIMALOUT= and DUALOUT= options, respectively.

```
/* Input Data Set for Integer Programming Problem */
/* Buy Stock in Lots of 100 Shares */
/* 1 Lot Minimum, 4 or 7 Lots Maximum */
/* Portfolio Equal to or Less Than $100,000 */
/* Find Optimal Number of Lots to Buy */
data weight4;
   input _id_ $10. gerber tandy genmil coned weyer ibm dec mobil tex
         cpl _type_ $ _rhs_;
   cards;
exp_return .0176 .0288 .0148 .021 .0092 .0103 .0182 .0172 .0121 .0146 max      .
beta       .5309 1.048 .1383 .102 .7231 .3954 .7157 .6856 .5786 .2068 le      10
lots       4138 4250 4313 4713 3775 12000 10475 4013 3588 3863 le      100000
upper      7    7    7    7    7    4    4    7    7    7    upperbd .
lower      1    1    1    1    1    1    1    1    1    1    lowerbd .
integer    1    2    3    4    5    6    7    8    9    10   integer .
;

   /* Solving the Integer Programming Problem */
proc lp data=weight4 imaxit=200 primalout=lp_out4 dualout=d_out;
run;
```

The output from PROC LP is not shown. The following sections print the primal and dual solutions.

Printing the Primal Solution Data Set

Before printing the primal solution data set, you may want to use a DATA step to eliminate unneeded observations and variables. In this example, the DATA step creates the LP_OUT4A data set containing the stocks and the optimal number of 100-lot shares to purchase for this integer programming problem.

```
      /* Tailoring Output Data Set for Printing */
data lp_out4a(keep= _var_ _value_
              rename= _var_=name);
   set lp_out4;
   if _n_ > 10 then delete;
run;

      /* Printing the Primal Solution */
proc print data=lp_out4a;
   title 'Integer Programming';
   title2 'Number of 100 Share Lots to Buy';
run;
```

Output 5.7
Primal Solution to
Integer
Programming
Problem

```
                 Integer Programming
             Number of 100 Share Lots to Buy

             OBS     NAME     _VALUE_

              1     GERBER       3
              2     TANDY        4
              3     GENMIL       1
              4     CONED        6
              5     WEYER        1
              6     IBM          1
              7     DEC          1
              8     MOBIL        1
              9     TEX          1
             10     CPL          1
```

Interpretation of output

Output 5.7 displays the optimal number of 100-share lots to purchase of each stock. What cannot be shown by this output are comparable measures of the expected return and the portfolio risk level (previously measured by portfolio β). These values can be calculated from the input data set (WEIGHT4) and the primal solution data set (LP_OUT4).

A value required to calculate the portfolio expected return and risk level is the optimal size of the portfolio. Notice in the code producing Output 5.7 that the LOTS constraint (limiting the size of the portfolio) is an inequality constraint with a maximum value of $100,000. Of the allocated $100,000, how much is used to create the portfolio? To answer this question, you must examine the dual solution data set, which is printed and interpreted in the next section.

Printing the Dual Solution Data Set

You use PROC PRINT to print the dual solution data set D_OUT. The dual solution data set contains the following items of interest:

□ the return of the portfolio

□ the optimal size of portfolio

□ the optimal level of portfolio risk.

Note that these measures of portfolio risk and return are not comparable measures in previous linear programming stock selection problems. Previous portfolio return measures were linear combinations of the individual stock returns and the optimal portfolio weights. Previous portfolio risk measures were linear combinations of the individual stock risk (CAPM βs) and the optimal portfolio weights.

```
/* Printing the Dual Solution */
/* Optimal Solution Size of the Portfolio */
proc print data=d_out;
    title 'Linear Programming';
    title2 'Return, Risk, and Size of Portfolio';
run;
```

Output 5.8
Dual Solution to Integer Programming Problem

```
                            Linear Programming
                      Return, Risk, and Size of Portfolio

        OBS    _ROW_ID_      _TYPE_        _RHS_       _VALUE_

         1    exp_return    OBJECT          0.39          0.39
         2    beta          LE             10.00          9.84
         3    lots          LE         100000.00      99719.00
```

Interpretation of output

Output 5.8 displays the dual solution to the integer programming problem. The variable (column) headings are interpreted as follows:

□ The OBS variable identifies the observation number.

□ The _ROW_ID_ variable identifies the rows. These rows correspond to those in the input data set, WEIGHT4.

□ The _TYPE_ variable corresponds to the input data set values for the observations. EXP_RETURN is the objective function to be maximized, and BETA and LOTS are inequality (less than or equal to) constraints.

□ The _RHS_ variable corresponds to the right-hand-side variable value in the input data set WEIGHT4.

□ The _VALUE_ variable contains the optimal dual solution values.

Note the following:

□ The expected portfolio return is 0.39.

□ The portfolio risk level is 9.84 (of the possible 10).

□   The optimal portfolio size is $99,719 (of the possible $100,000).

The expected portfolio return and the portfolio risk level are not comparable to previous measures of risk and return. The next section shows you how to calculate comparable values.

Calculating Comparable Risk and Return Measures

The constraint requirements of the integer programming problem do not allow the right-hand-side coefficients to be set so that comparable portfolio risk and return measures are generated in the primal or dual solutions.

You can use the DATA step and PROC TRANSPOSE to generate these values. You proceed as follows:

□   Use PROC TRANSPOSE to transpose the input data set for the integer programming problem.

□   Use the DATA step to eliminate unneeded observations and variables, rename variables, and merge the input and primal solution data sets.

□   Use the DATA step to calculate the individual stocks' contributions to comparable risk and return measures.

□   Use PROC MEANS to sum the individual stocks' contributions to comparable risk and return measures.

Tailoring the Input Data Set

You can use PROC TRANSPOSE and the DATA step to tailor the input data set.

```
     /* Transpose Input Data Set */
proc transpose data=weight4 out=wt1;
run;
```

The transposition transforms rows to columns and columns to rows. After transposing, you can use a DATA step to eliminate unneeded observations and variables. You rename the variables with a RENAME statement. Then you use PROC PRINT to print the tailored input data set.

```
data wt2(drop=col4 col5 col6);
   set wt1;
   if _n_ > 10 then delete;
   rename _name_=name col1=return col2=beta col3=lots;
run;

   /* Printing the Tailored Data Set */
proc print data=wt2;
   title 'Integer Programming';
   title2 'Transposed and Tailored Input Data Set';
run;
```

Output 5.9
Tailored Input Data
Set

```
                    Integer Programming
              Transposed and Tailored Input Data Set

        OBS    NAME     RETURN    BETA     LOTS

         1     GERBER   0.0176   0.5309     4138
         2     TANDY    0.0288   1.0480     4250
         3     GENMIL   0.0148   0.1383     4313
         4     CONED    0.0210   0.1020     4713
         5     WEYER    0.0092   0.7231     3775
         6     IBM      0.0103   0.3954    12000
         7     DEC      0.0182   0.7157    10475
         8     MOBIL    0.0172   0.6856     4013
         9     TEX      0.0121   0.5786     3588
        10     CPL      0.0146   0.2068     3863
```

Interpretation of output

Output 5.9 displays the tailored input data set, which is ready for merging with the tailored primal solution data set LP_OUT4A. The variables RETURN, BETA, and LOTS contain the expected stock returns, the βs, and the cost of 100-share lots of each stock (as of December 31, 1986), respectively.

Merging the Input and Primal Solution Data Sets

You merge the tailored input and primal solution data sets in a DATA step. The merged data set can be printed with PROC PRINT.

```
    /* Merging Input and Primal Solution Data Sets */
data wt3;
    merge lp_out4a wt2;
run;

proc print data=wt3;
    title 'Integer Programming';
    title2 'Merged Data Set';
run;
```

Output 5.10
Merged Data Set

```
                    Integer Programming
                      Merged Data Set

     OBS    NAME    _VALUE_    RETURN    BETA     LOTS

      1    GERBER      3       0.0176   0.5309     4138
      2    TANDY       4       0.0288   1.0480     4250
      3    GENMIL      1       0.0148   0.1383     4313
      4    CONED       6       0.0210   0.1020     4713
      5    WEYER       1       0.0092   0.7231     3775
      6    IBM         1       0.0103   0.3954    12000
      7    DEC         1       0.0182   0.7157    10475
      8    MOBIL       1       0.0172   0.6856     4013
      9    TEX         1       0.0121   0.5786     3588
     10    CPL         1       0.0146   0.2068     3863
```

Performing the Calculations

To calculate the comparable measures of risk and return, you first need to create a variable containing each stock's fraction of the portfolio. This fraction is used later to calculate each stock's contribution to the portfolio risk and return.

You use the portfolio size from the dual solution data set to calculate these fractions in a DATA step.

```
data wt4;
   set wt3;
   amt=99719;
   fraction=_value_*lots/amt;
   risk=fraction*beta;
   exp_ret=fraction*return;
run;
```

After creating each stock's contribution to portfolio risk and return, you sum them with PROC MEANS.

```
/* Sum the Individual Stock Contributions */
proc means data=wt4 sum;
   var risk exp_ret;
   title2 'Comparable Measures of Risk and Return';
run;
```

Output 5.11
Comparable
Measures of Risk
and Return

```
                     Integer Programming
            Comparable Measures of Risk and Return

                 Variable        Sum
                 ----------------------
                 RISK          0.4862172
                 EXP_RET       0.0188888
                 ----------------------
```

Interpretation of output

In Output 5.11, the first observation (labeled RISK) is the CAPM portfolio β, calculated as a linear combination of individual stock βs and their portfolio weights. The second observation (labeled EXP_RET) is the expected return of the portfolio (1.89 percent), calculated as a linear combination of individual stock returns and their portfolio weights.

Portfolio Creation with Short Sales Allowed

Thus far, the linear and integer programming problems for portfolio selection have not allowed short sales. The amounts to be invested in each stock have been constrained to non-negative values. Lintner (1971) suggested a constraint that allows short sales but requires investors to hold in escrow the amount sold short until the outcome is known. This constraint is that the absolute values of the portfolio weights must sum to unity.

Solving the Linear Programming Problem

You can create an input data set in a DATA step for linear programming problems to incorporate the constraint that the portfolio weights sum to unity. You modify the input data set by listing each stock twice: once with positively signed return and risk measures for buying and once with negatively signed return and risk measures for selling short. In the INPUT statement, the suffix of 1 indicates that the stock is bought, while a suffix of 2 indicates that the stock is sold short.

Note that you may expect returns of different magnitudes from buying and holding a stock versus selling a stock short. In that case, you want to adjust the price coefficients (expected returns) in the objective function of the input data set to reflect those differences. In lieu of any specific differences in the magnitude of expected returns, the examples in this section are based on the same magnitudes of returns with opposite signs: positive for buying and holding and negative for short sales.

The objective function is still to maximize expected return, and, for this example, the constraints on the portfolio weights are as follows:

□ Weights must be chosen so that the portfolio risk level (β) is less than or equal to unity.

□ The individual portfolio weights are allowed to vary between -1 and +1.

□ The absolute value of the portfolio weights must sum to unity.

Under these constraints, the input data set for PROC LP is as shown in the following DATA step. Note that the / line-pointer control in the INPUT statement forces a new record to be read into the input buffer and forces the pointer to return to the beginning of that record. That is, each observation in the WEIGHT5 data set contains two lines of data. The / line-pointer control indicates that the first data line of each observation ends with the variable WEYER2, and the second data line begins with the variable IBM1.

```
data weight5;
   input _id_ $10. gerber1 gerber2 tandy1 tandy2 genmil1 genmil2
         coned1 coned2 weyer1 weyer2 / ibm1 ibm2 dec1 dec2 mobil1
         mobil2 tex1 tex2 cpl1 cpl2 _type_ $ _rhs_;
   cards;
exp_return .0176 -.0176 .0288 -.0288 .0148 -.0148 .021 -.021 .0092 -.0092
.0103 -.0103 .0182 -.0182 .0172 -.0172 .0121 -.0121 .0146 -.0146 max      .
beta       .5309 -.5309 1.048 -1.048 .1383 -.1383 .102 -.102 .7231 -.7231
.3954 -.3954 .7157 -.7157 .6856 -.6856 .5786 -.5786 .2068 -.2068 le        1.0
sum_wts       1     1     1     1     1     1     1     1     1     1
1      1     1     1     1     1     1     1     1     1      eq        1
available     1     1     1     1     1     1     1     1     1     1
1      1     1     1     1     1     1     1     1     1      upperbd   .
;
```

The PROC LP statements to solve this problem are shown in the following code. You can tailor the primal output data set LP_OUT5 to delete stocks with weights of 0. The amounts to invest in stocks with nonzero weights in a $100,000 portfolio are printed using PROC PRINT in Output 5.12. The output from PROC LP is not shown.

```
proc lp data=weight5 primalout=lp_out5;
run;
quit;

data lp_out5a;
   set lp_out5;
   if _n_ > 20 then delete;
   if _value_ = 0 then delete;
   amount=_value_*100000;
   rename _var_ = asset;
run;

proc print data=lp_out5a;
  var asset amount;
   title 'Linear Programming';
   title2 'Amount to Invest in Each Stock';
run;
```

Output 5.12
Amounts to Invest in
Stocks with Nonzero
Weights

```
                      Linear Programming
                  Amount to Invest in Each Stock

             OBS     ASSET      AMOUNT

              1      TANDY1    94926.00
              2      CONED1     5074.00
```

Interpretation of output
In Output 5.12, the stocks with nonzero portfolio weights and the amount to invest in each are listed. Both stocks have a suffix of 1, indicating that they should be bought.

▶ *Caution* . . . . *For Each Stock Either Buy and Hold or Sell Short, But Not Both*
Be aware that when using the Lintner constraint, it may be possible (but unlikely) for the solution to include a nonzero weight for purchases and for short sales. For each stock, you should follow either the buy-and-hold investment strategy or the selling-short strategy, but not both. In the rare case that the solution weights indicate following both strategies for an individual stock, you should respecify the problem. ▲

Optimal Solutions for Other Risk Levels

The WEIGHT5 data set created for Output 5.12 can be modified to constrain the portfolio risk level to different values. For example, you can constrain portfolio β to .75 or less with the following DATA step. Note that all other constraints in the WEIGHT5 data set are unchanged.

```
data weight5b;
   set weight5;
   if _id_ = 'beta' then _rhs_ = .75;
run;
```

You can use PROC LP to solve this linear programming problem with the following statements:

```
proc lp data=weight5b primalout=lp_out5b;
run;
quit;
```

The primal solution is stored in the LP_OUT5B data set. The output from these statements is not shown.

For this linear programming problem, the solution percentages of the portfolio to invest in each stock for various risk levels are shown in the following table:

Beta <=	Stocks to Invest in		Expected Return
-.25	CONED1=57.34%	WEYER2=42.66%	0.8116%
-.15	CONED1=69.46%	WEYER2=30.54%	1.1776%
-.05	CONED1=81.58%	WEYER2=18.42%	1.5437%
0	CONED1=87.64%	WEYER2=12.36%	1.7267%
.05	CONED1=93.70%	WEYER2= 6.30%	1.9097%
.15	CONED1=94.93%	TANDY1= 5.07%	2.1396%
.25	CONED1=84.36%	TANDY1=15.64%	2.2220%
.50	CONED1=57.93%	TANDY1=42.07%	2.4282%
.75	CONED1=31.50%	TANDY1=68.50%	2.6343%
1.00	CONED1= 5.07%	TANDY1=94.93%	2.8404%

The column labeled "Beta <=" lists a variety of values for which the portfolio β is less than or equal to. A positive β implies that the stock moves with the market. That is, if the market goes up, the portfolio return also goes up, and if the market goes down, the return goes down. The market β is 1.0. On average, the return of a portfolio with β of 1.0 moves in the same direction and magnitude as the market. On average, the return of a portfolio with β less than 1.0 and greater than 0, moves in the same direction as the market but with a smaller magnitude.

A portfolio with β of 0 is still risky in that the level of its future returns is unknown in advance, and returns of the portfolio are uncorrelated with the market. You may still be able to reduce the risk of holding portfolios with β of 0 by further diversification.

A portfolio with a negative β implies the stock (or the portfolio) moves against the market. That is, if the market goes up, the portfolio return goes down, and if the market goes down, the portfolio return goes up.

The column labeled "Stocks to Invest in" lists the optimal stocks (for this set of constraints and assumptions) to buy and hold or to sell short and the percentage of the portfolio to invest in each stock. In this example, Consolidated Edison stock is bought and held in every case. For portfolio βs of about .10 or less, the variable WEYER2 appears in the portfolio, and WEYER2 indicates that Weyerhauser stock is sold short. For portfolio βs of about .10 or more, Tandy Corporation stock is bought and held.

The column labeled "Expected Return" lists the expected portfolio return, and in terms of the linear program, the value of the objective function. As the portfolio β decreases, so does the expected return of the portfolio. Typically, investors require higher expected returns for accepting greater risks. The risk and return values in the table illustrate the trade-off investors face: greater return is possible, **if** one is willing to accept additional risk. Each investor must decide the optimal trade-off of risk and return.

Setting Bounds on the Optimal Weights

You can set different upper and lower bounds on the amount to buy or sell short for each stock. For example, you may want to modify the previous example by setting an upper bound of 25 percent of the portfolio for buying each stock, and an upper bound of 10 percent for short sales of each stock. For this example, the input data set WEIGHT6 is as follows:

```
data weight6;
    input _id_ $10. gerber1 gerber2 tandy1 tandy2 genmil1 genmil2
          coned1 coned2 weyer1 weyer2 / ibm1 ibm2 dec1 dec2 mobil1
          mobil2 tex1 tex2 cpl1 cpl2 _type_ $ _rhs_;
    cards;
exp_return .0176 -.0176 .0288 -.0288 .0148 -.0148 .021 -.021 .0092 -.0092
.0103 -.0103 .0182 -.0182 .0172 -.0172 .0121 -.0121 .0146 -.0146 max      .
beta        .5309 -.5309 1.048 -1.048 .1383 -.1383 .102 -.102 .7231 -.7231
.3954 -.3954 .7157 -.7157 .6856 -.6856 .5786 -.5786 .2068 -.2068 le        1.0
sum_wts     1    1    1    1    1    1    1    1    1    1
1    1    1    1    1    1    1    1    1    1    eq        1
upper       .25  .1   .25  .1   .25  .1   .25  .1   .25  .1
.25  .1   .25  .1   .25  .1   .25  .1   .25  .1   upperbd  .
;
```

The PROC LP statements to solve this linear programming problem are as follows:

```
proc lp data=weight6 primalout=lp_out6;
run;
quit;
```

You can tailor the primal output data set LP_OUT6 to delete stocks with weights of 0 in a DATA step. The amounts to invest in stocks with nonzero weights in a $100,000 portfolio are printed using PROC PRINT in Output 5.13. The PROC LP output is not shown.

```
data lp_out6a;
   set lp_out6;
   if _n_ > 20 then delete;
   if _value_ = 0 then delete;
   amount=_value_*100000;
   rename _var_ = asset;
run;

proc print data=lp_out6a;
  var asset amount;
   title 'Linear Programming';
   title2 'Amount to Invest in Each Stock';
run;
```

Output 5.13
Amounts to Invest in
Stocks with Nonzero
Weights

```
                            Linear Programming
                        Amount to Invest in Each Stock

                    OBS      ASSET      AMOUNT

                     1      GERBER1      25000
                     2      TANDY1       25000
                     3      CONED1       25000
                     4      DEC1         25000
```

Interpretation of output

In Output 5.13, the stocks with nonzero portfolio weights and the amount to invest in each are listed. All stocks listed have a suffix of 1, indicating that they should be bought.

Optimal Solutions for Other Risk Levels

You can modify the WEIGHT6 data set created for Output 5.13 to constrain the portfolio risk level to different values. To perform this task, you follow the example code used to generate the table that appears in the section "Optimal Solutions for Other Risk Levels."

The solution percentages of the portfolio to invest in each stock for various risk levels is shown in the following table:

Table 5.1
Portfolio Risk,
Weights, and
Expected Return

Beta <=	Stocks to Invest in			% Return
-.25	TANDY2 = 10.0% WEYER2 = 10.0% TEX2 = 10.0%	GENMIL1 = 25.0% DEC2 = 10.0% CPL1 = 7.3%	CONED1 = 25.0% MOBIL2 = 2.7%	0.2717%
-.15	TANDY2 = 10.0% WEYER2 = 10.0% CPL1 = 18.2%	GENMIL1 = 25.0% DEC2 = 1.8%	CONED1 = 25.0% TEX2 = 10.0%	0.6275%
-.05	GERBER = 0.2% WEYER2 = 10.0% CPL1 = 25.0%	GENMIL1 = 25.0% MOBIL2 = 4.8%	CONED1 = 25.0% TEX2 = 10.0%	0.9687%
0	GERBER1 = 4.3% WEYER2 = 10.0% CPL1 = 25.0%	GENMIL1 = 25.0% MOBIL2 = 0.7%	CONED1 = 25.0% TEX2 = 10.0%	1.1117%
.05	GERBER1 = 8.8% WEYER2 = 10.0%	GENMIL1 = 25.0% TEX2 = 6.2%	CONED1 = 25.0% CPL1 = 25.0%	1.2470%
.15	GERBER1 = 9.0% CONED1 = 25.0%	TANDY11 = 6.0% WEYER2 = 10.0%	GENMIL1 = 25.0% CPL1 = 25.0%	1.4989%
.25	TANDY1 = 18.0% WEYER2 = 7.0%	GENMIL1 = 25.0% CPL1 = 25.0%	CONED1 = 25.0%	1.7144%
.40	GERBER1 = 8.1% CONED1 = 25.0%	TANDY1 = 25.0% CPL1 = 16.9%	GENMIL1 = 25.0%	2.0043%
.50	GERBER1 = 25.0% CONED1 = 25.0%	TANDY1 = 25.0% DEC1 = 7.8%	GENMIL1 = 17.2%	2.0816%
.55	GERBER1 = 25.0% CONED1 = 25.0%	TANDY1 = 25.0% DEC1 = 16.5%	GENMIL1 = 8.5%	2.1111%
1.00	GERBER1 = 25.0% DEC1 = 25.0%	TANDY1 = 25.0%	CONED1 = 25.0%	2.1400%

The column labeled "Beta <=" lists a variety of values for which the portfolio β is less than or equal to. The column labeled "Stocks to invest in" lists the optimal stocks (for this set of constraints and assumptions) to buy and hold or to sell short and the percentage of the portfolio to invest in each stock.

For example, given the constraints of this problem, if the portfolio β is to be less than or equal to 0, then the investor should buy and hold common stocks of Gerber (4.3 percent of the portfolio), General Mills (25 percent), Consolidated Edison (25 percent), and CPL (25 percent) - while selling short the common stocks of Weyerhauser (10 percent), MOBIL (0.7 percent), and Texaco (10 percent).

The column labeled "Return" lists the expected returns for these portfolios. Note that as the portfolio β decreases, so does the expected return; this illustrates the trade-off between risk and return. As the portfolio β changes, so do the stocks to buy and hold, the stocks to sell short, the optimal percentages, and the expected portfolio return. Each investor must decide for himself the optimal trade-off of risk and return.

▶ *Caution* . . . . **Continue Analysis Until You Are Satisfied**
You are encouraged to experiment and explore many different constraints. Only when you are fully satisfied with the realistic nature of the input values and the constraints should you use the solution values to plan your investment strategies. ▲

Chapter Summary

This chapter has discussed stock selection for creating a portfolio subject to various constraints using PROC LP. Linear and integer programming problems were presented, discussed, solved, and interpreted. The objective function of the programming problems was to maximize returns. Equality and inequality constraints included risk level, weight summation equal to unity, and upper and lower bounds.

Learning More

□ For more information on the DATA step, see *SAS Language: Reference, Version 6, First Edition; SAS Language and Procedures: Usage, Version 6, First Edition; SAS Language and Procedures, Usage 2, Version 6, First Edition.*

□ For more information on PROC REG, see *SAS/STAT User's Guide, Version 6, Fourth Edition, Volume 1* and *Volume 2.*

□ For more information on PROC MEANS, PROC PLOT, PROC PRINT, and PROC TRANSPOSE, see *SAS Procedures Guide, Version 6, Third Edition* and *SAS Language and Procedures, Usage 2.*

□ For more information on PROC LP, linear programming, and integer programming, see *SAS/OR User's Guide, Version 6, First Edition.*

References

Black, F.; Jensen, M.; and Scholes, M. (1972), "The Capital Asset Pricing Model: Some Empirical Tests," *Studies in the Theory of Capital Markets*, ed. Michael Jensen, New York: Praeger, pp. 79-121.

Dantzig, G.B. (1963), *Linear Programming and Extensions*, Princeton: Princeton University Press.

Dorfman, R.; Samuelson, P.; and Solow, R. (1958), *Linear Programming and Economic Analysis*, New York: Dover Publications.

Elton, E. and Gruber, M. (1987), *Modern Portfolio Theory and Investment Analysis, Third Edition*, New York: John Wiley & Sons, Inc.

Evans, J. and Archer, S. (1968), "Diversification and the Reduction of Dispersion: An Empirical Analysis," *The Journal of Finance*, Vol. 23, pp. 761-767.

Hadley, G. (1962), *Linear Programming*, Reading, MA: Addison-Wesley.

Lintner, J. (1971), "The Effect of Short Selling and Margin Requirements in Perfect Capital Markets," *Journal of Financial and Quantitative Analysis*, Vol. 6, No. 5, 1971, pp. 1173-1195.

Markowitz, H. (1991), *Portfolio Selection: Efficient Diversification of Investments*, Cambridge, MA: Blackwell, Inc.

Chapter 6 The Markowitz Model, Portfolio Creation with Nonlinear Programming

Introduction

A formal model for creating efficient portfolios was developed by Harry Markowitz (1952 and 1991). The efficient frontier of portfolios is the set of portfolios that offer the greatest return for each level of risk (or equivalently, portfolios with the lowest risk for a given level of return). His model quantified risk so that investors could analyze risk-return choices. Moreover, risk quantification enabled investors to measure risk reduction generated by diversification.

This chapter shows you how to use the DATA step (with the CORR procedure), the NLP procedure in SAS/OR, and SAS/IML for portfolio creation with the Markowitz Model. The remainder of this section reviews the basic concepts of the Markowitz Model.

In the Markowitz model, the return of a stock is the *mean return* (also called the arithmetic mean). The risk for a stock is the standard deviation of stock returns. The *portfolio return* (R_p) is the weighted returns of the individual stocks. For portfolio creation in cases where short sales are not allowed, portfolio weights, X_i, are between 0 and 1, and they sum to 1. The portfolio return is calculated as follows:

$$R_p = x_1 R_1 + x_2 R_2 + \ldots + x_N R_N$$

$$R_p = \sum_{i=1}^{N} x_i R_i$$

The portfolio risk, σ_p, for the two-stock portfolio is defined as follows:

$$\sigma_p = \left(x_1^2 \sigma_1^2 + x_2^2 \sigma_2^2 + 2 x_1 x_2 \sigma_{12} \right)^{1/2}$$

The variables in the nonlinear risk equation are defined as follows:

σ_1^2 is the variance of the return of stock 1.

σ_2^2 is the variance of the return of stock 2.

σ_{12} is the covariance between the returns of stock 1 and stock 2. Note that, in some applications, it is useful to define σ_{12} in terms of the individual stock risks and the correlation between the individual stock returns, ρ_{12}.

$$\sigma_{12} = \rho_{12} \sigma_1 \sigma_2$$

By using the Markowitz Model, investors solve for portfolio weights that minimize the portfolio risk. Typically, investors constrain the portfolio risk equation to provide a desired level of return. The Markowitz Model is nonlinear and, therefore, it may be difficult to solve in some cases.

Portfolio Creation Using the DATA step and PROC CORR

Suppose you were considering constructing two-stock portfolios from the following three common stocks: Consolidated Edison (CONED), Mobil Corporation (MOBIL), and Texaco (TEX). (These stock returns are contained in the RETURN3 data set constructed in Chapter 4, "The Capital Asset Pricing Model (CAPM)," in the example code producing Output 4.7.) What two-stock combinations yield the greatest return for any given level of risk? In other words, what is the efficient frontier of two-stock portfolios?

This intuition-building section uses the DATA step and PROC CORR to calculate the risk and return of portfolios. PROC PLOT is used to plot the risk and return of portfolios.

Calculating Means and Covariances of Stock Returns

You can use the following PROC CORR statements to calculate the arithmetic (mean) returns and the covariance matrix of the stocks. The COV option in the PROC CORR statement calculates and prints the covariances. The OUTP= option in the PROC CORR statement creates a new SAS data set containing the Pearson correlations, arithmetic means, standard deviations, and number of observations. If the COV and the OUTP= options are specified, then the output data set also contains the covariances. In this example, the output data set is named COV_OUT1.

```
proc corr data=return3 cov outp=cov_out1 nosimple;
   var coned mobil tex;
   title 'Markowitz Model';
run;
```

Only the covariance matrix portion of the output is shown in Output 6.1.

Output 6.1
Covariance Matrix of CONED, MOBIL, and TEXACO Common Stock Returns

```
                        Markowitz Model

              3 'VAR' Variables:  CONED    MOBIL    TEX

                     Covariance Matrix     DF = 107

                      CONED          MOBIL

      CONED     0.0025956449    -.0000939720    Rate of Return for Con Edison
      MOBIL     -.0000939720     0.0060380402    Rate of Return for Mobil Corporation
      TEX       -.0004572243     0.0041149896    Rate of Return for Texaco
```

```
                        Markowitz Model

                     Covariance Matrix     DF = 107

                      TEX

      CONED     -.0004572243    Rate of Return for Con Edison
      MOBIL     0.0041149896    Rate of Return for Mobil Corporation
      TEX       0.0057175857    Rate of Return for Texaco
```

You use the following PROC PRINT statements to print the output data set COV_OUT1.

```
proc print data=cov_out1;
   title2 'Covariances, Means, and Correlations';
run;
```

Output 6.2
COV_OUT1 Data Set

```
                        Markowitz Model
                 Covariances, Means, and Correlations
```

OBS	_TYPE_	_NAME_	CONED	MOBIL	TEX
1	COV	CONED	0.003	-0.000	-0.000
2	COV	MOBIL	-0.000	0.006	0.004
3	COV	TEX	-0.000	0.004	0.006
4	MEAN		0.021	0.017	0.012
5	STD		0.051	0.078	0.076
6	N		108.000	108.000	108.000
7	CORR	CONED	1.000	-0.024	-0.119
8	CORR	MOBIL	-0.024	1.000	0.700
9	CORR	TEX	-0.119	0.700	1.000

Calculating the Mean Return of Two-Stock Portfolios

You can create many portfolios from two stocks. You can do this, for example, by holding 100 percent of one stock and 0 percent of the second stock, or 0 percent of one and 100 percent of the second, or any percentages in between. In the two-variable case, if one portfolio weight is known, the second is easily calculated: one minus the known weight. In general, the return of two-stock portfolios is calculated in the following equation:

$$R_P = xR_1 + (1 - x)R_2$$

In an iterative DO LOOP in a DATA step, you can add a variable, X, containing the portfolio weights to the COV_OUT1 data set. In this example, X goes from 0 to 1 by increments of .05. Note that the DROP= option is used to drop the variable _NAME_. Also, all observations other than those of _TYPE_ = MEAN are deleted.

```
data cov_out2(drop=_name_);
   set cov_out1;
   if _type_ ne 'MEAN' then delete;
   do x = 0 to 1 by .05;
      output;
   end;
   label x='Portfolio Weight';
run;
```

The two-stock portfolios generated from the three stocks used in this example are

□ CONED and MOBIL

□ CONED and TEX

□ MOBIL and TEX

In another DATA step, you can calculate the portfolio returns for these portfolios. The returns are stored in the MEAN1 data set.

```
data mean1;
   set cov_out2;
   pfol_m1=x*coned+(1-x)*mobil;
   pfol_m2=x*coned+(1-x)*tex;
   pfol_m3=x*mobil+(1-x)*tex;
run;
```

The portfolio returns of the MEAN1 data set are printed using PROC PRINT.

```
proc print data=mean1;
   title 'Markowitz Model';
   title2 '2-Stock Portfolio Returns';
run;
```

Output 6.3
Two-Stock Portfolio
Returns

```
                              Markowitz Model
                           2-Stock Portfolio Returns


   OBS   _TYPE_   CONED    MOBIL     TEX       X     PFOL_M1   PFOL_M2   PFOL_M3

    1    MEAN     0.021   0.017185  0.012056  0.00   0.017185  0.012056  0.012056
    2    MEAN     0.021   0.017185  0.012056  0.05   0.017376  0.012503  0.012312
    3    MEAN     0.021   0.017185  0.012056  0.10   0.017567  0.012950  0.012569
    4    MEAN     0.021   0.017185  0.012056  0.15   0.017757  0.013397  0.012825
    5    MEAN     0.021   0.017185  0.012056  0.20   0.017948  0.013844  0.013081
    6    MEAN     0.021   0.017185  0.012056  0.25   0.018139  0.014292  0.013338
    7    MEAN     0.021   0.017185  0.012056  0.30   0.018330  0.014739  0.013594
    8    MEAN     0.021   0.017185  0.012056  0.35   0.018520  0.015186  0.013851
    9    MEAN     0.021   0.017185  0.012056  0.40   0.018711  0.015633  0.014107
   10    MEAN     0.021   0.017185  0.012056  0.45   0.018902  0.016081  0.014364
   11    MEAN     0.021   0.017185  0.012056  0.50   0.019093  0.016528  0.014620
```

```
                              Markowitz Model
                           2-Stock Portfolio Returns


   OBS   _TYPE_   CONED    MOBIL     TEX       X     PFOL_M1   PFOL_M2   PFOL_M3

   12    MEAN     0.021   0.017185  0.012056  0.55   0.019283  0.016975  0.014877
   13    MEAN     0.021   0.017185  0.012056  0.60   0.019474  0.017422  0.015133
   14    MEAN     0.021   0.017185  0.012056  0.65   0.019665  0.017869  0.015390
   15    MEAN     0.021   0.017185  0.012056  0.70   0.019856  0.018317  0.015646
   16    MEAN     0.021   0.017185  0.012056  0.75   0.020046  0.018764  0.015903
   17    MEAN     0.021   0.017185  0.012056  0.80   0.020237  0.019211  0.016159
   18    MEAN     0.021   0.017185  0.012056  0.85   0.020428  0.019658  0.016416
   19    MEAN     0.021   0.017185  0.012056  0.90   0.020619  0.020106  0.016672
   20    MEAN     0.021   0.017185  0.012056  0.95   0.020809  0.020553  0.016929
   21    MEAN     0.021   0.017185  0.012056  1.00   0.021000  0.021000  0.017185
```

Interpretation of output

Output 6.3 lists the two-stock portfolio returns in the variables PFOL_M1-PFOL_M3. From the mean return values, you can see that CONED has the highest mean monthly return, followed by MOBIL and TEX. If the investor had perfect information about future returns, then they would simply pick the stock with the highest returns. But perfect information about future returns is unavailable; hence the motivation to diversify.

Thus, if all of the portfolios had equal risk, portfolio 1 would dominate because it is linear combinations of the two stocks with greatest mean returns. You can see this by plotting the portfolio returns versus the portfolio weight.

Plotting Portfolio Returns versus Portfolio Weight

You use PROC PLOT to plot the portfolio returns versus the portfolio weight. The results are shown in Output 6.4.

```
proc plot data=mean1 vpct=150;
   plot pfol_m1*x='1'
        pfol_m2*x='2'
        pfol_m3*x='3' / overlay;
   title2 'Portfolio Return versus Portfolio Weight';
run;
```

Output 6.4
Plotting the
Two-Stock Portfolio
Returns versus the
Portfolio Weight

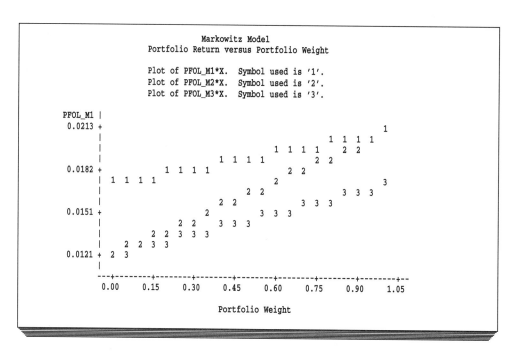

Interpretation of output

As shown in Output 6.4, portfolio 1 (combinations of CONED and MOBIL) has the greatest returns for all levels of the portfolio weight (with the exception of the case where it ties with portfolio 2 at 100 percent CONED and 0 percent TEX).

However, risk must also be considered. The next section shows you how to calculate portfolio risk for the two-stock case.

Calculating the Risk of Two-Stock Portfolios

You can calculate the risk levels of the two-stock portfolios in a DATA step using the MEAN1 data set and the values from the covariance matrix of the COV_OUT1 data set. The portfolio risk levels are calculated using the following equation, which was discussed in the introduction section of this chapter:

$$\sigma_p = \left(x_1^2 \sigma_1^2 + x_2^2 \sigma_2^2 + 2x_1 x_2 \sigma_{12} \right)^{1/2}$$

The following statements calculate the portfolio risk levels. The portfolio variances are calculated in assignment statements; then the portfolio risk levels (the standard deviations) are calculated using array processing in an iterative DO LOOP with the SQRT function. Lastly, PROC PRINT is used to print the values, as shown in Output 6.4.

```
        /* Calculating the 2-Stock Portfolio Risk Levels */
data risk1;
    set mean1;
    pfol_v1=x**2*.0025956+(1-x)**2*.0060380-2*x*(1-x)*.0000940;
    pfol_v2=x**2*.0025956+(1-x)**2*.0057176-2*x*(1-x)*.0004572;
    pfol_v3=x**2*.0060380+(1-x)**2*.0057176+2*x*(1-x)*.0041150;
```

```
                    /* Defining the Arrays */
             array pfol_v(3) pfol_v1-pfol_v3;
             array pfol_r(3) pfol_r1-pfol_r3;

                 /* Array Processing in the Iterative DO LOOP */
             do i=1 to 3;
                pfol_r(i)=sqrt(pfol_v(i));
             end;
          run;

                 /* Printing the 2-Stock Portfolio Risk Levels */
          proc print data=risk1;
             var x pfol_v1 pfol_r1-pfol_r3;
             title2 '2-Stock Portfolio Risk Levels';
          run;
```

Output 6.5
*Calculating
Two-Stock Portfolio
Risk Levels*

Markowitz Model
2-Stock Portfolio Risk Levels

OBS	X	PFOL_V1	PFOL_R1	PFOL_R2	PFOL_R3
1	0.00	.0060380	0.077705	0.075615	0.075615
2	0.05	.0054469	0.073803	0.071576	0.074607
3	0.10	.0048998	0.069999	0.067638	0.073704
4	0.15	.0043969	0.066309	0.063818	0.072912
5	0.20	.0039381	0.062754	0.060140	0.072233
6	0.25	.0035234	0.059358	0.056630	0.071670
7	0.30	.0031527	0.056149	0.053322	0.071227
8	0.35	.0028262	0.053162	0.050256	0.070906
9	0.40	.0025439	0.050437	0.047478	0.070708
10	0.45	.0023056	0.048016	0.045043	0.070634
11	0.50	.0021114	0.045950	0.043008	0.070685

Markowitz Model
2-Stock Portfolio Risk Levels

OBS	X	PFOL_V1	PFOL_R1	PFOL_R2	PFOL_R3
12	0.55	.0019613	0.044287	0.041433	0.070861
13	0.60	.0018554	0.043074	0.040370	0.071160
14	0.65	.0017935	0.042350	0.039863	0.071581
15	0.70	.0017758	0.042140	0.039930	0.072121
16	0.75	.0018022	0.042452	0.040570	0.072779
17	0.80	.0018726	0.043274	0.041756	0.073552
18	0.85	.0019872	0.044578	0.043444	0.074434
19	0.90	.0021459	0.046324	0.045578	0.075423
20	0.95	.0023487	0.048463	0.048098	0.076515
21	1.00	.0025956	0.050947	0.050947	0.077705

Interpretation of output

Output 6.5 lists the two-stock portfolio risk levels in the variables PFOL_R1-PFOL_R3. The variable X contains the portfolio weight values. The variable PFOL_V1 contains the variance (the square of the risk level) for the first portfolio.

As you examine each column of risk levels, you can see how the risk level changes as the portfolio weight changes. A naive approach to diversification is holding equal amounts of each stock in the portfolio (as shown in observation 11), which may not be the portfolio weight that minimizes the portfolio risk level. For example, portfolio 1 has minimum risk at observation 15 (.042140) where the portfolio is 70 percent CONED and 30 percent TEX.

The following table shows the portfolio risk levels for equally weighted and minimum risk portfolios:

Portfolio	Equal Weights Risk Level	Portfolio Mix	Minimum Risk Level	Portfolio Mix
1	.045950	50% CONED 50% MOBIL	.042140	70% CONED 30% MOBIL
2	.043008	50% CONED 50% TEX	.039863	65% CONED 35% TEX
3	.070685	50% MOBIL 50% TEX	.070634	45% MOBIL 55% TEX

For each weight, portfolio 2 has the lowest risk. If all two-stock portfolio returns were equal, then portfolio 2 would dominate. You can see this by plotting portfolio risk versus the portfolio weight.

Plotting Portfolio Risks versus Portfolio Weight

The set of two-stock portfolios with minimum risk can be more easily seen by plotting the risks versus the portfolio weight, X. The following PROC PLOT statements create this plot. The OVERLAY option in the PLOT statement specifies that the sets of portfolios be plotted on one plot. The plot is displayed in Output 6.6.

```
proc plot data=risk1 vpct=175;
   plot pfol_r1*x='1'
        pfol_r2*x='2'
        pfol_r3*x='3' / overlay;
   title2 'Portfolio Risk versus Portfolio Weight';
run;
```

Output 6.6
Plotting the
Two-Stock Portfolio
Risk Levels versus
the Portfolio Weight

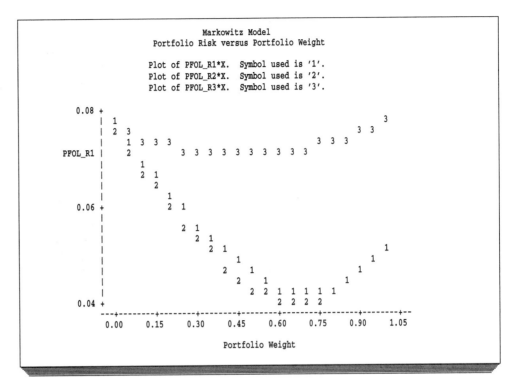

Interpretation of output

Output 6.6 displays the plot of two-stock portfolio risk levels versus the portfolio weight. Portfolio 2 (combinations of CONED and TEX) has the minimum risk for all values of portfolio weights.

Identifying Efficient Portfolios Using PROC PLOT

Efficient portfolios have the greatest return for any given level of risk. You can use the PLOT procedure to visually identify efficient portfolios of the RISK1 data set by plotting returns versus risks.

The following statements overlay the plots of the two-stock portfolios consisting of CONED and MOBIL (labeled 1), CONED and TEX (labeled 2), and MOBIL and TEX (labeled 3). The VAXIS= option enables you to specify the tick marks for the vertical axis. The resulting plot is shown in Output 6.7.

```
proc plot data=risk1 vpct=200;
   plot pfol_m1*pfol_r1='1'
        pfol_m2*pfol_r2='2'
        pfol_m3*pfol_r3='3' / overlay
                          vaxis=.012 to .021 by .003;
   title2 'Portfolio Return versus Portfolio Risk';
run;
```

Output 6.7
Plotting the
Two-Stock Portfolio
Returns versus the
Portfolio Risk Levels

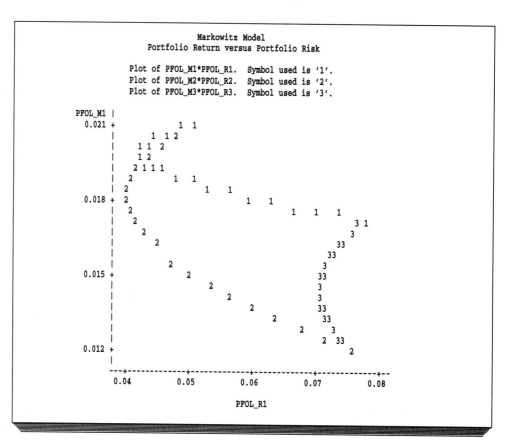

Interpretation of output

Output 6.7 displays the plot of two-stock portfolio risk levels versus returns. Returns are plotted on the vertical axis, and risk levels are plotted on the horizontal axis.

Each of the three sets of portfolios outline a curve. The end points of the curves (toward the right) are the nondiversified portfolios (100 percent of one stock and 0 percent of the other). Diversification reduces the risk levels. Portfolios on the top half of each curve dominate the portfolios on the bottom half of each curve because a greater return can be obtained for the same level of risk. In general, portfolios above and to the left dominate portfolios below and to the right.

The efficient frontier of portfolios are those with the greatest return for a given level of risk, that is, the upper left-most portfolios. Note that all portfolios labeled with 3s are dominated by those labeled with 1s and 2s.

Plotting A Subset of the Portfolios

You can plot a subset of the two-stock portfolios shown in Output 6.7 by first using a DATA step to eliminate most of the dominated portfolios and then by using PROC PLOT.

In the DATA step, portfolios with weight less than .61 are deleted. From Output 6.4, you can see that these are portfolios of lower return. From Output 6.6, you can see that these are portfolios of greater risk.

```
data risk2(drop=pfol_m3 pfol_r3);
   set risk1;
   if x < .61 then delete;
run;
```

In the PLOT statement of PROC PLOT, the portfolio returns are plotted versus the risk levels. Portfolios of CONED and MOBIL are plotted with the symbol *, while portfolios of CONED and TEX are plotted with the symbol @. The $ enables you to label the points with the portfolio weight X.

```
proc plot data=risk2 vpct=225;
    plot pfol_m1*pfol_r1='*' $ x
         pfol_m2*pfol_r2='@' $ x / overlay
                          vaxis=.0175 to .0214 by .0003;
    title2 'Return versus Risk';
    title3 'Selected Portfolios';
run;
```

Output 6.8
Plotting the
Two-Stock Portfolio
Risk Levels versus
the Portfolio
Returns

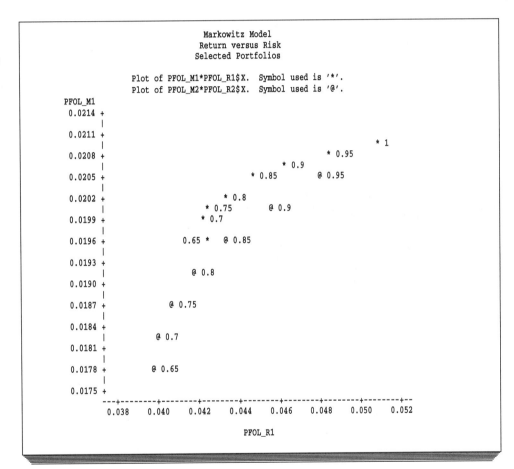

Interpretation of output

Output 6.8 plots the returns versus the corresponding risk levels for the subset of two-stock portfolios. For most points, the portfolio weight is plotted to the right of the plot symbols.

The right uppermost point (the 100 percent CONED portfolio) is shared by both sets of portfolios. The efficient frontier for the two-stock portfolios is portfolio 2 with weights from .65 to .8 and then portfolio 1 with weights .7 to 1.0.

However, if all three stocks are included, then additional portfolios can be created with lower risk for the same level of returns. For example, if investors construct a new three-stock portfolio consisting of 50 percent of portfolio 1 with weight .70 and 50 percent of portfolio 2 with weight .75, these portfolios would dominate all portfolios below and to the right. The portfolio weights for the individual stocks are calculated as follows:

$$(Portfolio\ 1\ with\ weight\ of\ .70).50 + (Portfolio\ 2\ with\ weight\ of\ .75).50$$
$$= (.70\ CONED + .30\ MOBIL).50 + (.75\ CONED + .25\ TEX).50$$
$$= .725\ CONED + .15\ MOBIL + .125\ TEX\quad .$$

Note that the efficient frontier slopes upward. More return can be obtained only as more risk is incurred. Different investors have different tolerance for risk; therefore, they may select different portfolios.

Portfolio Creation Using PROC NLP

The NLP procedure can be used to solve a wide variety of linear and nonlinear optimization problems, including the optimal portfolio weights from the nonlinear Markowitz model. With PROC NLP, you can also include boundary constraints and general linear constraints in the structure of the problem. This section shows you how to use PROC NLP to solve for the portfolio weights of the Markowitz model.

A Two-Stock Example

The following statements solve for the portfolio weights that minimize the two-stock portfolio risk of CONED and TEX, subject to the constraints that the weights are between zero and one, and that the weights sum to one. The results are shown in Output 6.9.

Explanation of syntax

PROC NLP
> invokes the NLP procedure. The OUTEST= option creates an output data set containing the solution values and other items of interest. In this example, the output data set is named NLP_OUT1.

MIN
> specifies the minimization of the listed variable. In this example, the variable to be minimized is RISK (the standard deviation of the portfolio returns), which is defined in programming statements within PROC NLP.
>
> Note that in PROC NLP you can also specify MAX and LSQ for objective function maximization and fitting least squares models, respectively.
>
> Also note that you can use most of the DATA-step functions and programming statements within PROC NLP.

PARMS
> specifies the parameters to be calculated. Starting values can be given to the parameters. By listing parameter starting values, you may substantially reduce computing time and the number of iterations. In this example, the parameters to be calculated are X1 and X2. The starting value of .5 is given to each of the parameters. (You can use the stock names as the parameter names; however, for data manipulations, parameter names like X1-Xn can simplify the programming statements.)
>
> You can also list more than one starting value for each parameter, which specifies an initial grid search. The feasible grid point (meeting all of the linear and boundary constraints) with the minimum objective function value is chosen as the initial estimate.

If you do not include starting values, PROC NLP will select starting values from the feasible region.

The next two statements are programming statements defining the portfolio variance and risk levels. You include all arithmetic operators in assignment statements when defining functions in PROC NLP.

BOUNDS

specifies the upper and lower bounds of the parameters. In this example, the parameters X1 and X2 are bounded to the interval 0 to 1, including the end points. You separate multiple boundary constraints with commas.

Note that the boundary constraints can be of the following forms:

□ *number* relation *variables* relation *number*

□ *number* relation *variables*

□ *variables* relation *number*

The relations between numbers and variables can be <=, <, >, =>, and =.

LINCON

specifies a list of linear equality or inequality constraints separated by commas. In this example, there is one linear constraint: the parameters sum to unity.

Note that the general linear constraints can be of many forms. The following are examples:

□ $\sum_{j=1}^{n} a_{ij}x_j$ relation b_i

□ *number* relation $\sum_{j=1}^{n} a_{ij}x_j$

□ $\sum_{j=1}^{n} a_{ij}x_j$ relation $\sum_{j=1}^{n} a_{ij}x_j$ relation . . . relation b_i

In these equations, the a_{ij} are the appropriate numbers, b_i are the right-hand-side values, and the relations between linear terms, variables, and numbers can be <=, <, >, =>, and =.

Note that linear constraints written simply with as few relations as possible are easier for diagnostic checking.

Example code

```
proc nlp outest=nlp_out1;
   min risk;
   parms x1=.5,
         x2=.5;
   var_p=x1*x1*.0025956+x2*x2*.0057176-2*x1*x2*.0004572;
   risk=var_p**.5;
   bounds 0 <= x1-x2 <= 1;
   lincon 1=x1+x2;
   title 'Markowitz Model';
   title2 'Quadratic Programming Portfolio Weights';
   title3;
run;
```

Output 6.9
Calculating
Two-Stock Portfolio
Weights Using
PROC NLP

```
                           Markowitz Model
                 Quadratic Programming Portfolio Weights

                    PROC NLP: Nonlinear Minimization

                      ❶  Optimization Start
                          Parameter Estimates


    ----------------------------------------------------------------
      Parameter    Estimate    Gradient    Lower BC    Upper BC


    ----------------------------------------------------------------
        1 X1       0.500000    0.024860         0      1.000000
        2 X2       0.500000    0.061156         0      1.000000


             Value of Objective Function = 0.0430081388
```

```
                           Markowitz Model
                 Quadratic Programming Portfolio Weights

                    PROC NLP: Nonlinear Minimization

                      ❷  Linear Constraints
                         ------------------

    [1] ACT    1.00000 =   +   1.0000 * X1 +   1.0000 * X2


                 First Order Lagrange Multipliers
                 -----------------------------------
                   Active              Lagrange
                   Constraint          Multiplier
                 -----------------------------------
                 Linear EC     [1]      -0.043008
```

```
                           Markowitz Model
                 Quadratic Programming Portfolio Weights

                    PROC NLP: Nonlinear Minimization

                      ❸  Projected Gradient
                         ------------------------
                     Free           Projected
                   Dimension        Gradient
                 ------------------------
                        1           -0.025665
```

```
                          Markowitz Model
                Quadratic Programming Portfolio Weights

                   PROC NLP: Nonlinear Minimization

           ❹  Newton-Raphson Ridge Optimization
                      Without Parameter Scaling
                  Number of Parameter Estimates 2
                      Number of Lower Bounds 2
                      Number of Upper Bounds 2
                    Number of Linear Constraints 1

Optimization Start: Active Constraints= 1  Criterion= 0.043
Maximum Gradient Element= 0.026

         Iter rest nfun act   optcrit  difcrit maxgrad  ridge   rho
           1    0    2   1    0.0399  0.00310 0.00461       0  0.865
           2    0    3   1    0.0398 0.000092 0.00002       0  0.997
           3    0    4   1    0.0398 1.962E-9  21E-13       0  1.000
Optimization Results: Iterations= 3 Function Calls= 5 Hessian Calls= 4
```

```
                          Markowitz Model
                Quadratic Programming Portfolio Weights

                   PROC NLP: Nonlinear Minimization

Active Constraints= 1  Criterion= 0.040 Maximum Gradient Element= 0.000
Ridge= 0.000

                  ❺   Optimization Results
                        Parameter Estimates
        ---------------------------------------------------------
          Parameter      Estimate     Gradient    Active BC
        ---------------------------------------------------------
          1  X1          0.669166     0.039820
          2  X2          0.330834     0.039820
```

```
                          Markowitz Model
                Quadratic Programming Portfolio Weights

                   PROC NLP: Nonlinear Minimization

        ❻  Value of Objective Function = 0.0398199853


               Active and Violated Linear Constraints
               --------------------------------------

   [1] ACT    1.0000 * X1 +   1.0000 * X2 -   1.0000 = -1.11022E-16
```

```
                          Markowitz Model
                Quadratic Programming Portfolio Weights

                   PROC NLP: Nonlinear Minimization
                              .
        ❼  First Order Lagrange Multipliers
           -----------------------------------
                Active              Lagrange
               Constraint          Multiplier
           -----------------------------------
            Linear EC      [1]       -0.039820
```

```
                          Markowitz Model
              Quadratic Programming Portfolio Weights

                   PROC NLP: Nonlinear Minimization

                    ❽  Projected Gradient
                   ------------------------
                      Free        Projected
                    Dimension     Gradient
                   ------------------------
                        1      2.101264E-12
```

Interpretation of output

The following list interprets items of interest from Output 6.9. The numbers of the list correspond to the callout numbers in the output.

❶ Optimization Start

1. Parameter names X1 and X2. Note that X1 refers to CONED and X2 refers to TEX. Instead of X1 and X2, you can use CONED and TEX as the parameter names.

2. User-specified starting values.

3. Initial gradient values (first derivatives of the objective function with respect to the parameters being estimated, that is, $\frac{\partial RISK}{\partial X_1}$ and $\frac{\partial RISK}{\partial X_2}$, which measure the change in the objective function for changes in the parameter values). Note that at a local minimum, the gradient values are 0.

4. User-specified lower and upper bounds.

5. Initial value of the objective function (0.0430081388).

❷ Linear Constraints

1. Active constraints, denoted ACT. In this example, the linear constraint that the parameters sum to 1 is active.

2. First-order Lagrange Multipliers. In this example, if the active linear constraint could be adjusted to be less restrictive, then the objective function could be reduced by the value of the Lagrange Multiplier. For example, if both of the weights could be reduced to 0, then the objective function could be reduced to 0.

❸ Projected gradient value at the end of the optimization process. In this example, there is one free dimension because the parameters must sum to 1, hence X2 = 1 − X1.

❹ Newton-Raphson Ridge Optimization (Summary of the Optimization Iterations), number of parameter estimates, lower and upper bounds, the number of constraints, the iteration history, and the number of calls.

❺ Optimization Results, Parameter Estimates. This section includes the final parameter estimates (X1 = 0.669166, and X2 = 0.330834) and the gradient values.

❻ Value of the objective function at the end of the optimization process (0.0398199853), and value of the linear constraint at the end of the optimization process. In this example, the linear constraint written as X1 + X2 − 1 is equal to -1.11022E-16 (which is 0 for all practical purposes).

❼ First-order Lagrange Multiplier for the active constraint at the end of the optimization process (-0.039820).

❽ Projected gradient in the free dimension is 2.101264E-12 (which is 0 for all practical purposes).

The optimization process indicates that the optimal portfolio weights for minimizing the risk of the two-stock portfolio are 66.92 percent CONED and 33.08 percent TEX. As a check, you may want to compare these portfolio weights to those listed in Output 6.5 (in the variable PFOL_R2).

Printing the OUTEST= Data Set

You use PROC PRINT to print the OUTEST= data set NLP_OUT1, created in Output 6.9. The following statements print the NLP_OUT1 data set, as shown in Output 6.10.

```
proc print data=nlp_out1;
   title2 'NLP_OUT1 Data Set';
run;
```

Output 6.10
OUTEST= Data Set,
NLP_OUT1

```
                        Markowitz Model
                        NLP_OUT1 Data Set


    OBS    _TECH_    _TYPE_    _NAME_      X1         X2        _RHS_

     1     NRRIDG    INITIAL             0.50000    0.50000    0.04301
     2     NRRIDG    PARMS               0.66917    0.33083    0.03982
     3     NRRIDG    GRAD                0.03982    0.03982      .
     4     NRRIDG    NABC                0.00000    0.00000      .
     5     NRRIDG    UPPERBD             1.00000    1.00000      .
     6     NRRIDG    LOWERBD             0.00000    0.00000      .
     7     NRRIDG    NALC                1.00000    1.00000      .
     8     NRRIDG    EQ       ACTIVE     1.00000    1.00000    1.00000
     9     NRRIDG    PROJGRAD            0.00000      .          .
    10     NRRIDG    LAGRANGE           -0.03982      .          .
    11     NRRIDG    HESSIAN  X1         0.02536   -0.05130    1.00000
    12     NRRIDG    HESSIAN  X2        -0.05130    0.10377    2.00000
    13     NRRIDG    PROJHESS            0.11587      .        1.00000
```

Interpretation of output

Output 6.10 lists the PROC NLP OUTEST= data set, NLP_OUT1. The data set contains _TECH_ (the optimizing technique used, Newton-Raphson Ridge Method), _TYPE_, _NAME_, parameter values, and _RHS_ (the right-hand-side values).

If you use the OUTEST= output data set from one invocation of PROC NLP as an INEST= input data set for another invocation of PROC NLP, the OUTEST= data set also contains the boundary and linear constraints specified in the first invocation of PROC NLP. You should avoid specifying the same constraints a second time.

Using an INEST= Input Data Set

For some NLP problems, you may want to use an INEST= input data set for PROC NLP. The form of the input is similar to that in the SAS/OR LP procedure (discussed in Chapter 5, "Portfolio Creation with Linear Programming.")

In particular, for larger and more complex nonlinear programming problems, you may want to specify the parameter bounds and starting values, as well as the general linear constraints, in a DATA step and then specify the objective function with programming statements in PROC NLP.

For the nonlinear programming problem solved in Output 6.10, the following statements create the INEST= data set.

Explanation of syntax

DATA

names the data set. In this example, the data set is named IN_NLP1. The TYPE= option indicates the SAS data set type for specially structured SAS data sets. For use as an input data set in PROC NLP, the data set should be TYPE=EST.

INPUT

describes the arrangement of values in an input record and assigns input values to corresponding SAS variables. In this example, the data set IN_NLP1 is used to calculate the solution values of the portfolio weights for CONED and TEX. The IN_NLP1 data set also contains the following:

□ a character variable, _TYPE_, that indicates the type of observation

□ parameter names for *n* numeric variables used in the PARMS statement of PROC NLP

□ a numeric variable _RHS_ (right-hand-side values), needed only if linear constraints are used.

CARDS

indicates that the data lines follow the statement. The four lines that follow the CARDS statement contain the parameter starting values (PARMS), the lower and upper bounds (LOWERBD and UPPERBD), and the linear constraints (EQ). You can include inequality constraints with the _TYPE_ of LE and GE, for less than and greater than constraints, respectively. The right-hand-side value is needed only for the linear constraint and is listed as a missing value (.) in the other observations. Note that the linear constraint is

$$(1 \times \text{CONED}) + (1 \times \text{TEX}) = 1$$

Example code

```
data in_nlp1(type=est);
   input _type_ $8. coned tex _rhs_;
   cards;
parms    .5  .5  .
lowerbd  0   0   .
upperbd  1   1   .
eq       1   1   1
;
```

The PROC NLP statements that solve the nonlinear programming problem are as follows. The INEST= option in the PROC NLP statement specifies IN_NLP1 as the input data set. The output from these statements is not shown.

```
proc nlp inest=in_nlp1;
   min risk;
   parms coned tex;
```

```
        var_p=coned*coned*.0025956+tex*tex*.0057176-2*coned*tex*.0004572;
        risk=var_p**.5;
run;
```

Using SAS/IML Optimizing Subroutines

You can also use SAS/IML optimizing subroutines to solve quadratic programming problems, like the Markowitz model, as well as other nonlinear optimizing problems. The following PROC IML statements solve the Markowitz model of Output 6.10:

```
        /* Invoking the IML Procedure */
proc iml;

        /* Defining Portfolio Risk */
start risk(x);
    y1=x[1]#x[1];
    y2=x[2]#x[2];
    var_p=y1#.0025956+y2#.0057176
        -2#x[1]#x[2]#.0004572;

    risk=sqrt(var_p);

return(risk);
finish risk;

        /* Listing the Constraints */
        /* Lower Bounds, Upper Bounds, Sum to One Linear Constraint */
con = ( 0  0  .  .,
        1  1  .  .,
        1  1  0  1);

        /* Starting Values */
x0 = (.5, .5);

        /* Calling the NLPQN (Quasi-Newton) Subroutine */
CALL NLPQN(rc,xr,"risk",x0,{0,2},con);
print rc xr;
quit;
```

For additional information on quadratic programming with PROC IML, see pages 143-145 of *SAS/IML Software: Usage and Reference, Version 6, First Edition.*

Including a Constraint on Portfolio Returns

You may want to include a return constraint in the nonlinear programming problem of Output 6.10. For example, you may want to minimize the portfolio risk subject to a minimum acceptable level of expected return. The average returns for CONED and TEX from Output 6.3 are used as the expected future (monthly) returns. For your analysis, you should use the future returns that your analysis indicates.

Suppose you wanted to minimize risk of the two-stock portfolio of CONED and TEX, subject to the constraint that expected returns must be at least .0195 (in addition to the constraints that the portfolio weights are between 0 and 1, and that they sum to 1). You can solve this nonlinear programming problem with the following PROC NLP statements.

The statements are the same as those shown previously for using an INEST= data set, with the exception of the additional general linear constraint, listed as the observation with _TYPE_ of GE. The results are shown in Output 6.11.

```
data in_nlp2(type=est);
    input _type_ $8. coned tex _rhs_;
    cards;
parms    .5      .5      .
lowerbd  0       0       .
upperbd  1       1       .
eq       1       1       1
ge       .021    .0121   .0195
;

proc nlp inest=in_nlp2 outest=nlp_out2 noprint;
    min risk;
    parms coned tex;
    var_p=coned*coned*.0025956+tex*tex*.0057176-2*coned*tex*.0004572;
    risk=var_p**.5;
run;

proc print data=nlp_out2;
    title2 'Quadratic Programming Portfolio Weights';
    title3 'Expected Return Must Be 1.95% or More';
run;
```

Output 6.11
Solving the
Quadratic
Programming
Problem with a
Minimum Constraint
on Expected Returns

```
                              Markowitz Model
                  Quadratic Programming Portfolio Weights
                  Expected Return Must Be 1.95% or More

    OBS   _TECH_    _TYPE_     _NAME_     CONED      TEX      _RHS_

     1    NRRIDG    INITIAL               0.83146   0.16854   0.04276
     2    NRRIDG    PARMS                 0.83146   0.16854   0.04276
     3    NRRIDG    GRAD                  0.04867   0.01364     .
     4    NRRIDG    NABC                  0.00000   0.00000     .
     5    NRRIDG    UPPERBD               1.00000   1.00000     .
     6    NRRIDG    LOWERBD               0.00000   0.00000     .
     7    NRRIDG    NALC                  2.00000   2.00000     .
     8    NRRIDG    EQ         ACTIVE     1.00000   1.00000   1.00000
     9    NRRIDG    GE         ACTIVE     0.02100   0.01210   0.01950
    10    NRRIDG    LAGRANGE             -0.03397   3.93489     .
    11    NRRIDG    HESSIAN    CONED      0.00531  -0.02622   1.00000
    12    NRRIDG    HESSIAN    TEX       -0.02622   0.12935   2.00000
```

Interpretation of output

Output 6.11 contains the following items: initial and final parameter values, the gradient values, the upper and lower bounds, the active constraints, the Lagrange multiplier, and the Hessian values. The solution values for the portfolio weights of this example are 83.146 percent CONED and 16.854 percent TEX, as shown in observation 2.

Listing the Efficient Frontier

You can define the efficient frontier of portfolios for any given set of assets by minimizing portfolio risk for different levels of return.

To list risk-minimizing portfolios for different levels of return of the problem solved in Output 6.11, you need to change the right-hand-side (_RHS_) value for the greater-than (GE) inequality return constraint, as shown in the following DATA step.

```
data in_nlp3(type=est);
   set in_nlp2;
      if _type_ = 'ge' then _rhs_ =.0190;
run;
```

After changing the right-hand-side value, you must also change the name of the INEST= data set option in the PROC NLP statement to match the new data set name. For the preceding DATA step, the new INEST= data set for PROC NLP is named IN_NLP3.

By selecting different right-hand-side values for the return constraint, you can trace the efficient frontier of portfolios. Each row of the following table contains the results of a separate invocation of PROC NLP with different right-hand-side values for the return constraint. The columns of the following table list the

□ right-hand-side value of the required return constraint

□ optimal percentages of the portfolio to invest in CONED and TEX

□ risk level of the resulting portfolios.

Return =>	% CONED	% TEX	Risk
.0210	100.000	0.000	.050947
.0205	94.382	5.618	.047767
.0200	88.764	11.236	.045012
.0195	83.146	16.854	.042763
.0190	77.528	22.472	.041104
.0185	71.910	28.090	.040108
.0180	66.917	33.083	.039820
.0175	66.917	33.083	.039820
.0170	66.917	33.083	.039820

For this example, right-hand-side values of portfolio returns in the range .0121 to .021 are feasible, because .0121 is the expected return on a portfolio of 100 percent TEX, and .021 is the expected return on a portfolio of 100 percent CONED. For this example, right-hand-side values for the return constraint outside of this range are infeasible. Note that when the right-hand-side value of the (greater than or equal to) return constraint is reduced below .0180, it is no longer active, and the optimal portfolio weights remain unchanged.

The efficient frontier of portfolios for these two stocks are the first seven rows of this table. Notice that return and risk are positively related along the efficient frontier. Intuitively, this seems reasonable; typically, investors accept greater risk only if offered greater returns.

Calculating Dollar Amounts to Invest

For the dollar value of your portfolio, you can use a DATA step and the optimal portfolio weights to calculate the dollar amounts to invest in each stock. For example, suppose you wanted to invest $100,000 in the portfolio of CONED and TEX using the optimal weights from Output 6.11. The following statements perform this task:

```
data amt_out2(drop=_TECH_ _NAME_);
    set nlp_out2;
    if _TYPE_ ne 'PARMS' then delete;
    coned_a=round(coned*100000, .01);
    tex_a=round(tex*100000, .01);
    total=sum(of coned_a tex_a);
run;

proc print data=amt_out2;
    var coned_a tex_a total;
    title2 'Amount to Invest in Each Stock';
    title3;
run;
```

Output 6.12
Optimal Amounts to Invest in Each Stock

```
                        Markowitz Model
                  Amount to Invest in Each Stock

        OBS     CONED_A      TEX_A      TOTAL

         1      83146.07    16853.93    100000
```

Interpretation of output
The amounts shown in Output 6.12 are the optimal amounts to invest in CONED and TEX to minimize risk, given an expected return of 1.95 percent and given the constraints listed in the code producing Output 6.11. The variable TOTAL is included as an accounting check.

A Ten-Stock Example

You can solve Markowitz models with hundreds (or even thousands) of variables using PROC NLP. The following statements solve a ten-stock example, where the ten stocks are the same stocks used in previous chapters (GERBER, TANDY, GENMIL, CONED, WEYER, IBM, DEC, MOBIL, TEX, and CPL).

The parameters are listed as X1-X10 for ease in array processing when calculating amounts to invest in each stock in later examples. The parameters are constrained to the range of 0 to 1, and they must sum to 1. Lastly, the expected return must be at least 1.9 percent. The variances, covariances, and mean returns (used as expectations of future returns) are calculated by PROC CORR. (See Output 6.2.)

The results from these statements are stored in the OUTEST= data set NLP_OUT4. The first ten observations of the NLP_OUT4 data set are printed in Output 6.13.

```
proc nlp outest=nlp_out4 noprint;
    parms x1 - x10;
    var=   x1*x1*.0065845 + x2*x2*.0161666 + x3*x3*.0034068
         + x4*x4*.0025956 + x5*x5*.0061889 + x6*x6*.0030980
```

```
        + x7*x7*.0081904 + x8*x8*.0060380 + x9*x9*.0057176
        + x10*x10*.0028676
        + 2*x1*x2*.0012481 + 2*x1*x3*.0008390 + 2*x1*x4*.0008552
        + 2*x1*x5*.0014933 + 2*x1*x6*.0011241 + 2*x1*x7*.0008087
        + 2*x1*x8*.0016392 + 2*x1*x9*.0010154 + 2*x1*x10*.0007377
        + 2*x2*x3*.0024433 + 2*x2*x4*.0006034 + 2*x2*x5*.0043589
        + 2*x2*x6*.0021623 + 2*x2*x7*.0055136 + 2*x2*x8*.0018761
        + 2*x2*x9*.0019255 + 2*x2*x10*.0008840
        + 2*x3*x4*.0011501 + 2*x3*x5*.0013081 + 2*x3*x6*.0002182
        + 2*x3*x7*.0005988 - 2*x3*x8*.0004289 - 2*x3*x9*.0008492
        + 2*x3*x10*.0011713
        + 2*x4*x5*.0006618 + 2*x4*x6*.0002583 + 2*x4*x7*.0003856
        - 2*x4*x8*.0000940 - 2*x4*x9*.0004572 + 2*x4*x10*.0017717
        + 2*x5*x6*.0017847 + 2*x5*x7*.0033916 + 2*x5*x8*.0018391
        + 2*x5*x9*.0009703 + 2*x5*x10*.0010631
        + 2*x6*x7*.0017977 + 2*x6*x8*.0009574 + 2*x6*x9*.0007195
        + 2*x6*x10*.0002032
        + 2*x7*x8*.0023587 + 2*x7*x9*.0014764 + 2*x7*x10*.0008061
        + 2*x8*x9*.0041150 + 2*x8*x10*.0000495 - 2*x9*x10*.0001139;
   risk=sqrt(var);
   min risk;
   bounds 0 <= x1-x10 <= 1;
   lincon 1=x1+x2+x3+x4+x5+x6+x7+x8+x9+x10,
          .019 <=  .0176*x1+.0288*x2+.0148*x3+.0210*x4+.0092*x5
                  +.0103*x6+.0182*x7+.0172*x8+.0121*x9+.0146*x10;
run;

proc print data=nlp_out4 (obs=10);
   title2 'Quadratic Programming Portfolio Weights';
   title3 'Ten-Stock Example';
run;
```

Output 6.13
Portfolio Weights
for Ten-Stock
Markowitz Model
Example

```
                           Markowitz Model
                 Quadratic Programming Portfolio Weights
                          Ten-Stock Example

   OBS  _TECH_   _TYPE_   _NAME_     X1       X2       X3       X4       X5

    1   NRRIDG   INITIAL           0.00000  0.00000  0.00000  0.72052 -0.00000
    2   NRRIDG   PARMS             0.04798  0.05696  0.10175  0.52813 -0.00000
    3   NRRIDG   GRAD              0.03412  0.05822  0.02810  0.04144  0.03408
    4   NRRIDG   NABC              2.00000  2.00000  2.00000  2.00000  2.00000
    5   NRRIDG   ACTIVE            0.00000  0.00000  0.00000  0.00000  1.00000


   OBS    X6       X7       X8       X9       X10      _RHS_

    1   0.04914  0.00000  0.00000  0.00000  0.23035  0.04602
    2   0.04156  0.02778  0.12062  0.07522  0.00000  0.03714
    3   0.01842  0.03542  0.03326  0.02229  0.03147    .
    4   2.00000  2.00000  2.00000  2.00000  2.00000    .
    5   0.00000  0.00000  0.00000  0.00000  1.00000    .
```

```
                              Markowitz Model
                  Quadratic Programming Portfolio Weights
                             Ten-Stock Example

    OBS  _TECH_   _TYPE_    _NAME_     X1       X2       X3       X4       X5

      6  NRRIDG   UPPERBD            1.00000  1.00000  1.00000  1.00000  1.00000
      7  NRRIDG   LOWERBD            0.00000  0.00000  0.00000  0.00000  0.00000
      8  NRRIDG   NALC               2.00000  2.00000  2.00000  2.00000  2.00000
      9  NRRIDG   EQ        ACTIVE   1.00000  1.00000  1.00000  1.00000  1.00000
     10  NRRIDG   GE        ACTIVE   0.01760  0.02880  0.01480  0.02100  0.00920

    OBS    X6        X7        X8        X9       X10       _RHS_

      6  1.00000   1.00000   1.00000   1.00000   1.00000     .
      7  0.00000   0.00000   0.00000   0.00000   0.00000     .
      8  2.00000   2.00000   2.00000   2.00000   2.00000     .
      9  1.00000   1.00000   1.00000   1.00000   1.00000   1.00000
     10  0.01030   0.01820   0.01720   0.01210   0.01460   0.01900
```

Interpretation of output

In Output 6.13, the optimal portfolio weights are listed in the second observation with
TYPE of PARMS. For this example, the majority of the portfolio (52.813 percent) should
be invested in X4 (CONED). The remaining portion should be invested as follows: 4.798
percent in X1 (GERBER), 5.696 percent in X2 (TANDY), 10.175 percent in X3 (GENMIL),
4.156 percent in X6 (IBM), 2.778 percent in X7 (DEC), 12.062 percent in X8 (MOBIL),
7.522 percent in X9 (TEX), and 0 percent in X5 (WEYER) and X10 (CPL).

   Also listed are the gradient values (observation 3), the upper and lower bounds
(observations 6 and 7), and the constraints (observations 9 and 10). The projected gradient,
Lagrange multipliers, and Hessian values are not shown.

Calculating Dollar Amounts to Invest

For the dollar value of your portfolio, you can use a DATA step and the optimal portfolio
weights to calculate the dollar amounts to invest in each stock. For a $100,000 portfolio of
these stocks used in Output 6.13, the following statements perform this task.

   Note that array processing is used in an iterative DO LOOP with the DATA step, and
that the amounts are rounded to the nearest $.01. A variable named TOTAL (the sum of the
ten individual amounts) is included as an accounting check.

```
data amt_out3;
   set nlp_out4;
   if _TYPE_ ne 'PARMS' then delete;
   array xa(10) x1-x10;
   array a(10) a1-a10;
   do i=1 to 10;
      a(i)=round(xa(i)*100000, .01);
   end;
   total=sum(of a1-a10);
run;

data amt_out4;
   set amt_out3;
   rename a1=gerber a2=tandy a3=genmil a4=coned a5=weyer
          a6=ibm a7=dec a8=mobil a9=tex a10=cpl;
run;
```

```
proc print data=amt_out4;
    var gerber tandy genmil coned weyer ibm dec mobil tex
        cpl total;
    title2 'Amount to Invest in Each Stock';
    title3;
run;
```

Output 6.14
Optimal Amounts to
Invest in Each Stock
of the Ten-Stock
Example

```
                        Markowitz Model
                    Amount to Invest in Each Stock

  OBS    GERBER    TANDY    GENMIL     CONED    WEYER      IBM

   1    4797.64   5696.06  10175.26  52813.13      0    4156.46

  OBS     DEC     MOBIL      TEX      CPL     TOTAL

   1    2778.12  12061.53  7521.80     0     100000
```

Using an INEST= Input Data Set

For Markowitz models involving large numbers of stocks, you may want to use an INEST= input data set for PROC NLP because the use of an INEST= data set simplifies the remaining PROC NLP statements while also simplifying diagnostic checking. The following statements create an INEST= data set for the problem solved in Output 6.13.

The INEST= data set should be a TYPE=EST data set. The initial starting values are given as .1 for all stocks. If these initial starting values are infeasible, PROC NLP will calculate feasible starting values. The lower bounds are zero and the upper bounds are one. The right-hand-side value of the return inequality constraint is set at .019 (or 1.9 percent). The mean values of the stocks are used as expected future returns. For this problem, right-hand-side return inequality constraint values greater than .0288 or smaller than .0103 are infeasible.

```
data in_nlp4(type=est);
    input _type_ $8. x1-x10 _rhs_;
    cards;
parms    .1    .1    .1    .1    .1    .1    .1    .1    .1    .1    .
lowerbd   0     0     0     0     0     0     0     0     0     0    .
upperbd   1     1     1     1     1     1     1     1     1     1    .
eq        1     1     1     1     1     1     1     1     1     1    1
ge       .0176 .0288 .0148 .021 .0092 .0103 .0182 .0172 .0121 .0146 .019
;
```

Using this INEST= data set, the following PROC NLP statements solve the programming problem. Note that the BOUNDS and LINCON statements are omitted from these PROC NLP statements because they are accounted for in the INEST= data set. Also to save space, only the first and last lines of the portfolio variance are shown.

```
proc nlp inest=in_nlp4 outest=nlp_out5;
    parms x1 - x10;
    var=   x1*x1*.0065845 + x2*x2*.0161666 + x3*x3*.0034068
```

.
.
.

```
        + 2*x8*x9*.0041150 + 2*x8*x10*.0000495 - 2*x9*x10*.0001139;
     risk=sqrt(var);
     min risk;
  run;
```

The output from these statements is not shown.

Using an INQUAD= Input Data Set

For Markowitz models involving large numbers of stocks, you may want to use an INQUAD= input data set for PROC NLP, which greatly simplifies the PROC NLP statements. The INQUAD= data set should contain the variances and covariances of stock returns. The general quadratic function to be minimized, *f(x)*, is of the following form:

$$f(X) = .5\, X^T H X + g^T X + c$$

In this equation, X_i is the portfolio weights, T stands for transposition (in a transposed matrix, the rows become columns and the columns become rows), *H* is a symmetric matrix of variance and covariances, *g* is a vector of linear coefficient (all 0, for examples in this chapter), and *c* is a constant (0, for examples in this chapter).

If you use an INQUAD= data set, then you minimize one half of the portfolio variance with PROC NLP. Because the portfolio variance is the square of the portfolio standard deviation (the Markowitz measure of risk), a strongly monotonic transformation, the same portfolio weights minimize both functions. (Note that to calculate the portfolio risk level (the standard deviation), you need to multiply the objective function value by 2 and then take the square root.)

To create an INQUAD= input data set, first use PROC CORR to create a covariance matrix; then use a DATA step to tailor the covariance matrix. The following statements use the RETURN3 data set from Chapter 4, "The Capital Asset Pricing Model (CAPM)," to create an INQUAD= data set for the problem solved in Output 6.13.

```
    /* Renaming Variables to Match INEST= Data Set */
data return4;
   set return3;
   rename gerber=x1 tandy=x2 genmil=x3 coned=x4 weyer=x5 ibm=x6
          dec=x7 mobil=x8 tex=x9 cpl=x10;
run;

    /* Creating the Covariance Matrix */
proc corr data=return4 cov outp=cov_out1 nosimple noprint;
   var x1-x10;
run;

    /* Tailoring Covariance Matrix for Input to PROC NLP */
data cov_out2;
   set cov_out1;
   if _TYPE_ ne 'COV' then delete;
   _TYPE_ = 'QUAD';
run;
```

Using the INEST= data set created in the previous section and the INQUAD= data set created above, the PROC NLP statements that solve the programming problem are as follows. The output from these statements is not shown.

```
proc nlp inest=in_nlp4 inquad=cov_out2 outest=nlp_out6;
   min;
   parms x1-x10;
run;
```

Concatenating INEST= and INQUAD= Input Data Sets

If you are using Release 6.10 or higher SAS software, you can further simplify the PROC NLP statements by concatenating the INEST= and INQUAD= data sets. This concatenation enables you to use only an INQUAD= data set in the PROC NLP statement.

The following DATA step concatenates the IN_NLP4 and COV_OUT2 data sets.

```
data quad;
   set cov_out2 in_nlp4;
   keep _TYPE_ _NAME_ x1-x10 _RHS_;
run;
```

The PROC NLP statements that solve the programming problem of Output 6.13 (using the concatenated QUAD data set) are as follows. The output from these statements is not shown.

```
proc nlp inquad=quad outest=nlp_out7;
   min;
   parms x1-x10;
run;
```

Creating an Input Data Set and Constraints

You can create an input data set for PROC NLP with PROC CORR and a DATA step that contains the constraints and starting values. The following DATA step statements use array processing to set the upper and lower bounds, to set initial values for the solution weights (equal to the reciprocal of the number of stocks, 1/N), and to constrain the solution weights to sum to unity.

```
/* Creating the VAR-COV Matrix */
proc corr data=return4 cov outp=cov_out1 nosimple noprint;
   var x1-x10;
run;

/* Creating Initial Values and Constraints */
data quada(type=est);
   keep _type_ x1-x10 _rhs_;
   array x x1-x10;
   n=10;

   /* Setting Initial Values for Solution Weights */
   _type_='parms';
   _rhs_=.;
   do over x;
      x=1/n;
```

```
        end;
        output;

            /* Setting Lower Bounds */
        _type_='lb';
        do over x;
            x=0;
        end;
        output;

            /* Setting Upper Bounds */
        _type_='ub';
        do over x;
            x=1;
        end;
        output;

            /* Constraining Solution Values to Sum to Unity */
        _type_='eq';
        _rhs_=1;
        do over x;
            x=1;
        end;
        output;

    run;
```

You create the complete input data set for PROC NLP by merging the QUADA and COV_OUT1 data sets in a DATA step.

```
    data quadb;
        set cov_out1 (in=D) quada;
        keep _type_ _name_ x1-x10 _rhs_;
        if D then do;
            if _type_='COV' then _type_='QUAD';
            else if _type_ ne 'MEAN' then delete;
        end;
    run;
```

Now you can use the following PROC NLP statements to solve for the solution weights that minimize the portfolio risk:

```
    proc nlp inquad=quadb outest=est;
        min;
        parms x1-x10;
    run;
```

The results from these statements are not shown. For more details about using input data sets for PROC NLP (and many advanced uses of PROC NLP for the Markowitz Model), see the SAS Technical Paper, "Using PROC NLP for Risk Minimization in Stock Portfolios."

Listing the Efficient Portfolios

You can list the efficient portfolios by repeatedly varying the right-hand-side value of the expected return inequality constraint in the INQUAD= or INEST= data sets used as input by PROC NLP. The following DATA step creates a new INQUAD= data set QUAD1, with the right-hand-side value of .020 for the return inequality constraint.

```
data quad1;
   set quad;
   if _TYPE_ = 'ge' then _rhs_ =.020;
run;
```

After creating the QUAD1 data set, you use it as the INQUAD= data set for PROC NLP to find the optimal portfolio weights.

The following table lists the resulting portfolios for various right-hand-side return inequality constraint values for the ten stocks used in Output 6.13. Note that for the expected returns used in these examples, the feasible range of returns is .0103 to .0288, which are the minimum and maximum expected returns on the individual stocks.

Included in the table are the right-hand-side values, the portfolio weights, and the value of the objective function. The portfolio risk can be obtained by multiplying the objective function value by 2 to obtain the portfolio variance, and then taking the square root of the portfolio variance.

Table 6.1
Portfolio Weights

RHSValue of Inequality Constraint on Returns	X1 GERBER	X2 TANDY	X3 GENMIL	X4 CONED	X5 WEYER	X6 IBM	X7 DEC	X8 MOBIL	X9 TEX	X10 CPL	Objective Function Value
.0288	0	1.00	0	0	0	0	0	0	0	0	.00808331
.0280	0	.897	0	.103	0	0	0	0	0	0	.00657942
.0270	0	.769	0	.231	0	0	0	0	0	0	.00495925
.0260	0	.641	0	.359	0	0	0	0	0	0	.00362764
.0250	0	.513	0	.487	0	0	0	0	0	0	.00258457
.0240	0	.385	0	.615	0	0	0	0	0	0	.00183006
.0230	0	.269	0	.704	0	0	0	.027	0	0	.00135805
.0220	.008	.189	0	.686	0	0	0	.117	0	0	.00106108
.0210	.051	.116	.006	.642	0	0	.012	.173	0	0	.00088853
.0200	.050	.082	.067	.581	0	0	.027	.146	.047	0	.00077936
.0190	.043	.057	.102	.530	0	.043	.028	.122	.075	0	.00069069
.0180	.037	.032	.137	.478	0	.085	.029	.099	.102	0	.00061873
.0170	.030	.008	.171	.427	0	.127	.031	.076	.130	0	.00056347
.0160	.022	0	.192	.346	0	.173	.018	.054	.153	.042	.00052555
.0150	.013	0	.208	.254	0	.220	0	.031	.175	.099	.00050807
.0140	.010	0	.213	.223	0	.234	0	.021	.183	.116	.00050699
.0130	.010	0	.213	.223	0	.234	0	.021	.183	.116	.00050699
.0120	.010	0	.213	.223	0	.234	0	.021	.183	.116	.00050699

For this example, the efficient portfolios are those with returns of .0140 to .0288. When the right-hand-side value of the inequality return constraint is less than .0140, the inequality constraint is no longer active, and the portfolio weights remain constant.

Note that none of the stocks are included in all of the portfolios and that WEYER (X5) is not included in any of the portfolios. Also note that, along the efficient frontier, as the required expected return increases, so does the variance (and the risk) of the portfolio. Lastly, note that you may want to explore portions of the efficient frontier in greater detail, and you can do so by specifying additional intermediate values for the right-hand-side value of the return inequality constraint.

Plotting the Capital Market Line

The *capital market line* is the line which connects the expected return on the risk-free asset with the efficient frontier of portfolios, and it is just tangent to the efficient frontier. All points of the capital market line are linear combinations of the the risk-free asset and the tangency portfolio on the efficient frontier. The portfolios on the capital market line dominate all other portfolios. (Given the importance of this tangential portfolio, the section "Calculating the Tangential Portfolio with PROC NLP," later in this chapter, shows you how to use PROC NLP to calculate the solution values for the tangential portfolio weights.)

To plot the capital market line for the ten-stock example, follow these steps:

1. Create a data set containing the return and risk values for portfolios on the efficient frontier.

2. Calculate or forecast the expected return on the risk-free asset.

3. Add the expected return on the risk-free asset to the data set containing the return and risk values of portfolios on the efficient frontier. Note that risk on the risk-free asset is 0.

4. Use PROC PLOT or the SAS/GRAPH GPLOT procedure to plot the portfolio returns versus the portfolio risks and to include the risk-free asset.

5. Draw a line connecting the risk-free asset with the tangential portfolio on the efficient frontier (by hand if using PROC PLOT and with the ANNOTATE facility of PROC GPLOT).

You begin the process of plotting the capital market line by placing the efficient portfolio returns and variances in a data set named PLOT1.

If you have already calculated or forecasted the expected risk-free return, you may include that value as an observation in the data set. There are many ways that you can calculate or forecast the expected return on the risk-free asset. For approaches to calculating expected returns on assets, see Chapter 1, "Background Topics."

For this example, the mean value of past risk-free monthly returns (.007161) is used as the expected risk-free return. You can calculate this value using PROC MEANS and the RETURN3 data set.

The following DATA step creates the PLOT1 data set. Note that the portfolio risk level is calculated by multiplying the PROC NLP objective function values (from the previous table) by 2 and taking the square root.

```
data plot1;
   input return obj_fun @@;
   risk=sqrt(2*obj_fun);
```

```
cards;
.0288   .00808331   .0280   .00657942   .0270   .00495925
.0260   .00362764   .0250   .00258457   .0240   .00183006
.0230   .00135805   .0220   .00106108   .0210   .00088853
.0200   .00077936   .0190   .00069069   .0180   .00061873
.0170   .00056347   .0160   .00052555   .0150   .00050807
.0140   .00050699   .007161   0.0
;
```

The following PROC PLOT statements plot the portfolio returns versus the risk levels. The labeling option in the PLOT statement is used to label the points with their return values. The results are shown in Output 6.15.

```
proc plot data=plot1 vpct=225;
   plot return*risk='*' $ return;
   title2 'The Capital Market Line';
run;
```

Output 6.15
Plotting the Capital Market Line for the Ten-Stock Example

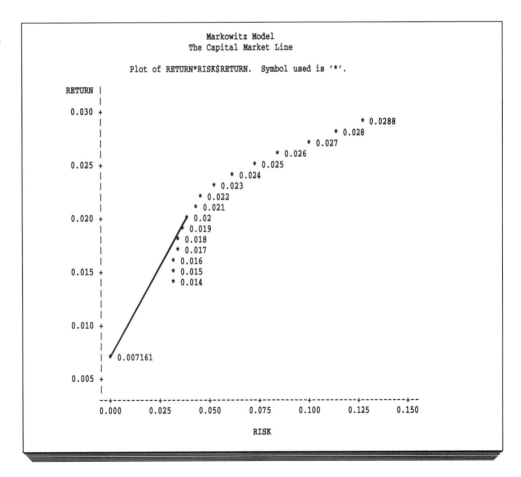

Interpretation of output

In Output 6.15, the return values are plotted versus the risk values of the ten-stock example. The plotted curve of portfolios is the efficient frontier for these stocks. The line representing the capital market line has been added to the plot. The efficient portfolio that is on the capital market line is the portfolio with expected return of .020, or 2.0 percent (for accuracy of the nearest .1 percent of expected returns). You may want to further explore the portion of the efficient frontier in the vicinity of the expected returns of 2.0 percent by specifying additional values of the right-hand-side value of the return inequality constraint.

Investors select the optimal portfolio along the capital market line based on their risk-return trade-off. Investors desiring less risk will select points closer to the risk-free asset by investing relatively greater percentages of their funds in the risk-free asset and the remainder in the tangential portfolio on the efficient frontier. Investors desiring relatively greater returns will select points closer to the tangential portfolio by investing relatively lesser percentages of their funds in the risk-free asset and the majority in the tangential portfolio on the efficient frontier.

Note that you can also perform this analysis with the data in Output 6.8.

Customizing a PROC PLOT Plot

You may want to customize a PROC PLOT by adding reference lines and axis values. A reference line can provide focus on one or more important points in the plot as well as provide a baseline reference. Specific axis values provide additional useful information to interpret points in the plot.

For example, the following options in the PLOT statement perform the customization of the plot in Output 6.15.

Explanation of syntax

HREF=
> adds a horizontal reference line. The portfolio risk level (the standard deviation, or the square root of the variance) of .03948 is the value specified for the horizontal reference line.

VREF=
> adds a vertical reference line. The expected portfolio return of .020 is the value specified for the vertical reference line.

VAXIS=
> specifies vertical axis values. The vertical axis values from .007 to .029 are specified by increments of .002.

Example code

```
proc plot data=plot1 vpct=225;
   plot return*risk='*' $ return / vref=.020 href=.03948
                                   vaxis=.007 to .029 by .002;
run;
```

Output 6.16
Customizing the Plot
of the Capital
Market Line

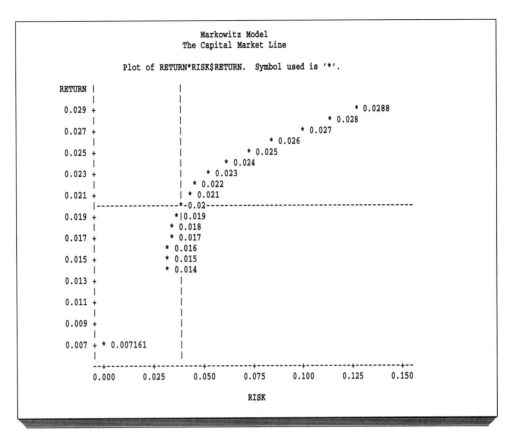

Calculating the Tangential Portfolio with PROC NLP

You can use PROC NLP to calculate the tangential portfolio described in the interpretation of Output 6.15. The return of the risk-free asset and the tangential portfolio (which is on the efficient frontier) define the capital market line. The capital market line is the ray emanating from the risk-free asset that is tangential to the efficient frontier, and it will have the maximum slope of all such rays that intersect or are tangent to the efficient frontier. See Elton and Gruber (1987) for details. This relationship implies that the tangential portfolio can be found by maximizing the following expression, $\dfrac{R_p - R_f}{\sigma_p}$, where R_p is the expected portfolio return, R_f is the expected risk-free return, and σ_p is the risk of the portfolio.

The following PROC NLP statements solve for the portfolio weights, the X_i that maximize this expression (OBJ) subject to the constraints that each X_i is between zero and one, and that the X_i sum to one. The NOPRINT option suppresses the printed output. To save space, only the first and last lines of the portfolio variance are shown.

```
proc nlp outest=nlp_out8 noprint;
   parms x1 - x10;
   var=   x1*x1*.0065845 + x2*x2*.0161666 + x3*x3*.0034068
```

.

.

.

```
          + 2*x8*x9*.0041150 + 2*x8*x10*.0000495 - 2*x9*x10*.0001139;
      risk=sqrt(var);
      r_f=.007161;
      num= .0176*x1+.0288*x2+.0148*x3+.0210*x4+.0092*x5+.0103*x6
          +.0182*x7+.0172*x8+.0121*x9+.0146*x10-r_f;
      obj=num/risk;
      max obj;
      bounds 0 <= x1-x10 <= 1;
      lincon 1=x1+x2+x3+x4+x5+x6+x7+x8+x9+x10;
   run;
```

Printing the Tangential Portfolio Weights

The following DATA step tailors the NLP_OUT8 data set by deleting all observations except the solution values for the portfolio weights:

```
   data amt_out5;
      set nlp_out8;
      if _TYPE_ ne 'PARMS' then delete;
   run;
```

The following PROC PRINT statements list the AMT_OUT5 data set containing the amounts to invest in a tangential portfolio with a total value of $100,000. The results are shown in Output 6.17.

```
   proc print data=amt_out5;
      var x1-x10;
      title 'Markowitz Model';
      title2 'Tangential Efficient Portfolio Weights';
   run;
```

Output 6.17
Portfolio Weights
for the Tangential
Portfolio

```
                               Markowitz Model
                     Tangential Efficient Portfolio Weights

O                                                              X
B     X       X       X      X   X X    X       X       X      1
S     1       2       3      4   5 6    7       8       9      0

1 0.028534 0.089837 0.023734 0.66193 0 0 0.052165 0.12694 0.016866 -1.3878E-17
```

Interpretation of output

In Output 6.17, the solution values are listed for the tangential portfolio weights. Note that X10 is 0 for practical purposes.

If you want to invest in a portfolio on the capital market line but with a lower level of risk, the amount invested in the tangential portfolio can be scaled back and invested in the risk-free asset instead. For example, a portfolio on the capital market line with half the risk level of the tangential portfolio can be constructed by investing 50 percent in the risk-free asset and 50 percent in the tangential portfolio (in the weights as shown in Output 6.17). At the other end of the capital market line, you can invest 100 percent of the portfolio in the risk-free asset and (virtually) eliminate risk.

After the tangential portfolio has been calculated, you should decide which portfolio (on the capital market line) is optimal for you based on your tolerance for risk and the available trade-off of risk and return. For an example of calculating dollar amounts to invest in each stock, see the example that generates Output 6.14.

Chapter Summary

This chapter has discussed the Markowitz model of portfolio creation. The first set of examples use PROC CORR and the DATA step to list portfolio risk and return levels. You use PROC PLOT to plot portfolio risk and returns to visually identify efficient portfolios. The second set of examples use PROC NLP and PROC IML to solve for optimal portfolio weights. Efficient portfolios were listed, and then plotted with the capital market line. Investors select their portfolio of choice from the capital market line.

Learning More

- □ For more information on the DATA step, see *SAS Language, Reference, Version 6, First Edition* and *SAS Language and Procedures, Usage 2, Version 6, First Edition.*

- □ For more information on SAS/IML, see *SAS/IML Software: Usage and Reference, Version 6, First Edition.*

- □ For more information on PROC NLP, see *The NLP Procedure: Release 6.10, Extended User's Guide* and the SAS Technical Paper, "Using PROC NLP for Risk Minimization in Stock Portfolios."

- □ For more information on PROC CORR, PROC PLOT, and PROC PRINT, see *SAS Procedures Guide, Version 6, Third Edition* and *SAS Language and Procedures, Usage 2, Version 6, First Edition.*

References

Elton, E. and Gruber, M. (1987), *Modern Portfolio Theory and Investment Analysis, Third Edition*, New York: John Wiley & Sons, Inc.

Jones, C. (1991), *Investments: Analysis and Management, Third Edition*, New York: John Wiley & Sons, Inc.

Markowitz, H. (1952), "Portfolio Selection," *Journal of Finance*, Vol. 7, pp. 77-91.

Markowitz, H., (1991), *Portfolio Selection: Efficient Diversification of Investments, Second Edition*, Cambridge, MA: Blackwell, Inc.

Chapter 7 Evaluating Portfolios

Introduction

As investors construct portfolios, they expect to receive the greatest return for the selected risk level. To perform the task of portfolio construction, investors predict future stock returns and risk levels, select stocks of interest, and then calculate solution values for portfolio weights. Chapters 2-6 discuss techniques for valuing stocks (DCF methodology in Chapter 2), sorting and clustering of stocks (sorting and clustering in Chapter 3), predicting stock returns and risk levels (the CAPM in Chapter 4), and methods of constructing portfolios (linear programming and nonlinear programming techniques in Chapters 5 and 6, respectively). This chapter shows you how to use SAS software to measure how well your portfolio performed.

Using portfolios constructed in previous chapters, you can measure portfolio performance and compare portfolios by

- comparing the portfolio ex ante expectations and their ex post realizations as a summary performance statistic

- comparing the portfolio return measures to the market portfolio return measures

- comparing portfolio ex ante expectations and their ex post realizations through α from a CAPM regression

- comparing portfolio returns per unit of risk using only systematic (nondiversifiable) risk with β from a CAPM regression

- comparing portfolio returns per unit of risk using total risk (both systematic and nonsystematic risk).

This chapter uses the following portfolios for comparison:

□ the portfolio created in Output 5.2 with PROC LP (linear programming), where portfolio β is constrained to be .7, the weights sum to 1, and all weights are constrained to be in the range 0 to 1

□ the portfolio created in Output 5.5 with PROC LP (linear programming), where portfolio β is constrained to be less than or equal to .7, the weights sum to 1, and all weights are constrained to be in the range .05 to .3333

□ the portfolio created in Output 5.7 with PROC LP (integer programming), where all 100-share lots are constrained to be in the range 1 to 7 (stocks less than $100/share) or 1 to 4 (stocks greater than $100/share)

□ the portfolio created in Output 6.13 with PROC NLP (nonlinear programming), where the minimum expected return is constrained to be at least 1.9 percent

□ the tangential portfolio created in Output 6.17 with PROC LP (nonlinear programming).

Comparing Expected and Actual Returns

Prior to investing, you compare portfolio risk and expected returns among portfolios and with the expected return of the market portfolio. After investing, you typically want to evaluate portfolio performance. To evaluate the performance of portfolios, you compare the expected portfolio returns with their actual returns. You also compare the actual portfolio returns with the market portfolio return. To make these comparisons, you calculate the expected returns and actual return measures for the comparison portfolios and the market portfolio.

This section shows you an approach to calculating expected returns, an approach to calculating actual return measures, and ways of comparing the resulting values. Note that Chapter 1, "Background Topics," discusses risk and return measures.

Creating a Data Set Containing the Portfolio Weights

Before calculating actual return measures, you want to create a data set containing the portfolio weights. There are five data sets (one for each portfolio) to tailor, transpose, and merge.

You can create a data set containing the portfolio weights by:

□ tailoring output data sets, that is, by deleting unneeded observations and variables.
   For this example, you tailor the output data sets LP_OUT1 (from Output 5.2), NLP_OUT4 (from Output 6.13), and NLP_OUT8 (from Output 6.17). Note that the output data sets, LP_OUT3 (from Output 5.6) and LP_OUT4 (from Output 5.7) have already been tailored to create the data sets LP_OUT3B (from Output 5.6) and WT4 (from Output 5.11), respectively.

□ transposing output data sets (where necessary) with the TRANSPOSE procedure.
   For this example, you transpose the PROC LP data sets LP_OUT1 (from Output 5.2), LP_OUT3A (from Output 5.6), and WT4 (from Output 5.11).

□ merging the tailored and transposed data sets in a DATA step.

The following code performs these tasks. The results are printed in Output 7.1.

Example code

```
     /* Tailoring the LP_OUT1 Data Set from Output 5.2 */
data lp_out1a(keep= _var_ _value_
               rename= _var_=name);
   set lp_out1;
   if _n_ > 10 then delete;
run;

     /* Transposing the Data Set LP_OUT1A */
proc transpose data=lp_out1a out=lp_out1b(drop=_name_ _label_
               rename=(col1=x1 col2=x2 col3=x3 col4=x4 col5=x5
                       col6=x6 col7=x7 col8=x8 col9=x9 col10=x10));
   var _value_;
run;

     /* Transposing the Data Set LP_OUT3A from Output 5.6 */
proc transpose data=lp_out3a out=lp_out3b(drop=_name_ _label_
               rename=(col1=x1 col2=x2 col3=x3 col4=x4 col5=x5
                       col6=x6 col7=x7 col8=x8 col9=x9 col10=x10));
   var _value_;
run;

     /* Transposing the Data Set WT4 from Output 5.11 */
proc transpose data=wt4 out=wt4a(drop=_name_ _label_
               rename=(col1=x1 col2=x2 col3=x3 col4=x4 col5=x5
                       col6=x6 col7=x7 col8=x8 col9=x9 col10=x10));
   var fraction;
run;

     /* Tailoring the LP_OUT4 Data Set from Output 6.13 */
data amtout3a(drop=_tech_ _type_ _name_ _rhs_ _iter_);
   set nlp_out4;
   if _TYPE_ ne 'PARMS' then delete;
run;

     /* Tailoring the LP_OUT8 Data Set from Output 6.17 */
data amtout5a(drop=_tech_ _type_ _name_ _rhs_ _iter_);
   set nlp_out8;
   if _TYPE_ ne 'PARMS' then delete;
run;

     /* Merging the Tailored and Transposed Data Sets */
data p_folio1;
   set lp_out1b lp_out3b wt4a amtout3a amtout5a;
run;
```

```
                    /* Printing the P_FOLIO1 Data Set */
              proc print data=p_folio1;
                 title 'Portfolio Evaluation';
                 title2 'Portfolio Weights';
              run;
```

Output 7.1
Listing of Portfolio
Weights in the
P_FOLIO1 Data Set

```
                              Portfolio Evaluation
                               Portfolio Weights

           OBS       X1         X2         X3         X4         X5

            1      0.00000    0.63214    0.00000    0.36786    0.000000
            2      0.05000    0.33330    0.05000    0.26670    0.050000
            3      0.12532    0.17161    0.04354    0.28546    0.038108
            4      0.04798    0.05696    0.10175    0.52813    0.000000
            5      0.05446    0.12241    0.00000    0.64696    0.000000

           OBS       X6         X7         X8         X9         X10

            1      0.00000    0.00000    0.00000    0.000000   0.000000
            2      0.05000    0.05000    0.05000    0.050000   0.050000
            3      0.12114    0.10574    0.04051    0.036220   0.038996
            4      0.04156    0.02778    0.12062    0.075218   0.000000
            5      0.00000    0.00704    0.16913    0.000000   0.000000
```

Interpretation of output

Output 7.1 lists the solution values for the portfolio weights of the five portfolios used for comparison. Each row represents a portfolio. The first row contains the portfolio weights of Output 5.2; the second row contains the portfolio weights of Output 5.5; and so on through the fifth row, which contains the portfolio weights of Output 6.17.

Each column represents portfolio weights for a particular stock. The stock variable names are changed to X1-X10 for ease in data manipulation. The variables X1-X10 refer to stock returns of GERBER, TANDY, GENMIL, CONED, WEYER, IBM, DEC, MOBIL, TEX, and CPL, respectively.

Calculating Expected Returns

There are many ways to calculate or predict expected portfolio returns, as discussed in Chapter 1. The examples in this chapter use the average of past returns as the expectation of future returns. Therefore, the expected return of the market portfolio is the arithmetic mean of the past market returns, while the expected portfolio returns are a linear combination of the expected individual stock returns.

This section first calculates the expected returns for the market portfolio, then the comparison portfolios from Chapters 5, "Portfolio Creation with Linear Programming," and Chapter 6, "The Markowitz Model, Portfolio Creation with Nonlinear Programming." Lastly, the chapter compares the expected returns.

Calculating Expected Returns for the Market and the Risk-Free Asset

You can use the TRANSPOSE procedure, the RETURN3 data set (introduced in Chapter 4, "The Capital Asset Pricing Model (CAPM)"), and a DATA step to calculate the expected returns of the market portfolio and the risk-free asset.

Tasks Performed by the Program

1. Use PROC TRANSPOSE to transpose the market returns (R_M) and the risk-free asset returns (R_F).

2. Use a DATA step to

   a. calculate the mean values with the MEAN function

   b. create a variable NAME to name the observations.

3. Use PROC PRINT to print the results, as shown in Output 7.2.

Example code

```
    /* Transposing the RETURN3 Data Set */
proc transpose data=return3 out=return3a;
   var r_m r_f;
run;

    /* Calculating Market Returns */
data return3b;
   set return3a;
   r=mean(of col1-col108);
   if _n_ = 1 then name = 'Market   ';
   if _n_ = 2 then name = 'Risk Free';
run;

    /* Printing Expected Market Return */
proc print data=return3b;
  var name r;
  title2 'Expected Returns';
run;
```

Output 7.2
Expected Returns for the Market Portfolio and the Risk-Free Asset

```
                       Portfolio Evaluation
                        Expected Returns

            OBS    NAME          R

             1     Market      0.014944
             2     Risk Free   0.007161
```

Interpretation of output

In Output 7.2, the expected market portfolio return is .014944, or about 1.5 percent, and the expected risk-free asset return is .007161, or about .72 percent. The expected market portfolio return is more than twice the magnitude of the expected risk-free asset return.

You want to compare these values with the expected returns of the comparison portfolios from Chapters 5 and 6. In general, you want to invest in portfolios with the highest return for any given level of risk.

Calculating Expected Returns for the Comparison Portfolios

In this example, the *expected individual stock returns* are the average monthly stock returns as calculated in Output 5.1. The weights for the linear combination are the solution values for the portfolio weights (X1 - X10), as shown in Output 7.1.

The following DATA step calculates the expected portfolio returns and creates a variable, NAME, that identifies each of the portfolios. PROC PRINT prints the results in Output 7.3.

```
data p_folio2;
   set p_folio1;
   r= .0176*x1+.0288*x2+.0148*x3+.021*x4+.0092*x5+.0103*x6
      +.0182*x7+.0172*x8+.0121*x9+.0146*x10;
   if _n_ = 1 then name = 'Ex_5.2  ';
   if _n_ = 2 then name = 'Ex_5.5  ';
   if _n_ = 3 then name = 'Ex_5.7  ';
   if _n_ = 4 then name = 'Ex_6.13 ';
   if _n_ = 5 then name = 'Ex_6.17 ';
run;

proc print data=p_folio2;
   var name r;
      title2 'Expected Portfolio Returns';
run;
```

Output 7.3
Expected Portfolio
Returns

```
                    Portfolio Evaluation
                 Expected Portfolio Returns

        OBS     NAME        R

         1      Ex_5.2    0.025931
         2      Ex_5.5    0.020900
         3      Ex_5.7    0.019014
         4      Ex_6.13   0.019000
         5      Ex_6.17   0.021107
```

Interpretation of output

Output 7.3 lists the expected returns of the comparison portfolios. Note that the portfolio constructed in Output 5.2 has the greatest expected return, .025931, or about 2.6 percent. The portfolio constructed in Output 6.13 has the lowest expected return of .019, or 1.9 percent.

These expected portfolio returns are based on the average monthly returns of each stock and their weight in the portfolios. If future stock returns behave similarly to past returns, then over time, the average, actual portfolio returns should approach the expected returns. You can compare these expected portfolio returns with actual portfolio returns and with the market portfolio.

Comparing Expected Returns

You can compare the expected returns of the market (shown in Output 7.2) with the expected returns of the comparison portfolios (shown in Output 7.3). The expected returns of the portfolios are contained in the P_FOLIO2 data set, and the expected market returns are contained in the RETURN3B data set. You can use a DATA step to concatenate the P_FOLIO2 and RETURN3B data sets. The results are printed with PROC PRINT in Output 7.4.

```
    /* Concatenating Data Sets */
data p_folio3;
    set p_folio2 return3b;
run;

    /* Printing Expected Returns */
proc print data=p_folio3;
    var name r;
    title2 'Expected Portfolio Returns';
run;
```

Output 7.4
Comparing
Expected Returns

```
                    Portfolio Evaluation
                 Expected Portfolio Returns

        OBS     NAME          R

         1      Ex_5.2      0.025931
         2      Ex_5.5      0.020900
         3      Ex_5.7      0.019014
         4      Ex_6.13     0.019000
         5      Ex_6.17     0.021107
         6      Market      0.014944
         7      Risk Free   0.007161
```

Interpretation of output

In Output 7.4, all of the five comparison portfolios have greater expected returns than the market portfolio. Simply comparing among the expectations, the future returns from investing in any of these portfolios appears good. However, for actual investing, you also want to compare risk measures and select the appropriate trade-off of risk and return.

Calculating Actual Return Measures

The actual portfolio returns are calculated only after the market, industry, and company-specific events have occurred that generate the actual returns. Returns are calculated as described in Chapter 1. Typically used summary measures of return are the arithmetic mean, wealth index, and geometric mean.

This section

□ introduces the RETURN4 data set, which contains the monthly returns of the market for 1987, the risk-free return (the return on 30-day US treasury bills), and the returns of the ten stocks used to construct the portfolios used for comparison

□ uses PROC TRANSPOSE to transpose the RETURN4 data set for ease in data manipulation

□ uses a DATA step to calculate the wealth index, the arithmetic mean, and the average compound return measure for the actual returns of the market portfolio

□ uses PROC IML to calculate the actual monthly returns for the comparison portfolios

□ uses a DATA step and the PROC IML output to calculate the actual return measures

□ uses PROC PRINT to print the actual return measures.

Creating the RETURN4 Data Set

You create the RETURN4 data set in the following DATA step. Note that the risk premium for the market portfolio (R_MKT) is created for later examples.

```
data return4;
   input r_m r_f gerber tandy genmil coned weyer ibm dec
         mobil tex cpl;
   retain date '01dec86'd;
   date=intnx('month',date,1);
   format date monyy.;
   r_mkt = r_m - r_f;
cards;
 .148 .00454  .057  .130  .123  .040  .270  .073  .385  .093  .049  .102
 .065 .00437  .019  .174  .049 -.067  .094  .092  .056 -.022 -.080 -.060
 .037 .00423  .040 -.118  .010 -.050  .089  .076  .061  .124  .103  .013
-.025 .00207 -.063 -.119 -.104  .020 -.027  .067  .055 -.007 -.094 -.039
 .004 .00438  .138 -.026  .190 -.012 -.107  .006 -.082 -.003  .114 -.090
 .038 .00402  .005  .045  .030  .059  .026  .016  .041  .091  .073  .088
 .055 .00455  .232  .087  .036 -.039  .021 -.009  .000  .032  .142 -.035
 .015 .00460 -.113  .027  .022  .043  .081  .053  .157  .030 -.076  .021
-.015 .00520 -.061  .088 -.009 -.006 -.054 -.105  .001 -.082 -.053 -.014
-.260 .00358 -.288 -.246 -.148 -.017 -.271 -.187 -.281 -.178 -.194 -.040
-.070 .00288 -.085 -.190 -.102 -.012 -.066 -.087 -.127 -.150 -.031 -.019
 .073 .00277  .070  .040  .128 -.006  .103  .043  .134  .159  .178  .023
;
```

Calculating Actual Market Return Measures

To calculate the actual arithmetic mean and the average compound return of the market portfolio, first use PROC TRANSPOSE to transpose the RETURN4 data set, then use a DATA step. Lastly, use PROC PRINT to print the returns, as shown in Output 7.5.

The following PROC TRANSPOSE statement uses the RETURN4 data set as input and places the transposed values in the RETURN4A data set.

```
proc transpose data=return4 out=return4a;
   var r_m r_f;
run;
```

The DATA step uses array processing to add 1 to the returns for ease in calculating the wealth index and the average compound return. The MEAN function is used to calculate the arithmetic mean. The observations containing the return measures for the market portfolio and the risk-free asset are named Market and Risk Free, respectively.

```
             /* Calculating the Market Return Measures */
data return4b;
    set return4a;
    t=12;
    array col(12) col1-col12;
    array ss(12) s1-s12;
    do i=1 to 12;
        ss(i) = col(i) + 1;
    end;
    wealth=(s1*s2*s3*s4*s5*s6*s7*s8*s9*s10*s11*s12);
    gm=((wealth)**(1/t))-1;
    gm_pct=gm*100;
    am=mean(of col1-col12);
    am_pct=am*100;
    if _n_ = 1 then name = 'Market   ';
    if _n_ = 2 then name = 'Risk Free';
run;

proc print data=return4b;
    var name gm gm_pct am am_pct wealth;
    title2 'Return Measures';
    title3 'Market Portfolio and Risk-Free Asset';
run;
```

Output 7.5
*1987 Market
Portfolio and
Risk-Free Asset
Return Measures*

```
                        Portfolio Evaluation
                          Return Measures
                  Market Portfolio and Risk-Free Asset

    OBS   NAME        GM        GM_PCT      AM       AM_PCT    WEALTH

     1    Market    .0002831   0.02831   .0054167   0.54167   1.00340
     2    Risk Free .0039321   0.39321   .0039325   0.39325   1.04822
```

Interpretation of output

Output 7.5 lists the market portfolio and risk-free asset return measures and the wealth index values. Returns from holding the market portfolio have an average compound return measure of .03 percent, and .54 percent as measured by the arithmetic mean. Holding the risk-free asset would have yielded a return of .39 percent as measured by the arithmetic mean and the average compound return.

You can compare these values with the actual returns from the portfolios. Obviously, portfolio returns greater than the market are preferred, and the greater the better.

In this example, the wealth index indicates that if you had invested $1 in the market portfolio at the beginning of the year, it would have grown to $1.0034 over the year. If you had invested $1 in the risk-free asset, it would have grown to almost $1.05 over the year.

Calculating Actual Portfolio Return Measures

You can calculate the actual (ex post) returns for the portfolios in a DATA step, similar to the one that produced Output 7.5. Then, you can merge the data sets containing the actual returns in another DATA step. However, if you are calculating returns for many portfolios, the IML procedure is much more efficient.

Intuitively, you proceed by multiplying the actual returns by the portfolio weights to obtain the month-by-month portfolio returns; then, the arithmetic and geometric measures of portfolio return can be calculated in a DATA step.

Using PROC IML

You can use PROC IML to calculate the actual monthly portfolio returns by performing the following steps:

□ Read in the data set of portfolio weights (P_FOLIO1 from Output 7.1) and the data set of the actual returns (RETURN4). These data sets become matrices that can be manipulated in PROC IML.

For this example, the P_FOLIO1 data set has 5 rows and 10 columns, while the RETURN4 data set has 12 rows and 10 columns. The P_FOLIO1 data set is read in as the **XX** matrix, while the appropriate columns of the RETURN4 data set are read in as the **RR** matrix.

□ Orient the matrices for the appropriate matrix operations. For this example, the matrix of portfolio weights is transposed.

The (5 X 10) **XX** matrix can be transposed to form the (10 X 5) **XT** matrix.

□ Multiply the conforming matrices to obtain the monthly portfolio returns, **RX**.

$$RX = RR \times XT$$

Note that the (12 X 10) **RR** matrix times the (10 X 5) **XT** matrix yields the (12 X 5) **RX** matrix.

□ Transpose the matrix of monthly portfolio returns for ease of use in the DATA step calculations.

$$RXT = T(RX)$$

Selected PROC IML Operators

You use the following list of PROC IML operators in the PROC IML statements to calculate the actual portfolio returns. These operators perform the following tasks:

□ *matrix* = t(*matrix*) creates a transposed matrix. In this example, the (5 X 10) **XX** matrix is transposed to create the (10 X 5) **XT** matrix.

□ *matrix* = *matrix**matrix multiplies conforming matrices. In this example, the (12 X 10) **RR** matrix is multiplied by the (10 X 5) **XT** matrix to create the (12 X 5) **RX** matrix. Note that the **RX** matrix is later transposed for ease of use in the subsequent DATA step.

□ *name* = *name1 name2 . . . nameN* creates a column vector of variable names. For this example, the column vector of variable names is VARNAME1, and the column vector names are R_ACT1 through R_ACT5.

Explanation of syntax
The following PROC IML statements calculate the actual portfolio returns:

PROC IML
: invokes the IML procedure.

USE
: makes the listed data set an active data set.

READ
: reads observations from the active data set into a PROC IML matrix.

  For this example, the P_FOLIO1 data set is the first active data set and all numerical variables are read in as the **XX** matrix. Each row of **XX** represents the portfolio weights for one of the comparison portfolios. Each column of **XX** represents the portfolio weights for one of the ten stocks.

  Later, the RETURN4 data set is made the active data set and the 10 columns containing the monthly stock returns are read in as the **RR** matrix. Note that the **RR** matrix has 12 rows and 10 columns. That is one row for each of the 12 months, and one column for each of the 10 stocks.

CREATE *SASdataset* FROM *matrix*
: creates a SAS data set from the designated matrix. For this example, two data sets are created. The first data set, ACTUAL1, is created from the RX matrix and is used in later examples. The second data set, ACTUAL2, is created from the RXT matrix and is used to calculate the actual monthly returns of the portfolios.

APPEND FROM *matrix*
: adds observations to the data set (created with the CREATE statement) from the specified matrix.

CLOSE *SASdataset*
: closes the newly created data set; that is, this statement informs PROC IML that all the observations have been read into the specified data set.

Example code

```
proc iml;
    /* Making P_FOLIO1 Current Data Set */
  use p_folio1;

    /* Reading in the Numerical Obs */
  read all var _num_ into xx;

    /* Creating the XT Matrix where */
    /* XT is the Transpose of the XX Matrix */
  xt=t(xx);

    /* Making RETURN4 Current Data Set */
  use return4;

    /* Reading in the Numerical Obs */
  read all var {gerber tandy genmil coned weyer ibm dec
               mobil tex cpl} into rr;

    /* Matrix Multiplication, Returns Times Weights */
  rx=rr*xt;
```

```
                    /* Transposing the RX Matrix to form the RXT Matrix */
                rxt=t(rx);

                    /* Creating a Column Name Vector */
                varname1='r_act1' : 'r_act5';

                    /* Creating the ACTUAL1 Data Set from RX Matrix */
                    /* Creating Variable Names for Columns */
                create actual1 from rx [colname= varname1];

                    /* Adding the Obs to the Data Set from RX Matrix */
                append from rx;

                    /* Closing the ACTUAL1 Data Set */
                close actual1;

                varname2='t1' : 't12';

                    /* Creating the ACTUAL2 Data Set from RXT Matrix */
                create actual2 from rxt [colname= varname2];
                append from rxt;
                close actual2;
            quit;
```

The ACTUAL2 data set is printed in Output 7.6 using PROC PRINT.

```
    proc print data=actual2;
        title2 'ACTUAL2, Weights Times Stock Returns';
    run;
```

Output 7.6
Actual Portfolio
Monthly Returns
from PROC IML
Calculations

```
                            Portfolio Evaluation
                      ACTUAL2, Weights Times Stock Returns

    OBS      T1          T2          T3          T4          T5          T6

     1     0.09689     0.085345   -0.092985   -0.067867   -0.020850    0.050150
     2     0.11160     0.047525   -0.026864   -0.044929   -0.003566    0.049234
     3     0.11559     0.029769   -0.000766   -0.019441    0.006155    0.043524
     4     0.07241    -0.022868   -0.002634   -0.013422    0.024320    0.055286
     5     0.06334    -0.024339   -0.023211   -0.005855   -0.004516    0.059631

    OBS      T7          T8          T9          T10         T11         T12

     1     0.040649    0.032886    0.053421   -0.16176    -0.12452     0.023078
     2     0.039546    0.029217    0.008880   -0.16588    -0.09988     0.053632
     3     0.039223    0.029096   -0.015106   -0.16810    -0.08555     0.056586
     4     0.013319    0.025531   -0.020212   -0.10351    -0.05919     0.053569
     5     0.003465    0.031150   -0.010294   -0.08888    -0.06191     0.032663
```

Interpretation of output

Output 7.6 lists the ACTUAL2 data set containing the actual monthly returns for the portfolios. Each row represents the actual monthly returns for individual portfolios. For example, the first row represents the monthly returns of the portfolio created in Output 5.2. Each column represents the actual monthly returns for individual months. For example, the first column represents the actual monthly returns for January 1987.

Calculating Portfolio Actual Return Measures

You can use a DATA step and the ACTUAL2 data set (from Output 7.6) to calculate the portfolio actual return measures. The results from these statements are printed in Output 7.7.

```
data actual3;
   set actual2;
   t=12;
   array tt(12) t1-t12;
   array ss(12) s1-s12;
   do i=1 to 12;
      ss(i) = tt(i) + 1;
   end;
   wealth=(s1*s2*s3*s4*s5*s6*s7*s8*s9*s10*s11*s12);
   gm=((wealth)**(1/t))-1;
   gm_pct=gm*100;
   am=mean(of t1-t12);
   am_pct=am*100;
   if _n_ = 1 then name = 'Ex_5.2   ';
   if _n_ = 2 then name = 'Ex_5.5   ';
   if _n_ = 3 then name = 'Ex_5.7   ';
   if _n_ = 4 then name = 'Ex_6.13  ';
   if _n_ = 5 then name = 'Ex_6.17  ';
run;

proc print data=actual3;
   var name gm gm_pct am am_pct wealth;
   title2 'Actual Portfolio Returns';
run;
```

*Output 7.7
Portfolio Actual
Return Measures for
1987*

```
                        Portfolio Evaluation
                       Actual Portfolio Returns

OBS    NAME        GM         GM_PCT       AM         AM_PCT     WEALTH

  1    Ex_5.2    -0.010611   -1.06106   -.0071300   -0.71300   0.87985
  2    Ex_5.5    -0.002864   -0.28639   -.0001234   -0.01234   0.96617
  3    Ex_5.7     0.000047    0.00470    0.0025820   0.25820   1.00056
  4    Ex_6.13    0.000700    0.07002    0.0018840   0.18840   1.00843
  5    Ex_6.17   -0.003349   -0.33492   -.0023970   -0.23970   0.96054
```

Interpretation of output

Output 7.7 lists the actual returns of the comparison portfolios and a wealth index, labeled WEALTH. You may want to compare the expected returns (from Output 7.3) with these actual returns. All of the comparison portfolios have lower actual returns than expected returns.

Using the arithmetic return measure, the portfolio created in Output 5.7 has the greatest return of the comparison portfolios. The wealth index indicates the wealth generated (or lost) by investing in the portfolio. If you had invested $1 in the portfolio at the beginning of the year, the wealth index indicates the value at the end of the year. For example, if you had invested $1 in the first portfolio (generated in Output 5.2), by the end of the year, you would have about $0.88. Only portfolios 3 and 4 (generated in Output 5.7 and Output 6.13) have greater ending wealth than the initial amount invested.

Concatenating Actual Return Measures

You can use a DATA step to concatenate the RETURN4B data set (containing the actual market return measures) and ACTUAL3 data set (containing the actual portfolio return measures) to create the ACTUAL4 data set. The results are shown in Output 7.8.

```
/* Merging Mkt and Portfolio Returns */
data actual4;
    set actual3 return4b;
run;

/* Printing Mkt and Portfolio Returns */
proc print data=actual4;
    var name gm gm_pct am am_pct wealth;
run;
```

Output 7.8
Concatenation of
Actual Return
Measures

```
                        Portfolio Evaluation
                        Actual Return Measures

   OBS   NAME         GM         GM_PCT      AM         AM_PCT     WEALTH

    1    Ex_5.2     -0.010611   -1.06106   -.0071300   -0.71300   0.87985
    2    Ex_5.5     -0.002864   -0.28639   -.0001234   -0.01234   0.96617
    3    Ex_5.7      0.000047    0.00470    0.0025820   0.25820   1.00056
    4    Ex_6.13     0.000700    0.07002    0.0018840   0.18840   1.00843
    5    Ex_6.17    -0.003349   -0.33492   -.0023970   -0.23970   0.96054
    6    Market      0.000283    0.02831    0.0054167   0.54167   1.00340
    7    Risk Free   0.003932    0.39321    0.0039325   0.39325   1.04822
```

Interpretation of output

Output 7.8 lists the actual return measures and the wealth index values for the market portfolio and the comparison portfolios. Although all of the comparison portfolios had greater expected returns than the market (as shown in Output 7.4), in actuality, ex post, only the portfolio created in Output 6.13 had an average compound return (GM) greater than the market. None of the comparison portfolios had greater arithmetic return measures than the market nor the risk-free asset.

Evaluating Portfolio Performance Using CAPM Regressions

You can use CAPM regressions of portfolio returns to evaluate portfolios by

◻ testing for consistent, nonmarket-related returns as measured by α, the intercept of CAPM regressions in risk premium form. Recall from Chapter 4 that α is expected to be 0. This approach to evaluating portfolio performance was suggested by Jensen (1968).

◻ comparing return per unit of systematic risk as measured by β, the slope parameter of the basic CAPM. This is the Treynor index used to compare portfolios by systematic risk (Treynor 1965).

Testing for Nonmarket-Related Returns

As discussed in Chapter 4, the CAPM in risk premium form relates the risk premiums of an individual stock ($R_{i,t} - R_{f,t}$) to the risk premiums of the market ($R_{M,t} - R_{f,t}$), as follows:

$$ R_{i,t} - R_{f,t} = \alpha_i + \beta_i \times \left(R_{M,t} - R_{f,t} \right) + \epsilon_{i,t} $$

The slope parameter, β_i, is a proportionality factor of asset i's dependence on the market's rate of return. As the market moves up (or down) by 1 percent, the portfolio returns are expected to move up (or down) by β percent.

The intercept parameter, α_i, measures the nonmarket portion of returns and over time is expected to be zero. A portfolio with a positive α_i indicates the portfolio has had consistent, positive nonmarket returns, while a portfolio with a negative α_i indicates the portfolio has had consistent negative nonmarket returns. In general, portfolios with positive α perform better than expected, while portfolios with negative α perform worse than expected.

Before testing for nonmarket returns, use a DATA step to:

◻ merge the RETURN4 data set (containing the market returns and the risk-free returns) with the ACTUAL1 data set (containing the portfolio returns)

◻ create the portfolio risk premiums using array processing.

Example code

```
     /* Merging Mkt and Portfolio Returns */
data return4c;
   merge return4 actual1;

      /* Using Arrays to Create Portfolio Risk Premiums */
   array r_act(5) r_act1-r_act5;
   array rp(5) rp1-rp5;
   do i=1 to 5;
      rp(i) = r_act(i)-r_f;
   end;
run;
```

You can use the REG procedure to fit the CAPM, test if α (the intercept) differs from zero, and create a data set containing the estimated parameters. The following statements perform these tasks; the output is not shown.

```
/* Fitting Portfolio CAPM Regressions */
proc reg data=return4c outest=capmest2;
    model rp1=r_mkt;
    model rp2=r_mkt;
    model rp3=r_mkt;
    model rp4=r_mkt;
    model rp5=r_mkt;
run;
```

The following table lists the fitted CAPM regressions, the individual t-tests of the estimated parameters, the historical and constrained portfolio βs, and the R-squares.

Portfolio	Observed α (t-statistic)	Observed β (t-statistic)	Expected and Constrained β	R-Sq.
Output 5.2	− .012062 (− .773)	.673561 (4.131)	.7 (Constrained)	.6305
Output 5.5	− .005102 (− .646)	.704849 (8.547)	.575222 (Expected)	.8796
Output 5.7	− .002392 (− .456)	.701491 (12.818)	.4862172 (Expected)	.9426
Output 6.13	− .002690 (− .349)	.432309 (5.373)	No comparable value calculated	.7427
Output 6.17	− .006866 (− .840)	.361384 (4.234)	No comparable value calculated	.6419

Note the following items of interest from the table:

□ All of the portfolios have estimated α values less than 0, and none of them are significant at the .05 level. Although it is not shown in the table, at the .05 level of significance, the critical *t*-value is 2.201 for 11 degrees of freedom.

□ All of the portfolios have estimated β values between 0 and 1, and all of them are significantly different from 0 at the .05 level.

Ex ante expectations of portfolio β may not match the ex post realizations. Based on historical returns (1978-1986), the CAPM βs for the portfolios of Output 5.2, 5.5, and 5.7 (as calculated in Output 4.11) were .7, .575222, and .4862172, respectively. The 1987 returns generated portfolio βs of .673561, .704849, and .701491, respectively. The differences occur partially because expectations of the future returns may differ from actual returns and partially because the portfolios may not be fully diversified. Note that no comparable β values were calculated for the portfolios generated in Outputs 6.13 and 6.17.

□ All of the portfolios have larger R-Squares than the individual stock CAPM regressions of Chapter 4. The individual stock CAPM regressions used data over 108 months, while the portfolio CAPM regressions used data over 12 months. In general, the more observations used in the regression analysis, the greater the precision of the estimated equation. For these portfolio regressions, the variation of the market returns accounted for much of the variation of the portfolio returns. In particular, note that the portfolio created in Output 5.7 has an R-Square of .9426, indicating that the model accounts for over 94 percent of the variation of the portfolio returns.

Comparing Return per Unit of Systematic Risk

Jack Treynor suggests evaluating portfolios based on their level of returns per unit of systematic risk. He calculates the following measure of return (as measured by the average portfolio risk premium over time) per unit of systematic risk (as measured by the portfolio CAPM β) for each portfolio (p):

$$\left[\overline{R}_p - \overline{R}_f\right] / \beta_p$$

In general, portfolios with the highest risk premium per unit of total risk perform the best. A portfolio with a Treynor Index value greater than that of the market portfolio has beaten the market. Note that the market portfolio has β of unity.

You can use a DATA step, the estimated CAPM parameters (contained in the CAPMEST2 data set), and the portfolio returns (contained in the ACTUAL4 data set created in Output 7.8) to evaluate portfolios by the Treynor Index. The following statements perform the calculations. The average monthly risk-free asset return for 1987 is .0039325 (from Output 7.5). The variable AM contains the average monthly returns for 1987 for the portfolios. The results are shown in Output 7.9.

```
    /* Merging Market and Portfolio Returns */
data return4d;
   merge capmest2(rename=(r_mkt=beta)) actual4;
   r_f=.0039325;
   if _n_ = 6 then beta=1;
   treynor=(am-r_f)/beta;
run;

    /* Printing the Treynor Index Values */
proc print;
   var name am r_f beta treynor;
   title2 'Treynor Index Values';
   title3;
run;
```

Output 7.9
Treynor Index
Values

```
                         Portfolio Evaluation
                         Treynor Index Values

      OBS     NAME        AM        R_F       BETA      TREYNOR

       1     Ex_5.2    -.0071300   .0039325   0.67356   -0.016424
       2     Ex_5.5    -.0001234   .0039325   0.70485   -0.005754
       3     Ex_5.7    0.0025820   .0039325   0.70149   -0.001925
       4     Ex_6.13   0.0018840   .0039325   0.43231   -0.004738
       5     Ex_6.17   -.0023970   .0039325   0.36138   -0.017515
       6     market    0.0054167   .0039325   1.00000    0.001484
```

Interpretation of output

Output 7.9 lists the average monthly returns for the portfolios, the average monthly risk-free return, the CAPM βs, and the Treynor Index values.

For this example, none of the portfolios have a positive value for the Treynor Index. In addition, none of the portfolios have an index value greater than the market portfolio index value. Therefore, you can conclude that none of the comparison portfolios performed well by the Treynor Index.

Evaluating Portfolio Performance Using Total Risk

William Sharpe (1966) suggests evaluating portfolios based on the portfolio risk premium per unit of total risk (standard deviation). He calculates the following measure for each portfolio (p):

$$\left[\overline{R}_p - \overline{R}_f \right] / \sigma_p$$

In general, portfolios with the highest risk premium per unit of total risk perform the best. A portfolio with a Sharpe Index value greater than that of the market portfolio has beaten the market.

For well-diversified portfolios, the rankings between the Treynor and Sharpe indexes will be similar. For poorly diversified portfolios, the rankings may be very different.

To calculate Sharpe Index values, you proceed as follows.

Tasks performed by the program

□ Use a DATA step to merge data sets. For this example, you merge the RETURN4 and RETURN4C data sets to create the RETURN4E data set.

□ Use PROC TRANSPOSE to transpose the data sets. For this example, you transpose the RETURN4E data set.

□ Use a DATA step to calculate the portfolio average risk premiums, the standard deviations, and the Sharpe Index values.

□ Use PROC PRINT to print the index values.

The results are shown in Output 7.10.

Example code

```
    /* Merging Data Sets */
data return4e;
   merge return4 return4c;
run;

    /* Transposing RETURN4E Data Set */
proc transpose data=return4e out=return4f;
   var rp1-rp5 r_mkt;
run;

    /* Calculating Sharpe Index Values */
data return4g;
```

```
        set return4f;
        mean = mean(of col1-col12);
        std = std(of col1-col12);
        sharpe=mean/std;
        if _n_ = 1 then name = 'Ex_5.2 ';
        if _n_ = 2 then name = 'Ex_5.5 ';
        if _n_ = 3 then name = 'Ex_5.7 ';
        if _n_ = 4 then name = 'Ex_6.13';
        if _n_ = 5 then name = 'Ex_6.17';
        if _n_ = 6 then name = 'Market ';
    run;

        /* Printing Sharpe Index Values */
    proc print data=return4g;
        var name mean std sharpe;
        title2 'Sharpe Index Values';
    run;
```

Output 7.10
Sharpe Index Values

```
                        Portfolio Evaluation
                        Sharpe Index Values

        OBS     NAME        MEAN        STD       SHARPE

         1     Ex_5.2    -0.011063    0.084817    -0.13043
         2     Ex_5.5    -0.004056    0.075145    -0.05397
         3     Ex_5.7    -0.001350    0.072243    -0.01869
         4     Ex_6.13   -0.002048    0.050157    -0.04084
         5     Ex_6.17   -0.006329    0.045101    -0.14034
         6     Market     0.001484    0.099987     0.01484
```

Interpretation of output

Output 7.10 lists the Sharpe Index values for the comparison portfolios and the market portfolio.

For this example, none of the portfolios have a positive value for the Sharpe Index. In addition, none of the portfolios have an index value greater than the market portfolio index value. Therefore, you can conclude that none of the comparison portfolios performed well by the Sharpe Index.

Note that the ranking of the comparison portfolios is equivalent for both indexes (portfolios from Output 5.7, 6.13, 5.5, 5.2, and 6.17).

Learning More

□   For more information on the DATA step, see *SAS Language, Reference, Version 6, First Edition* and *SAS Language and Procedures, Usage 2, Version 6, First Edition.*

□   For more information on SAS/IML software, see *SAS/IML Software: Usage and Reference, Version 6, First Edition.*

□   For more information on PROC REG, see *SAS/STAT User's Guide, Version 6, Fourth Edition, Volume 1* and *Volume 2.*

□ For more information on PROC PRINT and PROC TRANSPOSE, see *SAS Procedures Guide, Version 6, Third Edition* and *SAS Language and Procedures, Usage 2, Version 6, First Edition.*

References

Elton, E. and Gruber, M. (1987), *Modern Portfolio Theory and Investment Analysis, Third Edition*, New York: John Wiley & Sons, Inc.

Hagin, R. (1979), *Modern Portfolio Theory*, Homewood, Illinois: Dow Jones-Irwin.

Jensen, M. (1968), "The Performance of Mutual Funds in the Period 1945-1964," *Journal of Finance* (May), pp. 389-416.

Jones, C. (1991), *Investments: Analysis and Management, Third Edition*, New York: John Wiley & Sons, Inc.

Sharpe, W. (1966), "Mutual Fund Performance," *Journal of Business*, Vol. 39, No. 1, pp. 119-138.

Treynor, J. (1965), "How to Rate Management of Investment Funds," *Harvard Business Review*, Vol. 43, No.1, pp. 63-76.

Chapter 8 Valuing Stock Options

Introduction

This chapter discusses stock options, the binomial valuation approach, the Black-Sholes valuation approach, and applications of options pricing to other investment decisions. Note that you cannot value options using discounted cash flow (DCF) analysis because the risk of an option changes as the stock price changes, and an appropriate discount rate cannot be selected.

Stock options may be issued by the company itself (warrants) or issued by other investors (puts and calls). Options and some of their characteristics are listed below:

☐ A *call option* gives the holder a right to buy (or "call away") 100 shares of a common stock at a specified price before a specified expiration (or maturity) date. Investors buying *calls* expect the stock price to rise; they are "bullish" on the stock. Those selling calls (often called writers) are less bullish on the stock.

☐ A *put option* gives the holder a right to sell (or "put away") 100 shares of a common stock at a specified price before a specified expiration date. Investors buying *puts* expect the stock price to fall; they are "bearish" on the stock. Those selling puts are less bearish on the stock.

☐ A *warrant* is an option to purchase a stated number of shares of common stock at a specified price any time before a specified expiration date.

Puts and calls, typically, have lifetimes of three or six months, while warrants may last for years or have no expiration date. Options designated as "American" can be exercised at any time prior to the expiration date, while options designated as "European" can be exercised only at maturity (the expiration date). Hence, the more flexible American options are typically more valuable.

Options have the following advantages:

☐ Options provide leverage; that is, rather than buying and holding the stock, an investor can buy a call option at a fraction of the cost. Thus, the percentage gain can be magnified.

□ The buyer's maximum loss is known in advance. Options can be used as insurance against adverse market movements. For example, an investor can reduce the risk of a short sale by buying a call option.

□ Options expand the possible set of assets investors can buy, hold, and sell.

The following table lists the IBM common stock options for a given day as reported in the financial pages by major newspapers.

Table 8.1
IBM Stock Options on Chicago Exchange in mid-February

Option	Strike Price	February Volume	February Last Price	March Volume	March Last Price	April Volume	April Last Price
Call	40	no option		no option		10	13
Call	45	no option		no option		26	9
Call	50	1191	2 13/16	834	3 3/4	356	4 1/2
Call	55	3076	1/16	2377	1 1/16	2866	1 7/8
Call	60	80	1/16	2247	1/4	1275	11/16
Call	65	not traded		186	1/16	131	1/4
Call	70	not traded		no option		204	1/8
Put	45	no option		no option		44	3/8
Put	50	465	1/16	856	13/16	780	1 5/16
Put	55	3597	2 1/4	1952	3 1/8	709	3 3/4
Put	60	299	6 3/4	102	7	5	6 1/2

The first column lists the type of option (call or put); the second column, the *striking price* (the specified price at which the stock is to be exchanged, also known as an *exercise price*); and the remaining columns list the volume and last price for the appropriate expiration date (the Saturday following the third Friday of the exercise month). There are no options for some striking prices and expiration dates, while some options were not traded.

On the previous day's trading, IBM closed down 1 7/8 at 52 3/4, having traded at a high of 55 and a low of 52 1/2, while the previous 52-week high and low were 60 and 40 5/8, respectively. This gives some indication why call options priced at 40 and 45 and put options for 45 do not exist for the near future. Call options exist for striking prices of 65 and 70, but they were not traded. Given the volume of trading, the majority of investors expect IBM stock to trade at prices between 50 and 60 in the near future.

The traded options have values ranging from 1/16 of $1 per share (or $6.25 for 100 shares) to a high of 13 (or $1300 for 100 shares). In general, call options are more valuable the more time prior to their expiration, the higher the stock price, the lower the striking price, the greater the fluctuation of the stock's price, and the higher the risk-free rate of return.

Valuing Options Using the Binomial Method

Suppose that you are considering buying a call option on a stock that currently sells for $50 per share. In one year, you expect the stock price to either rise to $60 per share or fall to $40 per share. Note that buying the stock at $50 per share yields $10 profit per share (20 percent return) if the stock increases in value, but $10 loss per share (-20 percent return) if the stock decreases in value. Also suppose that the striking price of the option is $55 and the one-year rate of interest is 10 percent. What is the value of the call option?

If the stock is priced at $40 in one year, the call option to buy stock at $55 per share is worth $0 (because you can buy as many shares as you want at $40). If the stock is priced at $60 in one year, the call option is worth $5 ($60 minus the $55 striking price).

Now compare these pay offs with that of buying one share of stock (at $50) and borrowing $36.37 (that is, the present value of the lower value of the year-end stock price, $40/1.1) from the bank. In one year, the loan and interest must be repaid, $40 total (that is, $36.37 × 1.1). If the stock is priced at $40, you can repay the loan by selling the share of stock, and you lose $13.63 overall. (Note that $13.63 is the difference between the current share price and the amount borrowed.) If in one year the stock is valued at $60 per share, you can sell the share of stock, repay the loan, and still earn $10.

If you had invested $13.63 in call options, you would have lost the same if the stock price fell, but you would have earned more if the stock price rose. The $13.63 is a multiple of the value of the call option, as described in the following equation:

$$\text{Multiple} = \frac{Spread\ of\ option\ prices}{Spread\ of\ share\ prices} = \frac{5\ -\ 0}{60\ -\ 40} = \frac{1}{4}$$

The multiple is often called *delta* (and sometimes called the *hedge ratio* or the *option delta*), and for this example, buying one share of stock replicates buying four call options. Therefore, the value of four call options equals the difference between the value of the share ($50) and the bank loan ($36.37) divided by 4; or $13.63/4 is about $3.41. If the option sells for more than $3.41, you can profit by buying shares and selling four call options for each share bought. If the option sells for less than $3.41, you can profit by selling the stock and buying four calls for each share sold. Note that this logic says little about investors beliefs of risk concerning this stock.

You can also calculate the value of the option by assuming investors are indifferent about risk and calculating the expected future value of the option, then discounting it back to present value at the risk-free rate. If investors are indifferent to risk, the expected stock return must be equal to the rate of interest. The stock is assumed to either rise by 20 percent to $60 (the upside) or fall by 20 percent to $40 (the downside). You can calculate the probability of a price rise (P) as follows:

$$Expected\ return = (P \times upside\ \%\ change) + (1\ -\ P) \times downside\ \%\ change = interest\ rate$$

$$Expected\ return = (P \times 20) + (1\ -\ P) \times (-20) = 10$$

$$P = \frac{interest\ rate\ -\ downside\ \%\ change}{upside\ \%\ change\ -\ downside\ \%\ change}$$

$$P = \frac{10\ -\ (-20)}{20\ -\ (-20)} = \frac{3}{4} = 75\%$$

If the stock price rises, the call option will be worth $5. If the stock price falls, the call option will be worthless. The expected future value of the call option (in one year) is calculated as

$$Call\ Value = (P \times 5) + [(1 - P) \times 0] = (.75 \times 5) + (.25 \times 0) = \$3.75 \quad .$$

The discounted future value of the option is

$$Present\ Value = \frac{Future\ Value}{1 + interest\ rate} = \frac{\$3.75}{1.1} = \$3.41 \quad .$$

This example had only two future prices of the stock, but it could have had a distribution of future prices. You can use the general binomial method to value options if you know the standard deviation of (continuously compounded) annual returns of the stock (σ) and the time until expiration of the option, expressed as a fraction of a year (t). The formula uses e, the base of the natural logarithms (2.718 . . .) and is

$$1 + upside\ changes = u = e^{\sigma\sqrt{t}}$$

$$1 + downside\ changes = d = \frac{1}{u} \quad .$$

For the previous example the time period is one year, and the standard deviation of the discrete distribution of returns is .17321. (You may want to review Chapter 1, "Background Topics," for examples of calculating the standard deviation of a discrete distribution of expected returns.) For additional discussion on the binomial method see Brealey and Myers (1991) and Elton and Gruber (1987).

A Call Option Using the Binomial Method

You can use the DATA step to perform the binomial method calculations for valuing the option in the following statements. Note that this example uses the EXP and SQRT functions (for the exponential and square root transformations, respectively) and that the mean (MEAN), variance (VAR), and standard deviation (S) are calculated. For discussion of mean and variance calculations of a discrete distribution, see Chapter 1.

```
data binom1;
      /* Current and Future Prices */
   price=50;
   price_h=60;
   price_l=40;

      /* Striking Price of the Option, Fraction of Year, Interest Rate */
   sp=55;
   t=1;
   r=.10;

      /* % Downside Change, % Upside Change, Probability of Rise */
   p_down=(price_l-price)/price;
   p_up=(price_h-price)/price;
   p=(r-p_down)/(p_up-p_down);
```

```
        /* Mean, Variance, Standard Deviation */
   mean=p*p_up+(1-p)*p_down;
   var=p*((p_up-mean)**2)+(1-p)*((p_down-mean)**2);
   s=sqrt(var);

        /* Binomial Calculations */
   exponent=s*sqrt(t);
   up=exp(exponent);
   down=1/up;
   up_per=up-1;
   down_per=down-1;

        /* Gain, Expected Future Return, Present Value of Option */
   if price_h<sp then gain=0;
   else if price_h>sp then gain=price_h-sp;
   exp_ret=gain*p;
   pv_call=exp_ret/(1+r);
run;
```

You print variables in the BINOM1 data set with the PRINT procedure. The results are shown in Output 8.1.

```
proc print data=binom1;
   title 'Option Pricing';
   title2 'Binomial Model';
   title3 'Call Option';
run;
```

Output 8.1
Call Option Value
with Binomial
Pricing Model

```
                          Option Pricing
                          Binomial Model
                            Call Option

OBS PRICE PRICE_H PRICE_L SP T  R  P_DOWN P_UP   P  MEAN VAR    S

 1    50    60      40    55 1 0.1  -0.2  0.2 0.75 0.1 0.03 0.17321

OBS EXPONENT    UP      DOWN    UP_PER  DOWN_PER  GAIN  EXP_RET  PV_CALL

 1   0.17321  1.18911  0.84097  0.18911  -0.15903   5     3.75    3.40909
```

Interpretation of output

Output 8.1 lists the values of the input data, the intermediate calculations, and the value of the call option. The mean of the distribution of the returns is different from 0 because the interest rate is greater than 0 and risk neutrality is assumed (that is, the return is what matters). The present value of the call option is about $3.41, or $340.91 for 100 shares.

After calculating the option value based on your expectations of the future stock prices, you want to compare your calculated value with the market price of the option. **If** you are satisfied with your analysis and you believe you have found an undervalued option, then you want to consider purchasing that option. For example, if the market price of the above option is $2.00, then you may want to review your analysis; however, if you are satisfied with your analysis, then you may want to purchase this option. If you believe you have found an overvalued option, then you may want to consider writing (selling) that option or similar options. For example, if the market price for the above option is $4.50 and you are satisfied with your analysis, then you may want to consider writing similar options.

Multiple Call Options Using the Binomial Method

You can value multiple call options in one DATA step. For example, suppose there were several call option striking prices ($52.50, $55, and $57.50), several ranges of high and low prices ($60-$40, $65-$35, and $70-$30), and all other information remains the same from the previous example. What are the values for the call options? The following DATA step calculates the value of the call options. The results are printed with PROC PRINT in Output 8.2.

```
data binom2;
   input price price_h price_l sp @@;
   r=.10;
   t=1;

      /* % Downside Change, % Upside Change, Probability of Rise */
   p_down=(price_l-price)/price;
   p_up=(price_h-price)/price;
   p=(r-p_down)/(p_up-p_down);

      /* Mean, Variance, Standard Deviation */
   mean=p*p_up+(1-p)*p_down;
   var=p*((p_up-mean)**2)+(1-p)*((p_down-mean)**2);
   s=sqrt(var);

      /* Binomial Calculations */
   exponent=s*sqrt(t);
   up=exp(exponent);
   down=1/up;
   up_per=up-1;
   down_per=down-1;

      /* Gain, Expected Future Return, Present Value of Option */
   if price_h<sp then gain=0;
   else if price_h>sp then gain=price_h-sp;
   exp_ret=gain*p;
   pv_call=exp_ret/(1+r);

cards;
50 60 40 52.5   50 60 40 55   50 60 40 57.5
50 65 35 52.5   50 65 35 55   50 65 35 57.5
50 70 30 52.5   50 70 30 55   50 70 30 57.5
;

proc print data=binom2;
   var sp price_h price_l p exp_ret pv_call;
   title3 'Call Options';
run;
```

Output 8.2
Call Option Values
with Binomial
Pricing Model

```
                              Option Pricing
                              Binomial Model
                              Call Options


      OBS    SP    PRICE_H   PRICE_L      P      EXP_RET   PV_CALL

       1    52.5     60        40      0.75000    5.6250   5.11364
       2    55.0     60        40      0.75000    3.7500   3.40909
       3    57.5     60        40      0.75000    1.8750   1.70455
       4    52.5     65        35      0.66667    8.3333   7.57576
       5    55.0     65        35      0.66667    6.6667   6.06061
       6    57.5     65        35      0.66667    5.0000   4.54545
       7    52.5     70        30      0.62500   10.9375   9.94318
       8    55.0     70        30      0.62500    9.3750   8.52273
       9    57.5     70        30      0.62500    7.8125   7.10227
```

Interpretation of output

Output 8.2 lists the option striking prices (SP), the high price (PRICE_H), the low price (PRICE_L), the probability of a stock price rise (P), the expected return from the call options (EXP_RET), and the present value of the call options (PV_CALL). As the striking price increases, the expected return and the present value of the call option decreases. As the range between the high and low stock prices increases, the probability of a price rise decreases, while the expected return and the present value of the call options increase.

A Put Option Using the Binomial Method

You can also use the DATA step to calculate the value of a put option. The value of a European put (which can only be used at maturity) is

$$Value\ of\ put\ =\ value\ of\ call\ -\ value\ of\ stock\ +\ present\ value\ of\ striking\ price\qquad.$$

The value of American put options depends on when they are exercised. Sometimes it pays to exercise an American put option before maturity. For an extreme example, if the stock price falls to 0, the option can be used and the proceeds invested to earn additional returns.

Using the above equation, the previous example of valuing a call option can be modified to also yield the value of a put option. Suppose you were considering the purchase of a put option with a striking price of $55 and all other information remains the same as in the example producing Output 8.1. The following DATA step performs the calculations using the BINOM1 data set. The results are printed in Output 8.3.

```
data binom1;
   set binom1;
   pv_sp=sp/(1+r);
   if sp<price_l then pv_put=0;
   else pv_put=pv_call-price+pv_sp;
   output;
run;

proc print data=binom1;
   var pv_put;
   title3 'Put Option';
run;
```

Output 8.3
Put Option Value
with Binomial
Pricing Model

```
                        Option Pricing
                        Binomial Model
                          Put Option

                        OBS     PV_PUT

                         1      3.40909
```

Interpretation of output

In Output 8.3, the put option value is printed. In this example, note that the put option has the same value as the call option. This is because the present value of the striking price ($55/1.1 = $50) is equivalent to the current price of the asset ($50). Typically, these values differ.

Multiple Put Options Using the Binomial Method

You can calculate the value of multiple put options in one DATA step. The following DATA step calculates the value of put options with the same striking prices as the call options in the BINOM2 data set. The results are printed with PROC PRINT in Output 8.4.

```
data binom2;
   set binom2;
   pv_sp=sp/(1+r);
   if sp<price_l then pv_put=0;
   else pv_put=pv_call-price+pv_sp;
   output;
run;

proc print data=binom2;
   var sp price_h price_l p pv_call pv_put;
   title3 'Put Options';
run;
```

Output 8.4
Put Option Values
with Binomial
Pricing Model

```
                              Option Pricing
                              Binomial Model
                               Put Options

        OBS    SP    PRICE_H    PRICE_L      P      PV_CALL    PV_PUT

         1    52.5      60         40     0.75000    5.11364   2.84091
         2    55.0      60         40     0.75000    3.40909   3.40909
         3    57.5      60         40     0.75000    1.70455   3.97727
         4    52.5      65         35     0.66667    7.57576   5.30303
         5    55.0      65         35     0.66667    6.06061   6.06061
         6    57.5      65         35     0.66667    4.54545   6.81818
         7    52.5      70         30     0.62500    9.94318   7.67045
         8    55.0      70         30     0.62500    8.52273   8.52273
         9    57.5      70         30     0.62500    7.10227   9.37500
```

Interpretation of output

Output 8.4 lists the option striking prices (SP), the probability of a stock price rise (P), the present value of the call options, (PV_CALL), and the present value of the put options (PV_PUT). As the striking price increases, the present value of the put option increases. This makes sense because the buyer of the option is purchasing the right to sell the stock at the specified price. As the range between PRICE_H and PRICE_L increases, so does the value of the put option.

Extending the Binomial Method to Other Investments

You can extend the binomial option pricing method to other investments. Suppose you are considering two sets of machinery to produce a product, and the demand for the product may be high or low. For simplicity, assume that the initial costs are the same for the two sets, $20 million. The first set of machinery, set A, is specific to the product, producing lower individual cost items. The second set of machinery, set B, is less specific to the product, but it has the flexibility to produce other products. The pay offs in one year are listed in the following table:

Pay offs	Set A	Set B
High demand	$40 million	$35 million
Low demand	$10 million	$ 5 million

For any positive interest (discount) rate, the present value of Set A is greater than the present value of Set B. So, if you are committed to continuing production, no matter how high or low demand is, then Set A is chosen. If you also know that the salvage value of Set B is $16 million while the salvage value of Set A is nil, then you realize that Set B offers a put (sell) option with a striking price of the equipment's salvage value, $16 million.

Now the comparison appears very different. With Set A, if demand is high, you earn $40 million; if demand is low, you continue producing and you earn $10 million. However, with Set B, if demand is high, you earn $35 million; if demand is low, you can sell the assets for $16 million (as opposed to continuing to produce and earn $5 million). The put option acts like an insurance policy. In general, any set of pay offs that depend on the value of some underlying asset can be valued as a mixture of options on that asset.

You can use the DATA step and the binomial method to value the put option on the Set B machinery. The following DATA step performs this task, and PROC PRINT is used to print the results in Output 8.5.

```
data binom3;
      /* Current and Future Prices */
   price=20;
   price_h=35;
   price_l=5;

      /* Striking Price of the Option, Fraction of Year, Interest Rate */
   sp=16;
   t=1;
   r=.10;
```

```
                     /* % Downside Change, % Upside Change, Probability of Rise */
                   p_down=(price_l-price)/price;
                   p_up=(price_h-price)/price;
                   p=(r-p_down)/(p_up-p_down);

                     /* Mean, Variance, Standard Deviation */
                   mean=(p*p_up+(1-p)*p_down);
                   var=p*((p_up-mean)**2)+(1-p)*((p_down-mean)**2);
                   s=sqrt(var);

                     /* Binomial Calculations */
                   exponent=s*sqrt(t);
                   up=exp(exponent);
                   down=1/up;
                   up_per=up-1;
                   down_per=down-1;

                     /* Gain, Expected Future Return, Present Value of Option */
                   if price_h<sp then gain=0;
                   else if price_h>sp then gain=price_h-sp;
                   exp_ret=gain*p;
                   pv_call=exp_ret/(1+r);
                   pv_sp=sp/(1+r);
                   if sp<price_l then pv_put=0;
                   else pv_put=pv_call-price+pv_sp;
                   output;
                run;

             proc print data=binom3;
                /* var pv_put; */
                title2 'Binomial Model';
                title3 'Alternative Use Technology Put Option';
             run;
```

Output 8.5
Put Option Value of Alternative Technology Use with Binomial Pricing Model

```
                        Option Pricing
                         Binomial Model
               Alternative Use Technology Put Option

   OBS   PRICE   PRICE_H   PRICE_L   SP   T    R    P_DOWN   P_UP      P

    1     20       35         5      16   1   0.1   -0.75    0.75   0.56667

   OBS   MEAN    VAR      S      EXPONENT     UP      DOWN     UP_PER

    1     0.1   0.5525  0.74330   0.74330   2.10287  0.47554  1.10287

   OBS  DOWN_PER  GAIN   EXP_RET    PV_CALL    PV_SP     PV_PUT

    1   -0.52446   19   10.7667    9.78788   14.5455   4.33333
```

Valuing Options Using the Black-Scholes Method

The binomial approach to pricing options was used in previous examples to value options that expired after one year and had only two outcomes. The binomial approach can be used for shorter time periods; for example, six months, and then at the end of a year, there are four possible outcomes. If the stock prices are allowed to rise or fall every three months, then there would be eight possible outcomes at the end of a year. As the time periods become smaller and smaller, a continuous distribution of outcomes are possible, and the binomial options pricing method approaches the Black-Scholes method. See Black and Scholes (1973).

The Black-Scholes formula states that the present value of a call option is the product of the option delta times the share price minus the present value of a bank loan to purchase the share (at the end of the time period), or

$$\text{Option Value} = (delta \times price) \ - \ (bank\ loan)$$

$$\text{Option Value} = \left[N(d_1) \times Price \right] \ - \ \left[(Striking\ Price) \times e^{-rt} \times N(d_2) \right] \quad .$$

Note that the bank loan is discounted (continuously for the time period of one year) at the risk-free rate (r). The option delta is defined as the cumulative normal probability of d_1:

$$d_1 = \frac{log\,(Price\ /\ Striking\ Price)\ +\ rt\ +\ \sigma^2 t\,/\,2}{\sigma\,\sqrt{t}}$$

The remaining term, (d_2), is defined as $d_1 \ - \ \sigma\sqrt{t}$.

Lastly, note that the Black-Scholes method of pricing options is appropriate when the stock offers no dividend. For stocks paying dividends you should use the binomial method and value the option at each decision point (that is, just prior to the dividend payment date and at the end of the time period of interest).

A Call Option Using the Black-Scholes Method

The following DATA step calculates the value of the call option for the same conditions as the call option valued by the binomial method in Output 8.1. Note that the cumulative normal value is calculated by the PROBNORM function of the DATA step, while the LOG and EXP functions are used to make the natural logarithmic and exponential transformations. The results are printed with PROC PRINT in Output 8.6.

```
data option1;
     /* Current and Striking Price of the Option */
   price=50;
   sp=55;

     /* Standard Deviation, Fraction of Year, Interest Rate % */
   s=.17321;
   t=1;
   r=.10;
```

```
          /* Black-Scholes Option Pricing Calculations */
     d1=(log(price/sp)+(r*t)+(s**2*(t))/2)/(s*sqrt(t));
     d2=d1-(s*sqrt(t));
     delta_c=probnorm(d1);
     delta_p=delta_c-1;

     pv_sp=sp*exp((-r)*t);
     loan=pv_sp*probnorm(d2);

     pv_call=(price*delta_c)-loan;
     pv_put=pv_call+pv_sp-price;

     output;
run;

proc print data=option1;
   title2 'Black-Scholes Model';
   title3;
run;
```

Output 8.6
Black-Scholes
Method Option
Values

```
                              Option Pricing
                           Black-Scholes Model

   OBS    PRICE    SP      S       T     R      D1         D2        DELTA_C

    1      50      55   0.17321   1    0.1   0.11368   -0.059529    0.54525

   OBS    DELTA_P    PV_SP     LOAN    PV_CALL    PV_PUT

    1     -0.45475   49.7661  23.7018  3.56088   3.32694
```

Interpretation of output

Output 8.6 lists the input data, intermediate calculations, and the Black-Scholes values for put and call options. Given the current price of the stock ($50), the striking price of the options ($55), the variation of stock prices (standard deviation, labeled S, .17321), the time period involved (one year), and the annual interest rate (10 percent), the call option is worth about $3.56 per share, or $356.09 for 100 shares. The call option delta is .54525. Each call option is equivalent to a controlling 1/.54525, or about 1.8 shares.

Given the input information, the put option is worth about $3.33 per share, or $332.69 for 100 shares. The put option delta is -.45475. Instead of buying a put option, you sell .45475 shares of stock and buy a treasury bill (the risk-free asset) with the proceeds.

Note that the call option and the put option are no longer equivalent in value. This is because, with the continuous discounting used in the Black-Scholes method, the present value of the striking price ($49.7661) no longer equals the current price of the stock ($50) as it did in Output 8.1 and Output 8.3.

Multiple Options Using the Black-Scholes Method

You can value multiple call options in one DATA step. The following DATA step calculates the value of call and put options in the BINOM2 data set. The results are printed with PROC PRINT in Output 8.7.

```
data option2;
    set binom2;

    /* Black-Scholes Option Pricing Calculations */
    d1=(log(price/sp)+(r*t)+(s**2*(t))/2)/(s*sqrt(t));
    d2=d1-(s*sqrt(t));
    delta_c=probnorm(d1);
    delta_p=delta_c-1;

    pv_sp=sp*exp((-r)*t);
    loan=pv_sp*probnorm(d2);

    pv_call=(price*delta_c)-loan;
    pv_put=pv_call+pv_sp-price;

    output;
run;

proc print data=option2;
    var sp price_h price_l delta_c delta_p pv_call pv_put;
    title3 'Call Options';
run;
```

Output 8.7
Valuing Multiple Options Using the Black-Scholes Method

```
                           Option Pricing
                         Black-Scholes Model
                            Call Options

  OBS    SP    PRICE_H   PRICE_L   DELTA_C    DELTA_P    PV_CALL   PV_PUT

   1    52.5     60        40      0.64887   -0.35113    4.75810   2.26207
   2    55.0     60        40      0.54525   -0.45475    3.56078   3.32684
   3    57.5     60        40      0.44316   -0.55684    2.59865   4.62681
   4    52.5     65        35      0.62645   -0.37355    6.81981   4.32377
   5    55.0     65        35      0.56277   -0.43723    5.72773   5.49379
   6    57.5     65        35      0.50034   -0.49966    4.77933   6.80748
   7    52.5     70        30      0.62774   -0.37226    8.79837   6.30233
   8    55.0     70        30      0.58151   -0.41849    7.77703   7.54309
   9    57.5     70        30      0.53625   -0.46375    6.85983   8.88798
```

Interpretation of output

Output 8.7 lists the striking prices (SP), the high and low prices (PRICE_H and PRICE_L), the call option deltas (DELTA_C), the put option deltas (DELTA_P), and the present values of the call and put options (PV_CALL and PV_PUT), respectively. As the striking price increases, the option deltas decrease, and the present value of the call options decrease, while the present value of the put options increase. As the range between the high and low prices increases, so do the option values.

Note that all of the deltas for the call options are all positive and less than 1, indicating that each share of stock purchased would represent more than one call option, specifically, 1/DELTA_C. Also note that all of the deltas for the put options are all negative, indicating that instead of buying the put options, you sell DELTA_P shares of stock and buy U.S. Treasury bills (the risk-free asset) with the proceeds.

Learning More

□ For more information on the DATA step, see *SAS Language: Reference, Version 6, First Edition*; *SAS Language and Procedures: Usage, Version 6, First Edition*; and *SAS Language and Procedures, Usage 2, Version 6, First Edition*.

References

Black, F. and Scholes, M. (1973), "The Pricing of Options and Corporate Liabilities," *Journal of Political Economy*, Vol. 81, 637-654.

Brealey, R. and Myers, S. (1991), *Principles of Corporate Finance, Fourth Edition*, New York: McGraw-Hill, Inc.

Elton, E. and Gruber, M. (1987), *Modern Portfolio Theory and Investment Analysis, Third Edition*, New York: John Wiley & Sons, Inc.

Hagin, R. (1979), *Modern Portfolio Theory*, Homewood, Illinois: Dow Jones-Irwin.

Jones, C. (1991), *Investments: Analysis and Management, Third Edition*, New York: John Wiley & Sons, Inc.

Glossary

call option
the right to buy (or call away) 100 shares of a common stock at a specified price before a specified expiration (or maturity) date.

capital gains (losses)
the percentage amount by which the sale price of a stock exceeds (falls short of) the purchase price as shown in the equation for the ith stock purchased at time $t - 1$ and sold at time t:

$$\text{Capital Gain or Loss} = \frac{P_{i,t} - P_{i,t-1}}{P_{i,t-1}}$$

capital market line
the linear relationship of the average rate of return that is provided by the marketplace for various levels of risk. In the Sharpe model, the capital market line connects the risk-free rate of return and the return of the portfolio tangent to the efficient frontier of risky assets.

cross-sectional data
observations on multiple units in one time period. Examples of cross-sectional units are individuals, firms, and geographic aggregations. See also panel data and time series.

DATA step
a group of statements in a SAS program that begins with a DATA statement and ends with either a RUN statement, another DATA statement, a PROC statement, the end of the job, or the semicolon that immediately follows instream data lines. The DATA step enables you to read raw data or other SAS data sets and use programming logic to create a SAS data set, write a report, or write to an external file.

discount rate
the interest rate that is used in calculations of present value.

diversifiable risk
See nonsystematic risk.

dividends
cash and property that are distributed to corporate shareholders.

efficient frontier
the locus of all efficient portfolios.

efficient portfolio
a fully diversified portfolio that has either the greatest return for a given level of risk or the lowest risk for a given level of return.

estimation
the process of calculating parameter values for a model from sample data.

forecast
a numerical prediction of a future value for a time series.

missing value

a value in the SAS System indicating that no data are stored for the variable in the current observation. By default, the SAS System prints a missing numeric value as a single period (.) and a missing character value as a blank space.

nondiversifiable risk

See systematic risk.

nonsystematic risk

risk that is associated with factors other than the movement of the market portfolio (for example, industry- and firm-specific factors that affect stock returns). Nonsystematic risk is also known as diversifiable risk because owning additional assets reduces this risk.

observation

a row in a SAS data set. An observation is a collection of data values associated with a single entity, such as a customer or a state. Each observation contains one data value for each variable.

panel data

observations on two or more cross-sectional units over two or more time periods. See also cross-sectional data and time series.

present value

a calculation of the value of an asset or liability, taking into account the timing of payments and interest that can be earned. For example, the present value of one dollar one year from now is worth less than the present value of one dollar today.

put option

the right to sell (or put away) 100 shares of a common stock at a specified price before a specified expiration date.

return

dividends received and capital gains (or losses) that are realized from owning a share of stock, expressed as a percentage of the per-share stock price. Also known as yield.

risk-free asset

a default-free asset such as a short-term government security.

risk premium

the difference between the return of a stock and the return of the risk-free asset.

SAS data set

descriptor information and its related data values organized as a table of observations and variables that can be processed by the SAS System.

SAS program

a group of SAS statements that guide the SAS System through a process or series of processes.

SAS statement

a string of SAS keywords. SAS names, and special characters and operators ending in a semicolon that instructs the SAS System to perform an operation or gives information to the SAS System.

scatter plot

a two- or three-dimensional plot showing the joint variation of two (or three) variables from a group of observations. The coordinates of each point in the plot correspond to the data values for a single observation.

security market line

a linear relationship between the risk and the return of stocks; in equilibrium (when all information is reflected in the price of the stock), every stock will plot on this line.

selling short

selling a stock that you do not currently own with the expectation that its price will fall.

systematic risk

risk that is associated with the movements of the market portfolio. Systematic risk is also known as nondiversifiable risk because owning additional assets cannot reduce this risk.

time series

any univariate or multivariate data collected over time and arranged in temporal order. Time series can consist of discrete or continuous values.

total risk

the risk that is associated with all of the factors that affect stock returns.

warrant

an option issued by a corporation to purchase a stated number of shares of its stock at a specified price before a specified expiration date.

yield

See return.

Index

Your Turn

If you have comments or suggestions about *Stock Market Analysis Using the SAS System: Portfolio Selection and Evaluation*, please send them to us on a photocopy of this page or send us electronic mail.

For comments about this book, please return the photocopy to

> SAS Institute Inc.
> Publications Division
> SAS Campus Drive
> Cary, NC 27513
> **email:** yourturn@unx.sas.com

For suggestions about the software, please return the photocopy to

> SAS Institute Inc.
> Technical Support Division
> SAS Campus Drive
> Cary, NC 27513
> **email:** suggest@unx.sas.com